LEGENDARY LOCALS OF LAKE WORTH TEXAS

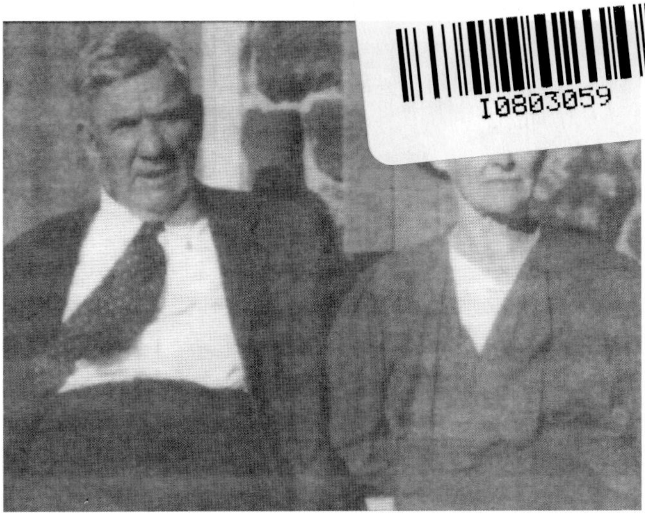

Page 1: James Hodgkins

James Hodgkins, considered by many as "The Father of Lake Worth," married Sara Greer in Benbrook in 1889. He built the area's first store, Lake Worth Trading Post, in 1906. Hodgkins, donated 100 acres for creation of the Lake Worth reservoir and donated five acres for the first school, hired the first teacher, and drove the first school bus. (Courtesy Archives Lake Worth Museum.)

LEGENDARY LOCALS

OF

LAKE WORTH

TEXAS

LAWANA MAULDIN AND JOE McDANIEL

LEGENDARY LOCALS

ISBN 978-1-4671-0158-5

Legendary Locals is an imprint of Arcadia Publishing
Charleston, South Carolina

Printed in the United States of America

Library of Congress Control Number: 2013957542

For all general information, please contact Arcadia Publishing:
Telephone 843-853-2070
Fax 843-853-0044
E-mail sales@arcadiapublishing.com
For customer service and orders:
Toll-Free 1-888-313-2665

Visit us on the Internet at www.arcadiapublishing.com

Dedication

The authors dedicate this book to Ken Brower and the memories of Ben Mauldin, and Rip and Lucyle Collins.

On the Front Cover: Clockwise from top left:
Zachary Lopez (Courtesy of Carla Bezner; see pages 103, 107), Eldon and Linda Pritchard (Courtesy of Linda Pritchard; see page 41), Glenn Sperry (Courtesy of Glenn Sperry; see pages 103, 108–112), Col. Forrest D. Giles (Courtesy of the Giles family; see pages 49, 53, 61), Dave Tatsak (Courtesy Dave Tatsak; see pages 61, 69, 70), LeAnn and Bill Davenport (Courtesy Bill Davenport; see pages 49, 57), Dr. Steve Whitaker (Courtesy of Ken Brower; see page 55), Paul Harmon (Courtesy of Paul Harmon; see pages 61, 64), Rue Dean Purdom (Courtesy of Donnie Purdom; see pages 103–105, 112).

On the Back Cover: From left to right:
Charlotte Wilson and grandson Ethan (Courtesy of Charlotte Wilson; see page 26), Murray Richey (Courtesy of Murray Richey; see page 40).

CONTENTS

ACKNOWLEDGMENTS

The number one acknowledgement for this book belongs to the grace of Jesus Christ, Son of God. Secondly, we wish to thank photographer Ken Brower, who not only photographed a number of images used but also scanned all images and provided much insight as to which ones were chosen for book.

Also, the authors thank Jason Humphrey, editor at Arcadia Publishing, who passed along much encouragement when moments of doubt crept in as to getting it completed on time. In addition, a huge thank-you to everyone who contributed in any way to this book.

INTRODUCTION

Lake Worth has a number of individuals, such as J.R. Foster, James Hodgkins, William Charbonneau, George Reynolds and his wife, Lucinda, who contributed greatly to the development of this area. They are, indeed, the legendary cornerstones for this small community.

The first established neighborhood, called Indian Oaks, acquired the street names through Lucinda Reynolds. Her husband sold land to Amon Carter, who bought over 600 acres and built his famous Shady Oaks Ranch. After Reynolds death, Lucinda sold more land to a developer in 1925 and had the honor of naming the streets. She chose Indian names likely to commemorate the ties of the white man with the Indians who had once settled in the area in the 1800s.

Comanche, Kiowa, Wichita, Tonkawa, and Hasinai tribes go back as far as the late 1700s when they settled in the North Texas region. With a tribal campground established near a creek in the early to mid-1800s, fish and water supplied nourishment needs. By the mid-1800s, white settlers moved into the area. This invasion stirred up the Comanches who raided nearby towns stealing horses and taking them back to their campgrounds. Any town residents that chased after the Comanches became engaged in a war of firearms and arrows.

One such battle, noted on a state marker, tells of the incident called The Independence Day Raid, which happened on July 4, 1869. A group of 11 Indians stole horses from nearby downtown Fort Worth and headed north and west of the city. A Tarrant County posse chased the Indians into Parker County where they found homes had been invaded, people had been shot, and two had been scalped. With other groups lending a hand to the posse, the Indians left behind their stolen horses and disappeared into the night on July 5. According to the Archives of the Texas Historical Commission, the marker, located at Mosque point, which overlooks the reservoir Lake Worth, contains valuable information about the incident.

Years after these battles, and years before George and Lucinda Reynolds and Amon Carter became involved in this area, swirls of concern in 1914 over prohibition dominated the national political scene. At the same time, others delighted in the completion of the largest reservoir in the southwest. Expecting it to take three years to fill, all were amazed that a three-week rainy season filled it up. After thoughts of other names, the officials chose the name Lake Worth. This reservoir brought about a better water supply for Fort Worth and presented an avenue for fun and adventure for many, including the village of people living close to this sparkling bit of pleasure.

Early settlers of this area opened up small businesses and some built cabins to rent or to have as a weekend home. Hodgkins, Charbonneau, and Foster each had their own developments and interests, including the development of a school system and self-appointed law enforcement. Hodgkins and Charbonneau donated land for churches and schools. Foster served on the school board and donated $5,000 to install lights on the high school football field. These and others earned the title of legendary locals.

Not everyone becoming legendary did so because of good things. As time went by, gambling often existed behind hidden doors of legal establishments such as nightclubs and restaurants. The Jacksboro Highway, which runs right through the city of Lake Worth, became the escape route of gamblers and the path for many gangsters as they sought out the next person to kill.

In spite of any negative action in or near this area, with the help of many honest citizens, the small village of Lake Worth developed. A number of churches and schools as well as several businesses emerged. Finally, in the early 1950s, Lake Worth became an incorporated city.

The Lake Worth Reservoir and beaches have gone through many changes over the last 100 years, but plans are underway to redevelop the beach area and work started recently to clean up the contaminated waters. The growth of the small town has continued with its history still in the making as schools, churches, and parks expand and businesses flourish. Many do volunteer work, but may go unnoticed by the general public. The intention of this book spotlights those and many other individuals.

Specific businesses, ministers, educators, medical personnel, dentists, lawyers, bankers, and accountants broaden the information found in this book. Military personnel, city dignitaries, firefighters, police officers, authors, artists, musicians, athletes, and selected others fill the pages as well. In addition, barbers, beauticians, retail sales persons for boats and knives, insurance agents, pharmacy managers, and pharmacy associates receive attention.

Others include a number of residents involved in places such as the L.O. "Bud" Irby Senior Citizen Complex, Lake Worth Museum, and the Mary Lou Reddick Library.

Some of the Lake Worth legendary locals are deceased, but many live today and go forth with the necessary tasks that bind a community together. There remain those not included who deserve recognition, but as space dictates, we honor some, with respect for the others.

CHAPTER ONE

Founders and Civic Leaders

The first people to settle the area that became the city of Lake Worth, Texas, saw more than vast prairies with groves of oak trees and a few creeks. They saw opportunities to meet the needs of a community that would prosper for years to come.

In 1878, Alexis Charbonneau developed the first thriving farm and ranch in the area. His son William Charbonneau became the first benefactor as he gave much of his family's land for the building of schools and businesses.

Another founder, James Hodgkins, considered the "Father of Lake Worth Business" opened the community's first store. He also founded the first school. J.R. Foster, an early successful businessman, made his mark with his financial contributions to the school district. By the turn of the century, George Reynolds started a successful cattle ranch that supplied his cattle company in downtown Fort Worth. This company still exists. His wife, Lucinda Reynolds, later sold land to create Indian Oaks, the community's first small neighborhood.

Myrtle Belle Fowlkes exhibited her indomitable spirit as a city employee and as a volunteer in several areas. Mayor Walter Bowen, with a heart for leadership, spurred Lake Worth to its greatest commercial growth. His wife, Pat Bowen, also contributed as a school board member and more.

J.T. Hinkle came to Lake Worth from River Oaks and became an advocate for youths, foreign aid, and the disabled. He also served in a number of other areas. As a public servant in Lake Worth, Gene Brooks used his leadership skills as a reserve police officer, city council member, and in additional ways. Others involved in the city's growth included Larry Thompson who directed the Chamber of Commerce for five years. His wife, Judi Thompson, supported his chamber activities. Linda Nelson, who managed the Lake Worth Economic Development Department for more than five years, contributed much to the commercial development of the city, while Dona Stuard uncovered much Lake Worth history. She also served on several boards.

Additional leaders include James and Diane Smith, effective members who served on local planning committees and various civic groups.

Al and Judy Jameson, prominent school supporters, opened several businesses. He served in other capacities as well. Curtis and Lee McKay contributed leadership in the fire department and city government. Virginia Ross served admirably as secretary for the Chamber of Commerce, and in other areas, as did Gary Goodman. He served on the city council and other capacities in Lake Worth. These forerunners, leaders, and others inspired the growth of Lake Worth, Texas.

James and Sara Hodgkins Family

James Hodgkins, the epitome of resourcefulness and hard work in the area that became Lake Worth, operated the first grocery store, provided the first postal service, and started the first law enforcement. Hodgkins, born in 1866, met and married Sara Greer in 1891. Before coming to northwest Tarrant County, he worked as a butcher and meat supplier in north Fort Worth. In addition, he served as a school board member for the North Fort Worth School District.

In 1906, Hodgkins bought 240 acres in an area now known as Lake Worth. He did not want to use Trinity River water for irrigation, so he dug freshwater wells by hand for his household as well as for his grown children's families and new settlers. Another of Hodgkins's generous actions involved the donation 100 acres for the land needed by Fort Worth to build the large reservoir of water eventually known as Lake Worth. During 1915, Hodgkins established Lake Worth Trading Post near the lake for a growing community. He sold groceries and rented tents, boats, fishing poles, and cabins to people who came to enjoy the lake. Later, he provided law enforcement and acquired the nickname "The Judge."

In 1922, because of the need for a school, Hodgkins donated five acres of land. Rosen Heights School opened in 1923 as a one-room building for grades one through eight. Hodgkins hired the first teacher, Betty Singleton, and paid her salary for the first school year. The school's name changed to Lake Worth School in the 1930s.

Hodgkins also provided and drove a vehicle to transport students to and from school. Into his 60s, he helped bring city bus transportation to the Lake Worth area. With an eye on his destiny, he set aside 2.25 acres of land for a family cemetery in 1936. He wanted an above ground burial when he died. His family honored this request after his death in 1942 and had his body placed in a raised tomb. Hodgkins Road and James Hodgkins Park honor the memory of this generous man's gifts and leadership. He, his wife, and unidentified children appear in this photograph. (Courtesy Archives Lake Worth Museum.)

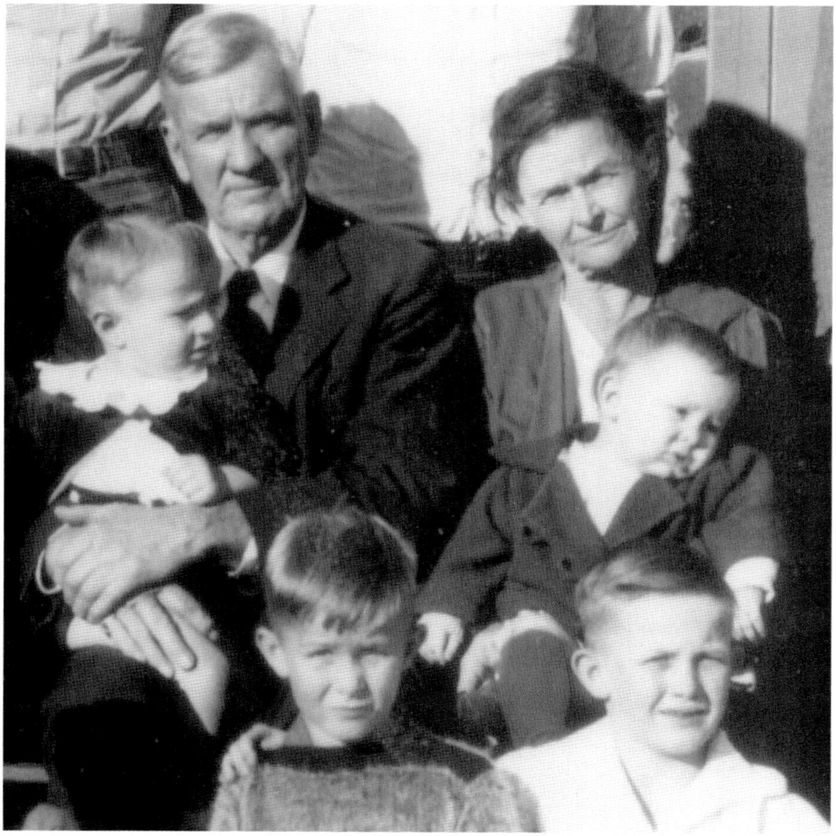

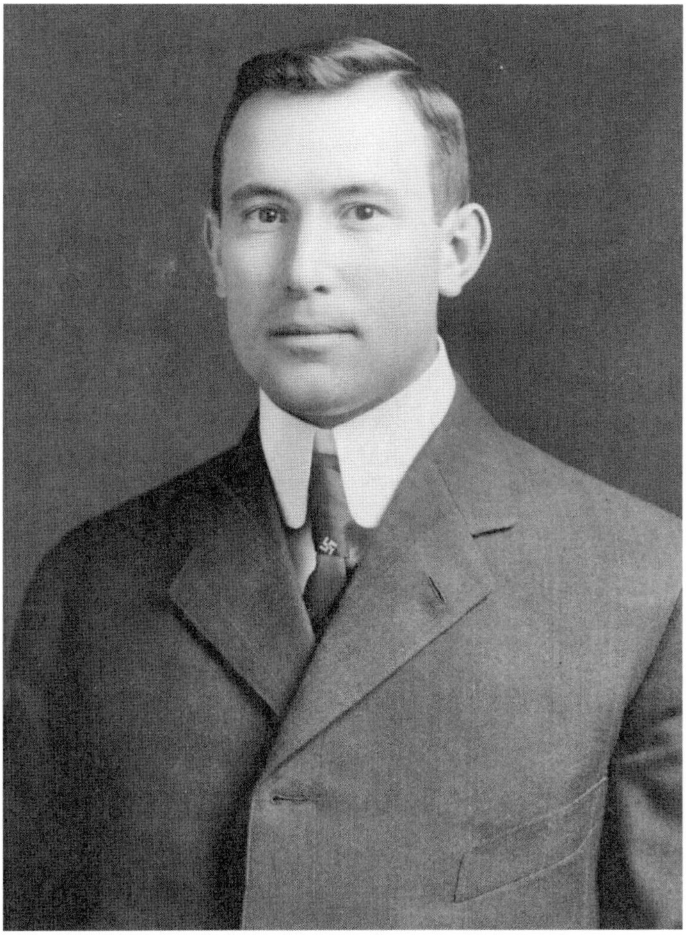

William Charbonneau

William Charbonneau gave land, time, and energy to Lake Worth's development. His parents, Alexis and Octavia Charbonneau were the first settlers in the area in 1878 and amassed so much land it encompassed much of the area now known as the city of Lake Worth. Shortly after the turn of the century, William Charbonneau operated the family farm and ranch. He married Loree Rogers. He raised and sold Percheron horses, which are workhorses much like Clydesdales. Large horseshoes, discovered in the 1970s under the original Lake Worth Methodist Church built on land that Charbonneau donated, gave evidence of Charbonneau's involvement with Percheron horses.

In 1911, he donated land for construction of the lake and more families moved into the area. A community developed near the lake and in the 1930s, and the local school building became too small for growing enrollment. Charbonneau donated land for a new school and soon became a school board member. Loree Charbonneau taught at the school, but that did not give them property privileges. In 1949, the board made a motion to request that Charbonneau keep his cattle off school property.

School enrollment continued to grow, and the city built another building in the early 1940s. By the early 1950s, with yet more growth, the school board voted to purchase additional acreage from Charbonneau. By September, construction began on the high school building that operated from 1953 to 1981. Up until the 1950s, Lake Worth school baseball players played on a field on the west side of the lake, two miles from the school. Charbonneau not only gave land for school property, but he helped build the field. He continued involvement in the community until his death in 1965. Names of a street and park in Lake Worth honor the family's name. (Courtesy Ben Mauldin.)

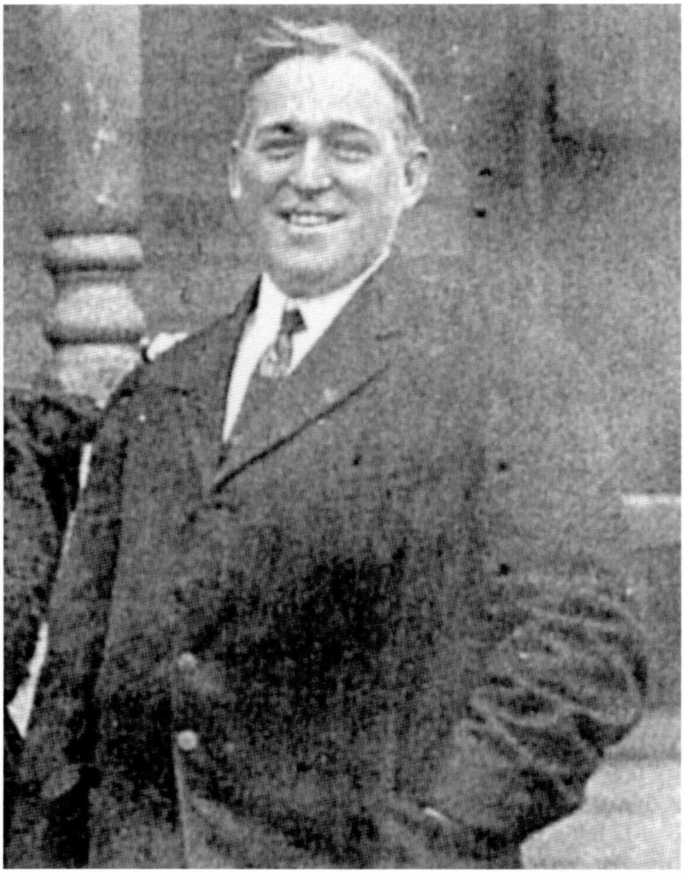

J.R. Foster

J.R. Foster, a prosperous local businessman, helped others to prosper. Born in Granbury in 1881, he had to quit school in the eighth grade to help support his family when his father died.

In 1902, Foster married Tessie Ella Bird. In 1922, Foster moved his family to the area now known as Lake Worth and opened a grocery store. He added an icehouse and delivered ice to customers' homes.

During 1930, Jacksboro Highway opened and Foster built a rock store to accommodate the traffic flow. It became a local landmark for more than 50 years. To compete with friendly business rival James Hodgkins, Foster added a gas station with four pumps, an icehouse, a feed store, a bait shop, a bait tank, a wood yard, and a water supply company. Known for letting customers buy on credit, he never shut off water service to late-paying customers.

By 1935, Foster's business prospered enough that he built a seven-room home of native sandstone and petrified wood, which now serves as the Lake Worth Museum. Foster later served as a school board member. When the school lacked funds for football field lights, Foster donated $5,000 for the lights. To honor him because of this generous donation, the school named the stadium after him. Foster did take time off from the community activities for deer hunting trips to the Davis Mountains.

He and his family attended Church of Christ services in Lake Worth. Eventually, the Church of Christ congregation outgrew an old store where they held services and Foster financed a new church building. Also, as chief air raid warden, Foster served in World War II.

A favorite hobby of Foster included racing his greyhounds throughout Texas. This hobby led him to build a greyhound track behind his store and sponsor his own races. He sold his store in 1945 and died a year later. His legacy lives on, even though the old rock building that housed his store no longer stands. Foster Drive, a street in Lake Worth, honors his name. (Courtesy David Woodall.)

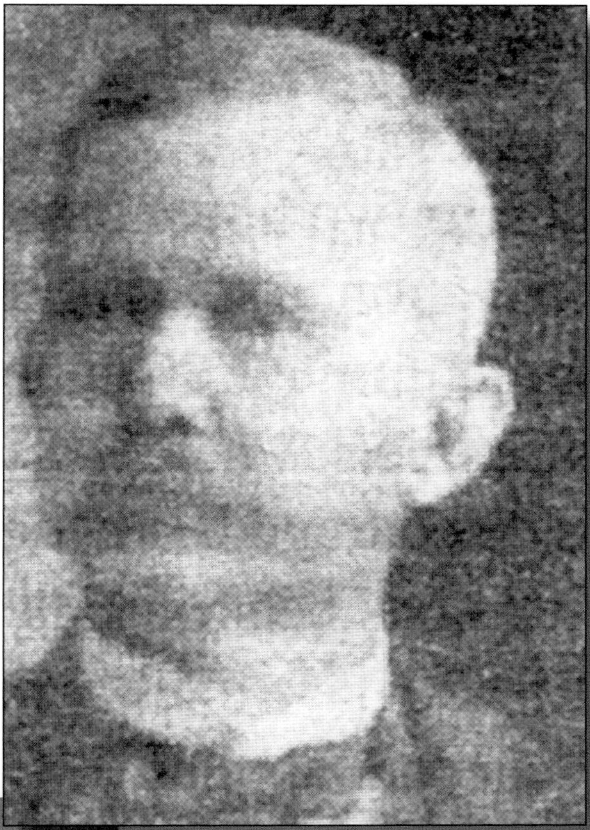

George and Lucinda Reynolds
George Reynolds married Lucinda "Bettie" Matthews in 1867. The couple bought, drove, and sold cattle all over Texas, New Mexico, and Colorado. By 1901, the Reynolds owned almost half a million acres of land throughout Texas. Reynolds relocated his cattle company to Fort Worth that year. He raised cattle for the company on the southern acreage of present-day Lake Worth.

In 1919, the Fort Worth Masons bought land from Reynolds to build a mosque. In 1923, Reynolds sold over 600 acres to Fort Worth businessman Amon Carter to create the legendary Shady Oaks Farm.

Lucinda Reynolds sold additional acreage in 1925 for development of Indian Oaks, Lake Worth's first neighborhood. Interestingly, she chose Indian names for the streets.

Reynolds Park—located on land they once owned—honors their memory. (Courtesy Archives Lake Worth Museum.)

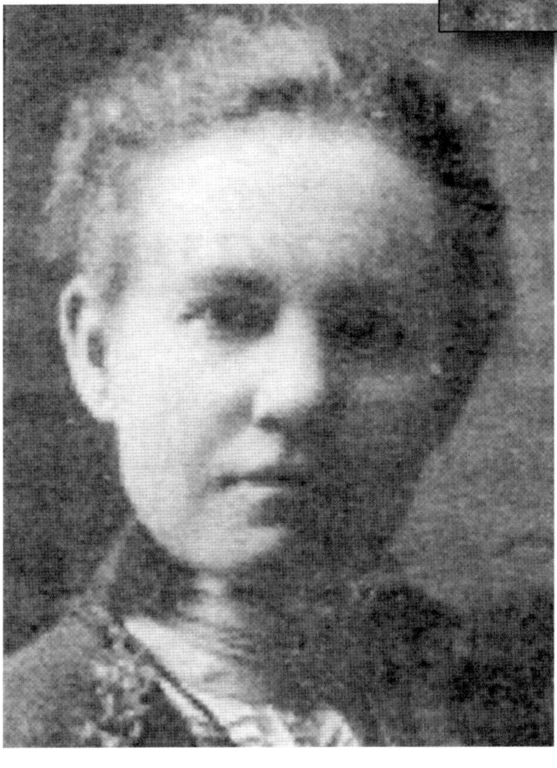

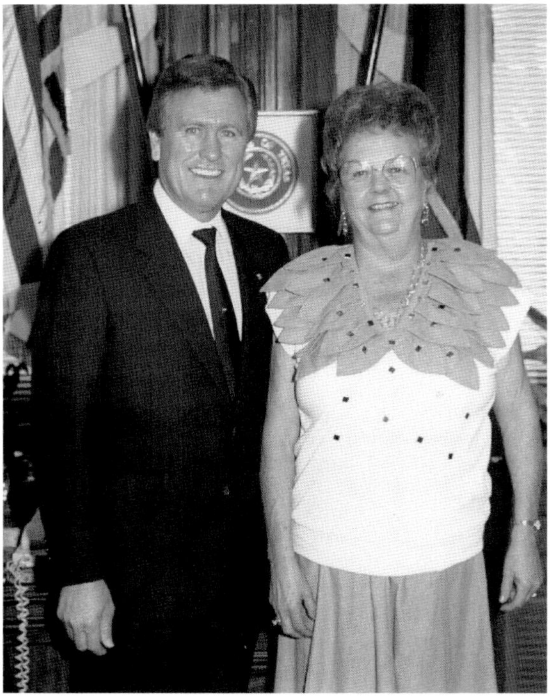

Myrtle Belle Fowlkes

Myrtle Belle "Myrt" Fowlkes worked as office manager for the City of Lake Worth in the 1950s, an era when well-known gangsters and gamblers ran amuck. She described it as very exciting, but scary times. She and her first husband, Neal Laverty, became active in the volunteer fire department where she helped start the Women's Auxiliary to the Fire Department. She worked as dispatcher for both the fire and police departments.

Fowlkes later married Jerry Sanders and moved away for a few years. After returning to Lake Worth in 1974, she became a member of the Kiwanis Club and helped establish the Christmas Express Program, which provides clothing, food, and toys for disadvantaged families. Elected to the school board after Sanders passed away in 1983, she remained on the board for nine years until 1998. Then she married Earl Fowlkes, an old boyfriend from age 12. After their marriage, she moved away for a while and then returned to Texas.

In 2003, Fowlkes was elected to the city council and served until 2013. While serving, she cycled on and off on the Economic Development Corporation as a very effective member. She also completed training for the Civilian Police Academy. This civic-minded resident, along with her husband, Earl, belonged to the Lions Club. Later, they both were appointed to the steering committee and helped establish the Lake Worth Area Historical Society. She served as president the second year and held that office for four years. Her tenacity proved a major force in getting the Lake Worth Museum established and opened.

Additionally, she served on the Bingo Committee in Austin, Texas, working to straighten out some difficulties they encountered. She is pictured above with Gib Lewis, who was Texas speaker of the house when this photograph was taken.

She always had a twinkle in her eyes for the city she moved to on January 1, 1940. Her stepfather Buddy Wyman, a respected Boy Scout leader in Lake Worth, set a fine example for her to follow in getting involved with the community, which she did so well. Fowlkes attended Lake Worth Methodist Church and Lake Worth's school, graduating in 1945. The dedication and love she poured into the community of Lake Worth will always be a huge part of the history of this small town where respect and love honor her name. (Courtesy Earl Fowlkes.)

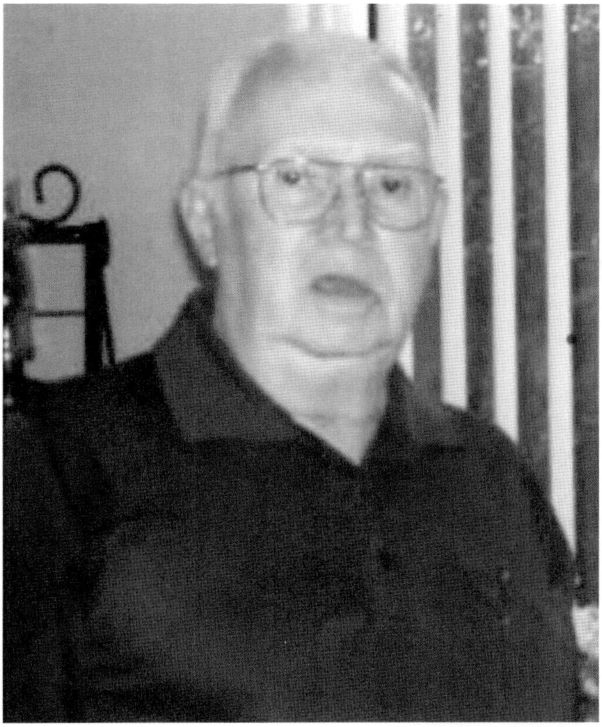

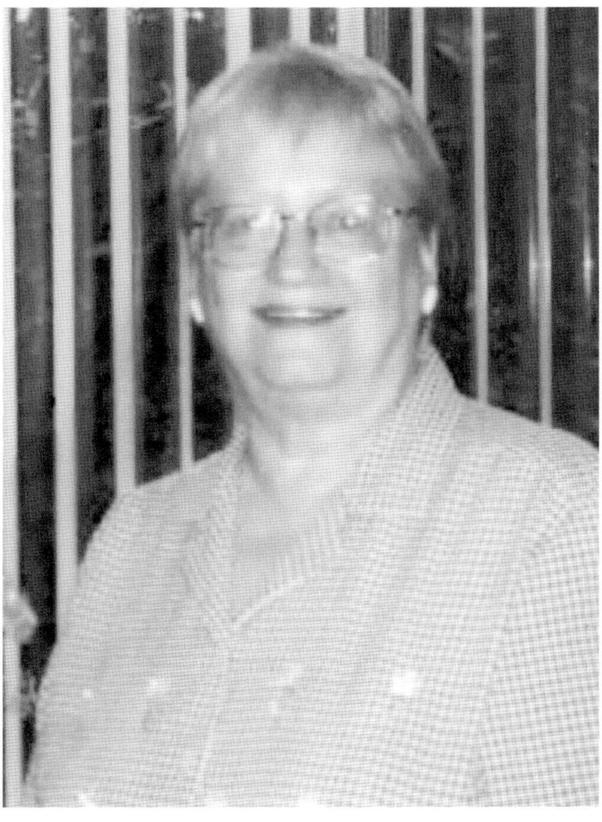

Curtis and Lee McKay
Curtis McKay served on the Lake Worth Volunteer Fire Department for 32 years. For 18 of those years, he led it as fire chief. He served on the city council from 1972 until 1982, and the community reelected him in 1984. He and his wife, Lee, stayed involved in activities at Lake Worth schools where their three children—Michele, Mike, and Mark—attended. Curtis McKay served as president of the Lake Worth Booster Club for one year.

Lee McKay served in the Ladies Auxiliary to the Fire Department. She teaches piano lessons to many of the area residents. She and her husband volunteered labor and donated items to the Lake Worth Area Historical Society and the Lake Worth Museum.

The couple has lived in Lake Worth for over 50 years, and the residents appreciate all they do. (Both photographs courtesy Lee McKay.)

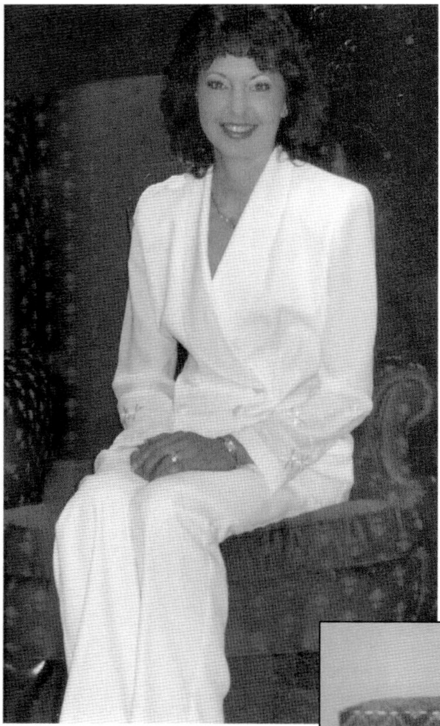

Dona Stuard

Dona Stuard played basketball and enjoyed being a member of the Flag Corps while in school in Lake Worth. At age 10, hit by a car, she spent the entire summer in a body cast recovering from a broken femur.

In 1985, she married James Henson and had a daughter named Samantha. In 1995, she married Gary Stuard, and they raised their combined families in Lake Worth. Stuard volunteered with the Lake Worth Band Patrons, serving as president for several years. She and family members ran the concession stand during football season. In addition, she served on the parks board, city council, economic development committee, and other committees.

Stuard uncovered much history about Lake Worth, which provided the Lake Worth Area Historical Society and the Lake Worth Museum with valued information. The second image exposes her humorous side. (Both photographs courtesy Dona Stuard.)

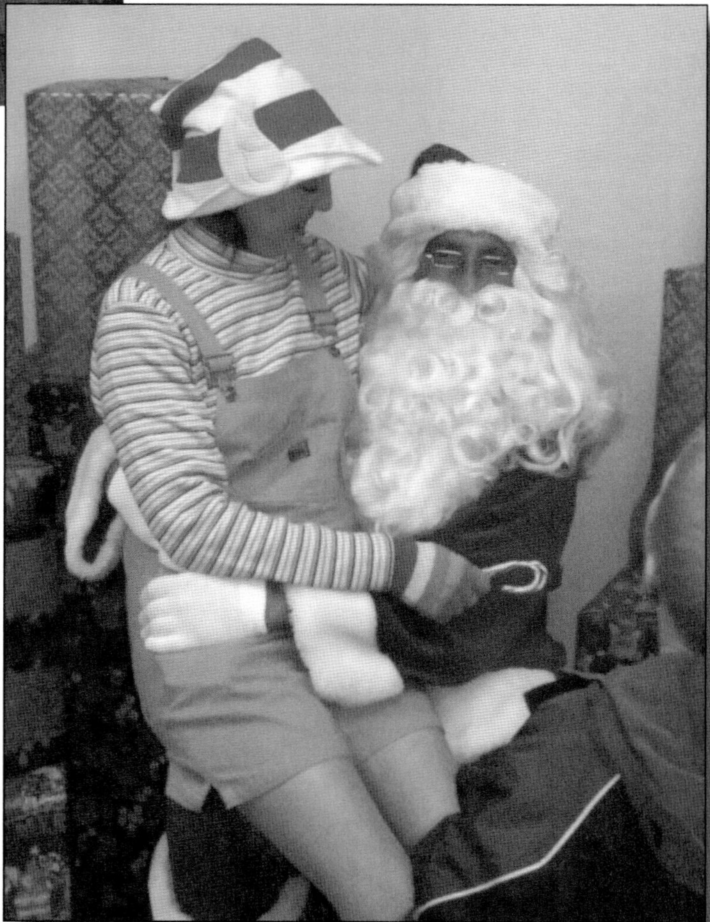

J.T. and Opal Hinkle

J.T. Hinkle and his wife, Opal, lived in Lake Worth for many years. She loved working in her yard and attending church with her husband, who had great compassion for people in need. He served in the Army for two years in the 1940s and later attained perfect attendance for 40 years in the River Oaks Lions Club. He held all club offices at different times, from director in 1956–1957 to chairman of the constitution and bylaws committee in 1987–1988. In 1971–1972, Hinkle was elected as district governor, the first year Texas had a lieutenant governor position.

In 1955–1956, he served as chairman and producer of the *Stars of Tomorrow Show.* This soon turned into a district project. Many contestants went on to become stars, such as Betty Buckley, a talented singer and actress. Hinkle received numerous awards while in the Lions Club, including four extension awards: Charter President of Lions Band, Chartering Blue Mound Lions Club, Chartering Mansfield Lions Club, and Chartering Cowtown Lions Club. Hinkle also attended many of the Lake Worth Lions Club meetings. In addition, he became involved in finding hospital beds for Greece. In the 1950s, he became project manager for a sports car racing event connected to the River Oaks Lions Club to raise money to give to the Young Men's Christian Association. He directed Crippled Children's Camp in the early 1970s.

Further youth involvement extended to Belize, where he arranged for three youths to come to America for eye surgery. He helped raise over $300,000 for medical supplies shipped to Belize to start the Eye, Ear, and Throat Clinic. Other achievements attributed to Hinkle's connection to the Lions Club are not included due to their vast number.

Hinkle served as secretary of Northwest YMCA and on the board of directors from 1956 to 1960. He founded the Lake Worth Animal Fair in 1983 and served as councilman for Lake Worth from 1983 to 1985. He received appointment by the speaker of the House of Representatives to serve on the Texas Council of Disabilities from 1989 to 1991. In 1991, elected as mayor of Lake Worth, he later served 20 years on the Board and Planning Committee. The Texas Lions Club honored Hinkle by inducting him into the hall of fame in 1992. Hinkle served as a deacon in his church from 1981 to 1986. He passed away in 1996. The community misses him greatly. (Courtesy Opal Hinkle.)

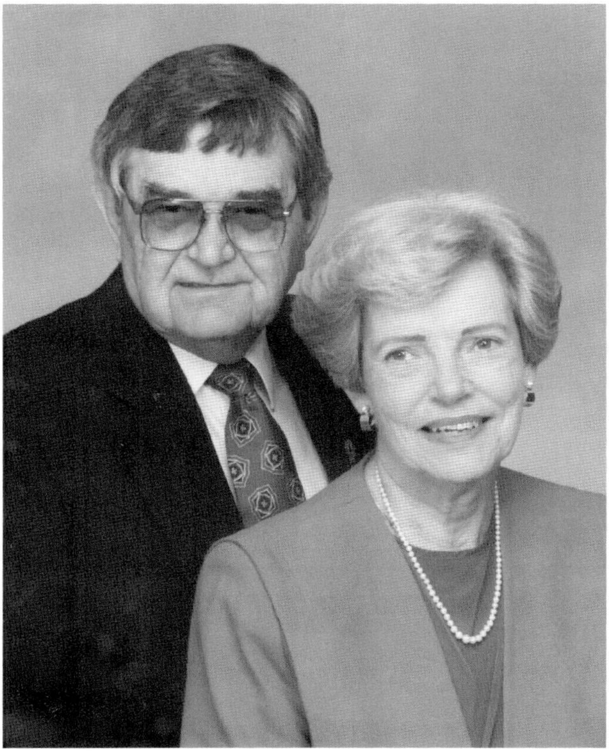

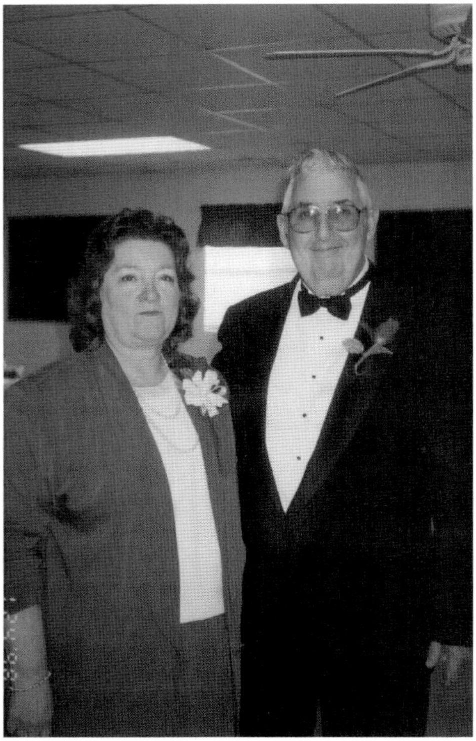

Virginia Ross

Virginia Ross became president of the Jaycees' Wives' Club in mid-1960s. She and her husband, Gary, both served on a number of boards and committees for The Lake Worth United Methodist Church.

In 1985 through 1987, she served as the executive director of Northwest Chamber of Commerce. She assisted in several events to promote growth in the city. Ross currently serves on the board of directors for Lake Worth Area Historical Society, and she works as an employee of Lake Worth's Mary Lou Reddick Library. (Courtesy Virginia Ross.)

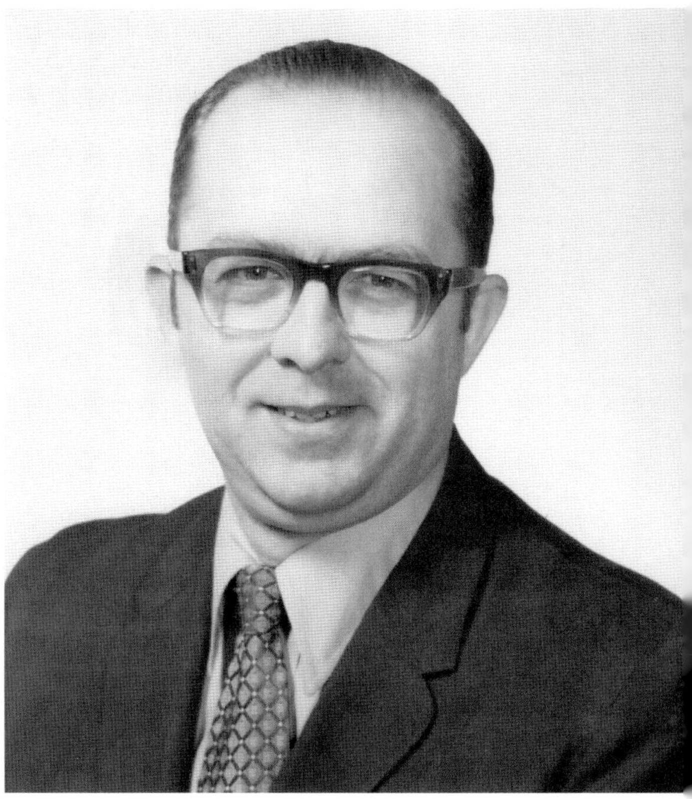

Gary Goodman

Gary Goodman moved to Lake Worth in 1941. He served as deacon for First Baptist Church of Lake Worth for 55 years. That statistic definitely qualifies him as a legendary local; however, his contributions extend well beyond that distinction. A registered professional engineer, Goodman held the position as chairman on the city's planning and zoning committee for 24 years. He also served on the Lake Worth School Board, 1960–1961. Additionally, his service included being president of the Economic Development Board. In 1996, his many hours of dedicated service earned him the Volunteer of the Year Award. (Courtesy Gary Goodman.)

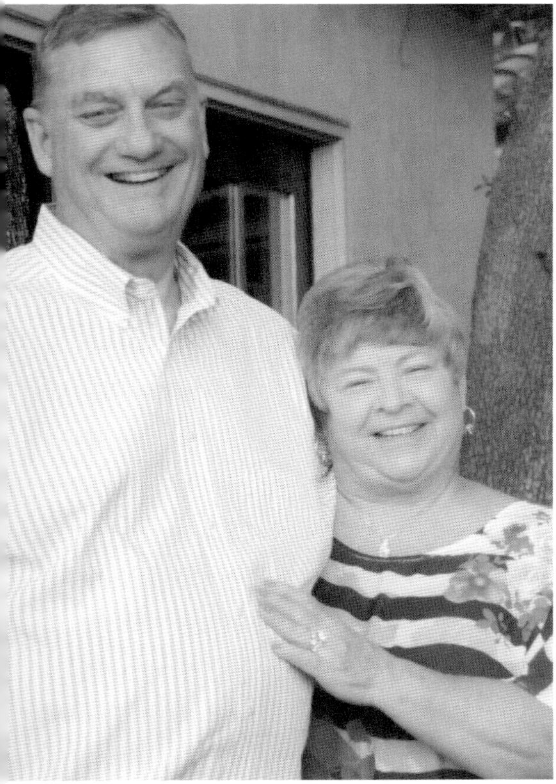

James and Diane Smith

James "Jim" Smith served six years on the Lake Worth School Board and became an active member of the Athletic Booster Club. He attended the Lake Worth Citizens' Police Academy and now participates in Lake Worth Citizens Response Team. Prior to his election to the city council, he served on the planning and zoning committee and became president for the 2013–2014 year. He also teaches school in the Eagle Mountain–Saginaw Independent School District. In addition, Smith had a distinguished military career.

Diane Smith, a registered nurse and once active in the Athletic Boosters Club, serves with her husband, James, on the Lake Worth Regional Coordinating Committee for the city of Fort Worth. The Smiths' collective involvement in military, civic, and educational endeavors resulted in special advantages for many. (Courtesy Smith Family.)

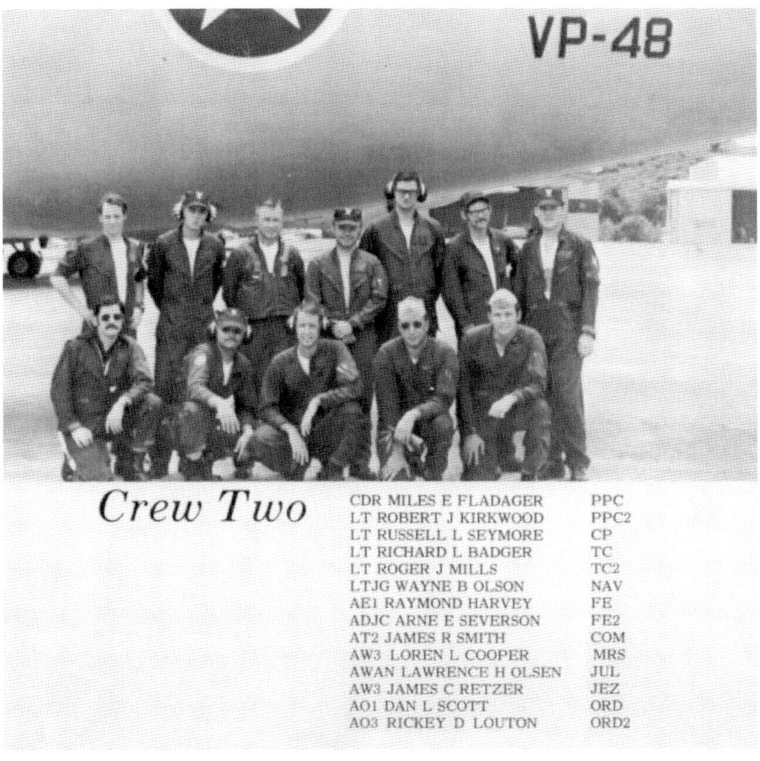

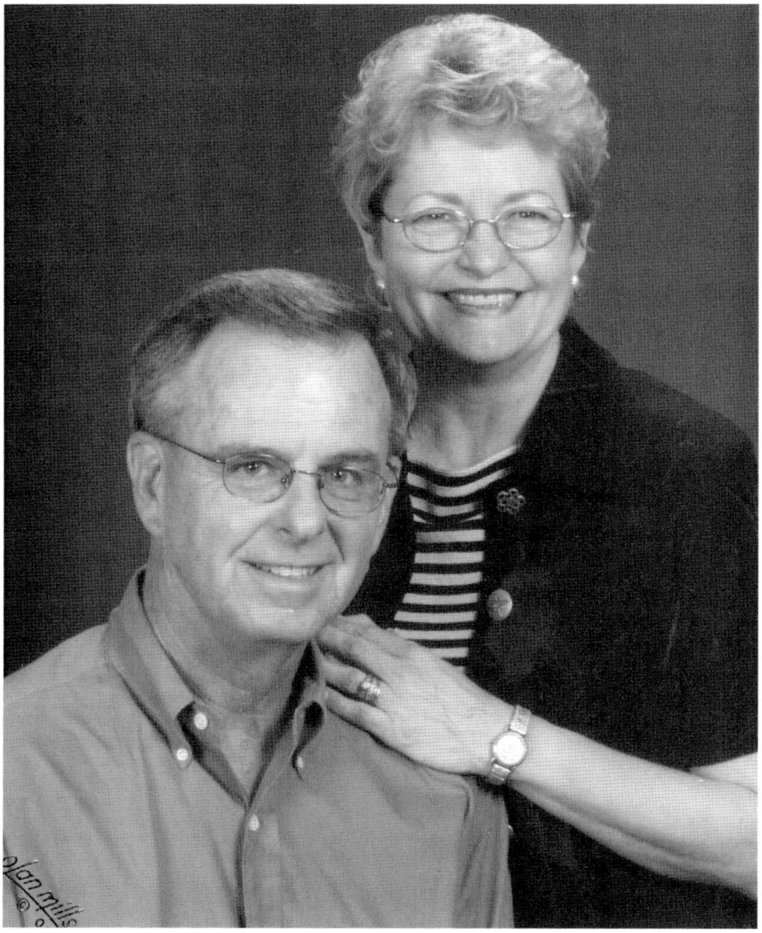

Pat and Walter Bowen

Pat Bowen has used her time, energy, and monetary means to support Lake Worth schools and the Ladies Auxiliary to the Fire Department. She served as an officer in both organizations. In addition, she served on the school board for two and half years, 1985–1987. She and her husband, Walter Bowen, shared their home with European foreign exchange students for the years 1987–1990. Two of the students graduated from Lake Worth High School, whereas the other younger student did not graduate from there.

They have three children of their own named Coy, Guy, and Misty. They also have six grandchildren. Pat Bowen currently shares an e-mail prayer ministry with her husband and considers herself a prayer warrior. In addition, she provides food for funerals and other occasions when needed. Her sincerity and enthusiasm for life is outstanding with her home often being the place for friends to gather.

Walter Bowen has a long history of civic involvement in Lake Worth. In 1970, as captain of the Volunteer Fire Department, he received the Fireman of the Year award along with Bill Schibler of White Settlement. Bowen has served on the Lake Worth City Council 40 years and once had a partnership in Sappington Printing Company. He received an associate of fire technology degree from Tarrant County Junior College in 1976 and took employment in the Denton Fire Department as a driver. Before becoming mayor of Lake Worth, Bowen served as mayor pro tem. He has been mayor since 1994. After retiring from Bell Helicopter in 2010, Bowen has stayed busy as an active church member and tending to his mayoral duties. He has lived in Lake Worth since the age of eight. Bowen, a huge patriotic supporter of the United States of America, often wears red, white, and blue. His warm personality endears him to many. (Courtesy Pat and Walter Bowen.)

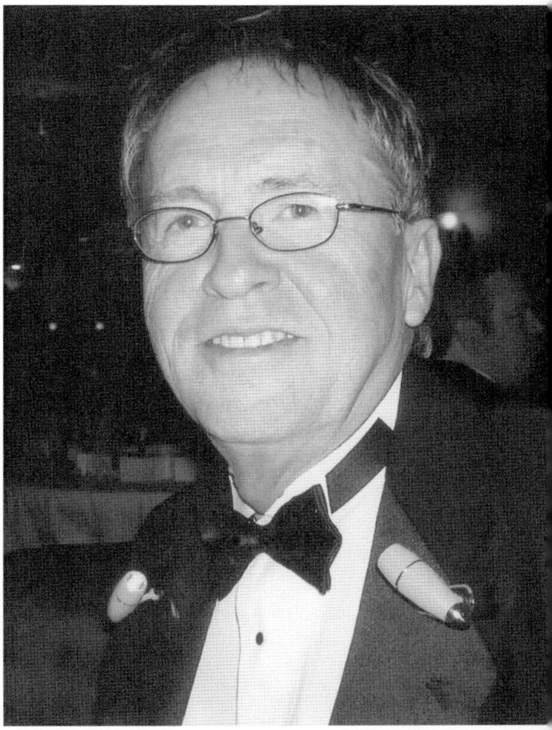

Larry Joe Thompson

After college graduation in 1968, Larry Thompson joined Vista Volunteers helping the underprivileged in Susanville and soon became a Vista administrator. After a few years, he transitioned to being a hospital administrator in Susanville, where he met his wife, Judi. An administrator in several hospitals throughout the United States for nearly 40 years, Thompson left that business and took the Northwest Chamber of Commerce director's position. He successfully directed the chamber from 2005 to 2010.

He loved people and enjoyed acting. Thompson died in 2010 from injuries incurred in a car accident caused by an intoxicated driver. His wife, a nurse, died of cancer a few years later. Family and friends miss them greatly. Thompson's photograph appears in the first image. Pictured below from left to right are Larry Thompson; his wife, Judi; his daughter Jennifer; and his son Jonathan. (Courtesy Thompson family.)

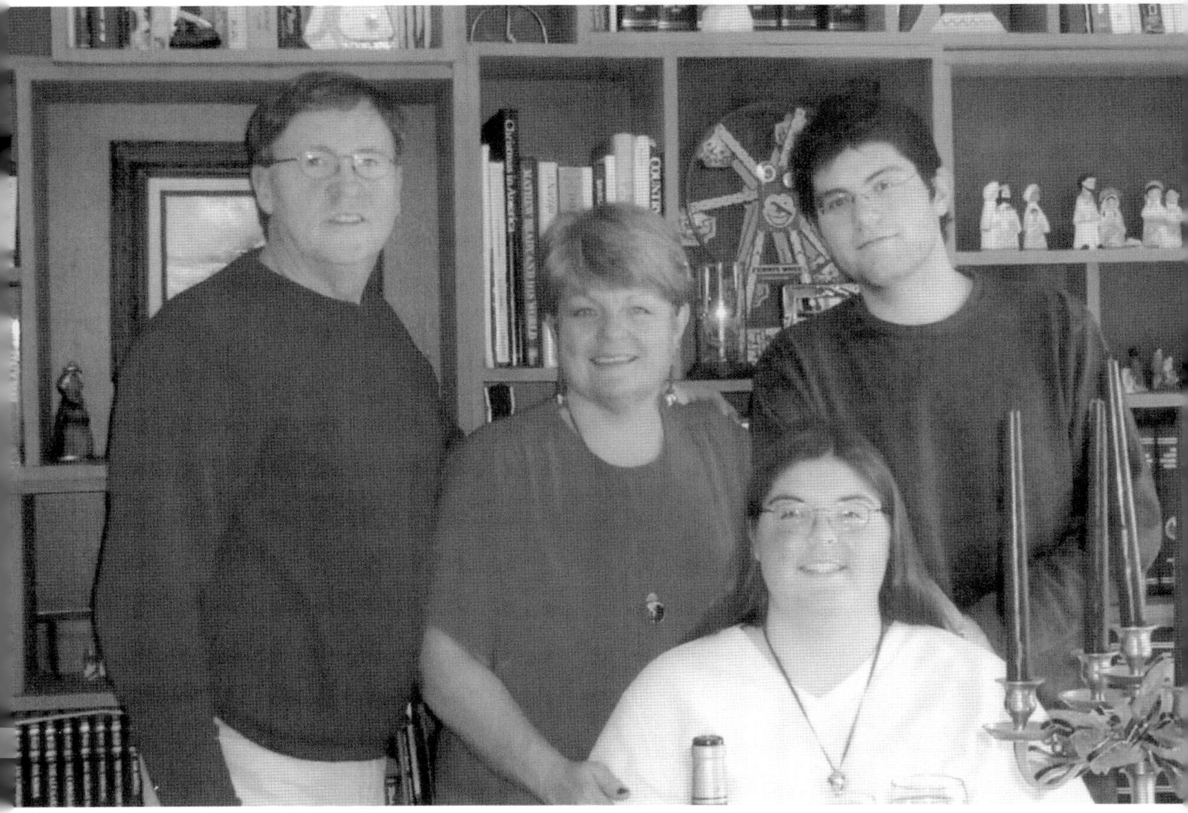

Al and Judy Jameson

Al Jameson and his wife, Judy, greatly impacted the city of Lake Worth. In the mid-1950s, they purchased the old Foster house, now the Lake Worth Museum. They purchased the home from William Charbonneau who owned much property in the area. After remodeling, it became the Jamesons' home. It originally had been built by J.R. Foster who also owned an icehouse, store, and gasoline station.

After Charbonneau's death, The Fort Worth National Bank Trust Department had charge of saving all his properties until they reached maximum worth. As that time appeared, the Jamesons bought small buildings from the Trust Department. He rented the buildings to various tenants, such as a shop teacher who started Mama's Pizza. Also, the Jamesons opened a flooring company in the 1960s in one of the buildings.

Jameson served on several important committees including one to locate land to build a church. He found success in dealing with Ethan Allen of the Fort Worth National Bank who controlled the land, and the merger of three churches became Northwest Church of Christ. He later became president of the Park Board. Also elected as president of the school board at a time when the district had great financial difficulty, Jameson and others successfully got things under control.

The old Lake Worth Skating Rink, purchased by the Jamesons, became the home of their expanded flooring business. Even though they had success with this business, they closed it, and Judy Jameson developed The Lake Worth Bizarre. This prosperous antique mall operated until the expansion of Highway 199 condemned the property and bought it out.

Having compassion for others likely led Jameson into getting two degrees in counseling. He worked in a hospital chain, worked in Saudi Arabia and other hospitals, as well as later having his own private practice. For the last seven years, he has traveled from Japan to Turkey serving as counselor for military members and their families returning from the war zones. At present, he has returned to private practice specializing in helping families with someone resisting needing assistance. The Jamesons now live in downtown Fort Worth in the historic Texas and Pacific Railroad Building. (Courtesy Al and Judy Jameson.)

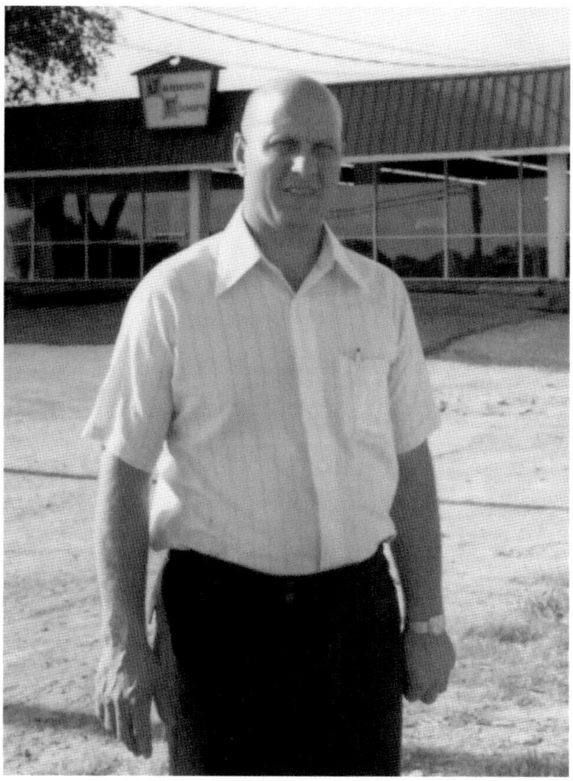

Gene Brooks

Eugene "Gene" Brooks's leadership abilities have served him well for many years and have taken him far and wide to other countries. He seized numerous opportunities in a variety of ventures including military-related endeavors. He became an experienced defense aerospace veteran with 34 years of leadership in exhibits, international air and trade shows, and marketing communications in various countries, including Australia and several other places.

In 1978, he joined General Dynamics as a logistics representative where he also did extensive traveling in other countries. While at General Dynamics, he additionally served as a Lake Worth reserve police officer for six years. Prior to working at General Dynamics, he served 10 years in the US Army.

Brooks probably holds one of the longest records of anyone who served on the Lake Worth City Council as his tenure spanned from 1990 to 2009. He felt one of his greatest accomplishments involved spearheading Resolution 500, which approved the widening of Highway 199 through Lake Worth, known also as the Jacksboro Highway. He also served on the Economic Development Committee, the Crime Control Committee, and as mayor pro tem.

As a member of Lakeside Baptist Church, Brooks enjoys serving as a greeter, usher, and member of the Missions Committee. He lives in Lake Worth with his wife of 35 years, Martha Worley Brooks. He enjoys golfing, fishing, motorcycle riding, and watching the Dallas Cowboys. (Courtesy Eugene Brooks.)

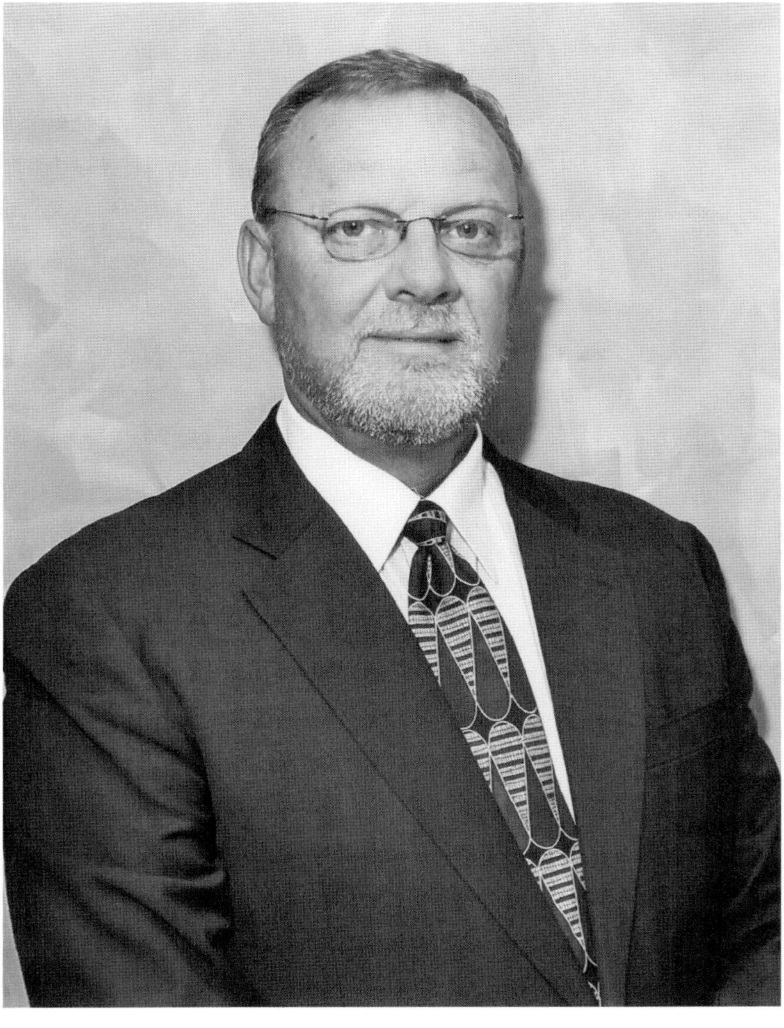

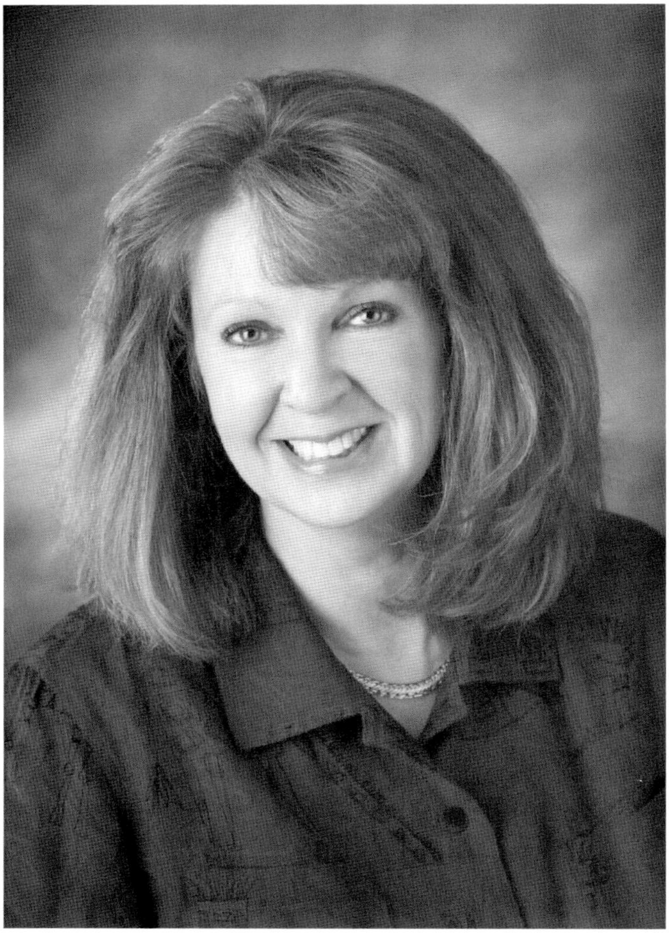

Linda Holland Nelson
Linda Holland Nelson managed the Economic Development Office with the City of Lake Worth from 2001 to 2006. During this time, Lake Worth had one of the fastest growing commercial areas for its size in Tarrant County with more than 750,000 square feet of new commercial development announced or completed. She worked closely with city staff, the area business community, and civic groups to promote economic growth in the city. Nelson received the 2002 Public Servant of the Year Award by Northwest Tarrant Chamber of Commerce, in part for her work with the Kids and Trees community project, spearheaded by the City of Lake Worth, along with the chamber and the Lake Worth Garden Club.

"My husband Steve and I visited Charbonneau Park recently, and the trees planted a decade ago by Effie Morris second graders and community volunteers have grown amazingly tall and strong," noted Nelson. "I've lived in a lot of places, but there's no place with as much heart as Lake Worth. I really miss the community spirit and the great friends that we made there."

Earlier in her career, Nelson managed the chairman's program for the US Chamber of Commerce, where she arranged media interviews, special events, and advanced logistics both in the United States and internationally. Although she has stayed busy with her career, Nelson has always enjoyed music.

While working on her master of arts degree in mass communications from the University of North Texas in Denton, she and a friend played guitar and sang her original songs at area clubs to help with tuition costs. Several years later, she won the top prize in the American Song Festival's open category amateur division for one of her compositions. She continues to write and enjoys photography, hiking, real estate investing, and gardening in her free time. (Courtesy Steve Nelson.)

CHAPTER TWO

Businesses

Developing a business takes foresight, energy, funds, and staying power. Many of the first businesses in and around Lake Worth developed because of the aforementioned necessities. For the most part, current day businesses appear in this chapter, and they too needed the same things as their ancestors to operate and maintain their chosen avenue for earning their living.

Some have inherited already operating businesses. Even so, without foresight and hindsight in many cases, the businesses still need energy, funds, and staying power. Although Lake Worth did not incorporate until the early 1950s, many businesses started much earlier. Chapter 1 highlighted a few of those. In this chapter, several businesses, such as Charlotte Wilson's Farmers Insurance, Brookshire's Pharmacy, and Russell's Feed Stores, will be discussed. Additional businesses include restaurants like Ginger Brown's Ole Tyme Restaurant and Bakery; the prominent realtor Billye Wright; her husband, Wayne; and their daughter Carol Wright Baskin.

Also, interesting information about businesses such as Estela's Hair Design and Garvin's Barber Shop presents a humorous side to some proprietors' personalities.

Information about a local business, Jack Burk's Irrigation and Landscape, exposes the spirit of a true innovator. Mary Sloss, owner of Lake Worth Florist, embraces past experiences to enhance the present-day setting just as Gunter Boat Sales does. Mark Gunter's father, Bill Gunter, paved the way for his son to learn a trade. The insurance profession, well represented in this chapter, includes longtime agent Mason Raine and his daughter April Taylor.

Another enterprising person, Frankie Robbins, prepared herself well for the position she now holds as head of an insurance agency. Her previous experience, from getting a college education to teaching school for a number of years, brought forward her dedication to whatever she chose to do.

Background information on the House of Blades' original owner, B.C. Adams, lends another dimension to the present-day ownership being Kenny Graff and his brother Chris. Their mother, Su Lee Adams, goes yearly to the Fort Worth Stock Show and sells their products. The importance of learning a trade early threads throughout the chapter with exception of one or two who learned their trade later in life.

Many businesses do not appear in this book, although several would have made a nice addition. Because of limited space and the necessity of obtaining information in a timely manner, some did not qualify. However, beyond the portrayals in this chapter, Lake Worth now has many restaurants, grocery stores, insurance agencies, shopping malls, and much more. Each offers a special service to the community.

Of the businesses not featured, some will in due time, become legendary if they have the staying power and other necessities to withstand the rigors of ownership. Many have done so in the past and one hopes many will continue in the future.

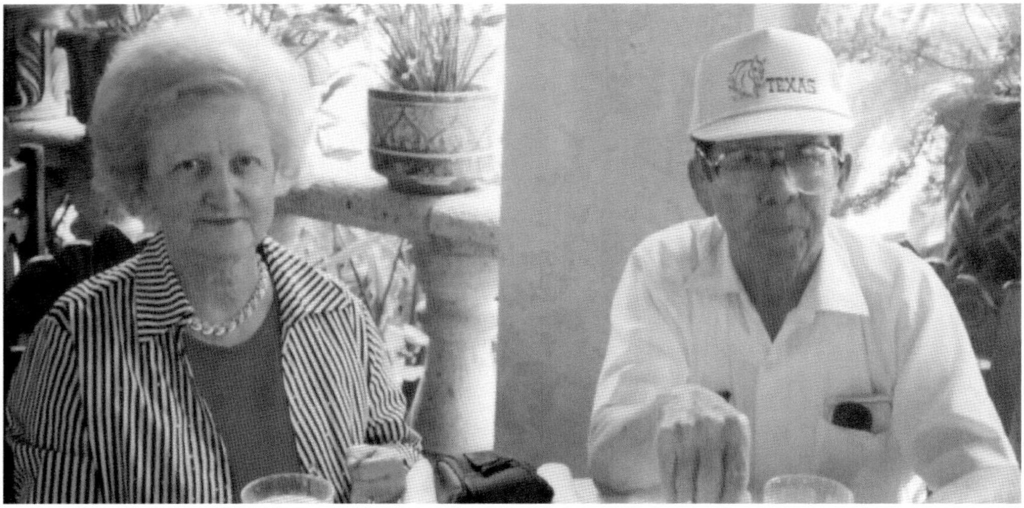

Charlotte Wilson

In 1968, Charlotte Wilson and her husband, Billy, joined Farmers Insurance Group. They started their agency from a home office. Later, they built a group of structures where they placed the agency. While Billy Wilson ventured into other businesses, sometimes with his wife's involvement, she has maintained the popular insurance office for over 40 years in the Lake Worth area.

Charlotte and Billy are pictured above at Joe T. Garcia's Restaurant in Fort Worth celebrating their daughter receiving her master's degree. Sometimes Wilson accompanies her husband to their farm in Comanche, Texas. The photograph below, taken at their farm, with grandchildren Ethan on back and Kacie in front, illustrates the trio's enjoyment riding on a four-wheeler. Wilson and her grandson Ethan are also on back cover. They enjoy the farm, but love living in Lake Worth. (Both photographs courtesy Charlotte Wilson.)

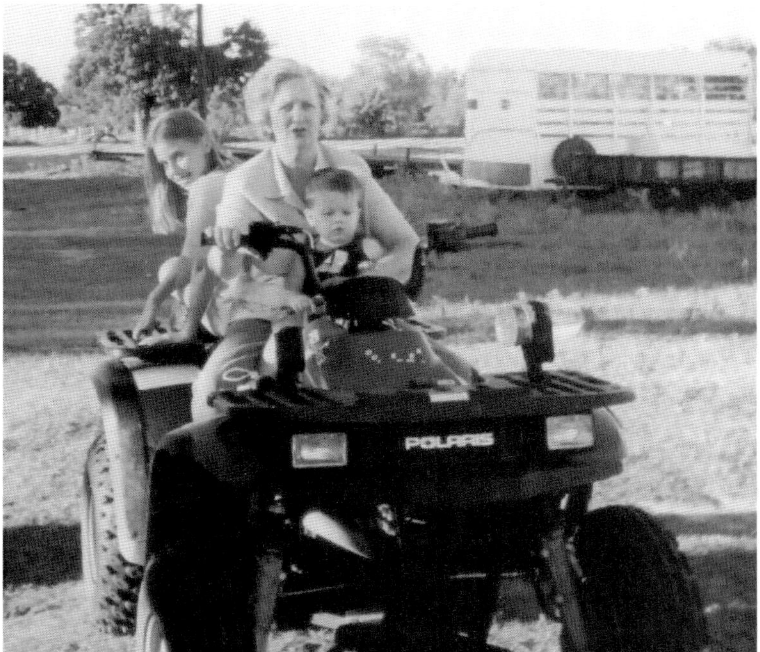

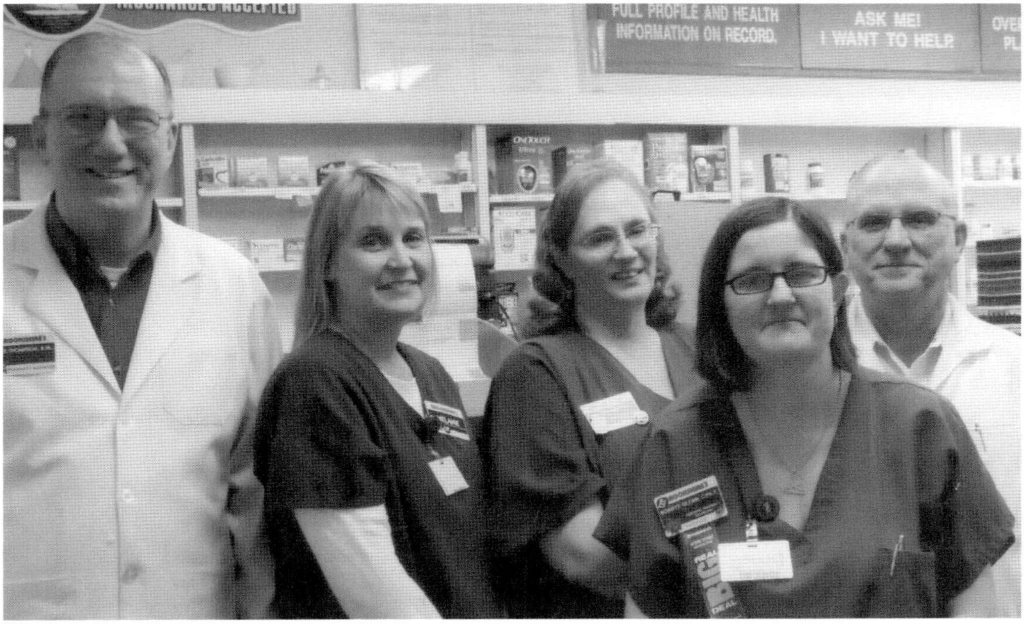

Bruce L. Thompson

Bruce L. Thompson, a registered pharmacist and native Fort Worthian, manages the Brookshire's Pharmacy No. 124 in Lake Worth, Texas. After receiving his pharmaceutical degree in 1973, he interned at Skillerns Drug in Arlington, Texas. He later accepted a full-time position with Town and Country Drug in the Wedgewood store. Further positions included the co-ownership of a new Town and Country location in Crowley, Texas, that combined sales of prescriptions drugs with hardware items. Thompson often traveled to purchase hardware items to add to the inventory at the new pharmacy. Unfortunately, he became ill after eating in a restaurant that left bread pudding out too long.

In 1997, Thompson accepted the management position of the pharmacy department at Winn-Dixie grocery store in Lake Worth. After a year, they purchased the business and prescription records from Lake Worth Pharmacy and added staffing, including Lesley Brown—also a registered pharmacist and native Texan helping with the management of the pharmacy. He attended college at Arlington State College and University of Austin where he began his pharmaceutical career in 1967. Brown served in the US Army Reserve from 1968 until 1974 and joined Brookshire's in 1998. He says that Lake Worth is his best job so far.

As certified pharmacy technicians, Melanie Lambert, Denise Gallagher (who moved to Lake Worth in 1982), and Bobby Glenn treat customers in a professional and friendly manner. In 2001, Brookshire's Grocery stores purchased many of Winn Dixie Grocery stores including the Lake Worth store, which was highly successful with the community. The pharmacy offers a number of special services, such as administering an assortment of vaccines. Brookshire's has a long-standing tradition of supporting history and heritage of each community that it serves, as is evidenced by the murals of early founders and the historical background of the area. The store décor also identifies the areas of the store with names like Pharmacy Point and Mainsail Market with a large variety of food offered.

Pictured from left to right are Bruce Thompson, Melanie Lambert, Denise Gallagher, Bobbye Glenn, and Lesley Brown. (Courtesy pharmacy staff.)

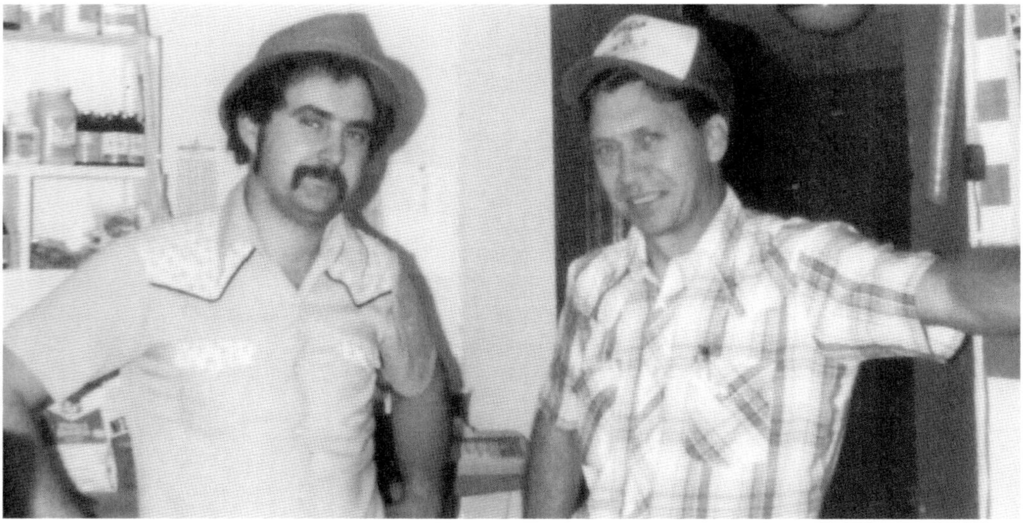

Kenny Russell

Kenny Russell started working with feed store products while in high school. Through the influence of agriculture teacher Gary Smith, Kenny took a job at Ruthardt's Feed, owned by Pete and Connie Ruthardt.

In 1997, the Ruthardts decided to retire. Russell took this opportunity to purchase the Sansom Park store, the Benbrook store, and the Camp Bowie West store. He added four other stores and two distribution warehouses, which made Russell Feed and Supply one of the largest independent feed operations in Texas.

The Sansom Park store, located close to the city limits of Lake Worth, serves many areas. People depend on Kenny Russell's Stores to give sound advice on feeding animals and how to get rid of pesky critters. For convenience, Russell built his corporate office a few doors down from the store. (Both photographs courtesy Kenny Russell.)

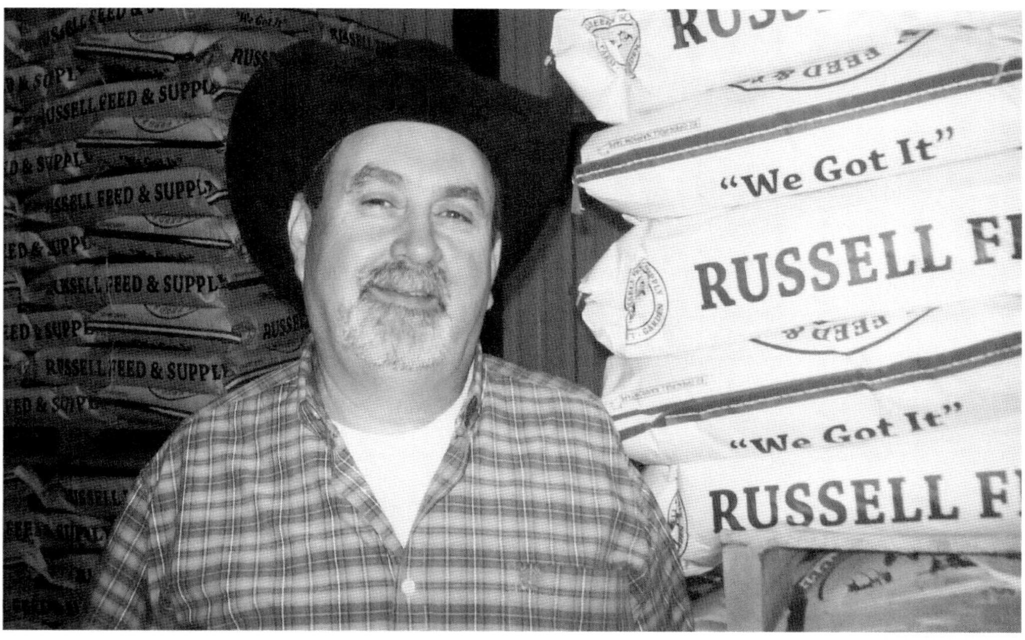

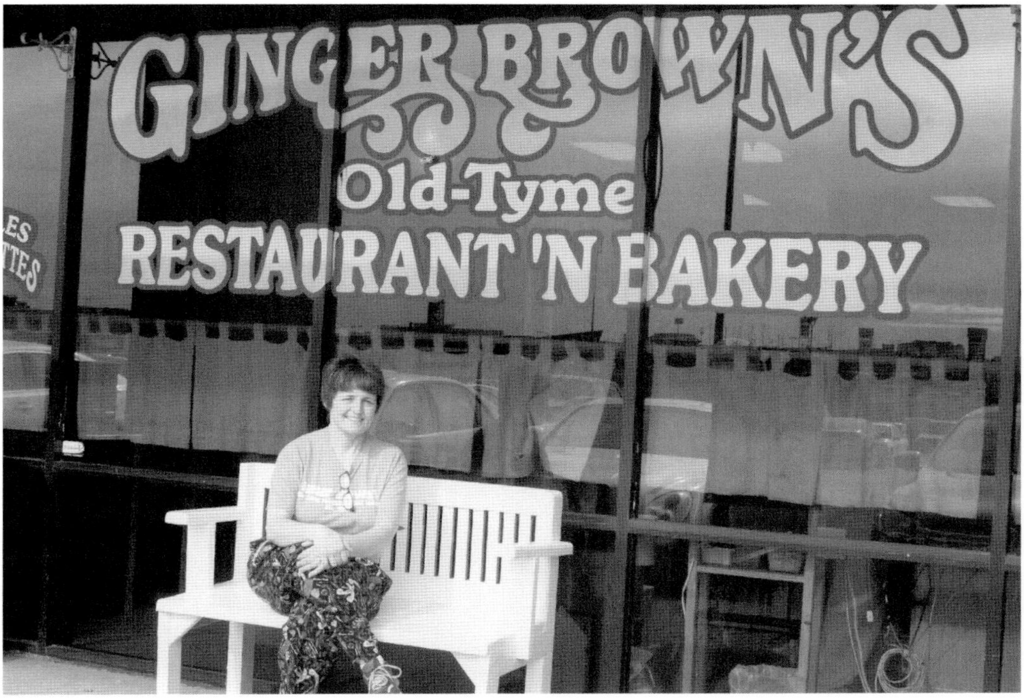

Ginger Brown
At age 20, Ginger Brown opened her restaurant in Lake Worth in 1985. She named it Ginger Brown's Old Tyme Restaurant and Bakery. On her menu, items like Smoky Mountain Chicken make one's mouth water. Some recipes became family treasures. With a variety of tasty entrees and desserts, her delicious cinnamon rolls that are served with every meal attract many customers. She has donated the rolls every other week for 10 years to the USO, often using her Cinnamon Roll Bus, featured here.

Brown recalls working in her father's restaurant as a girl of 10 or 12. This experience has served her well, but she says the best things that ever happened to her include the birth of her daughter and knowing the Lord. She has been in business 29 years and still maintains a large volume of customers. (Both photographs by Ken Brower.)

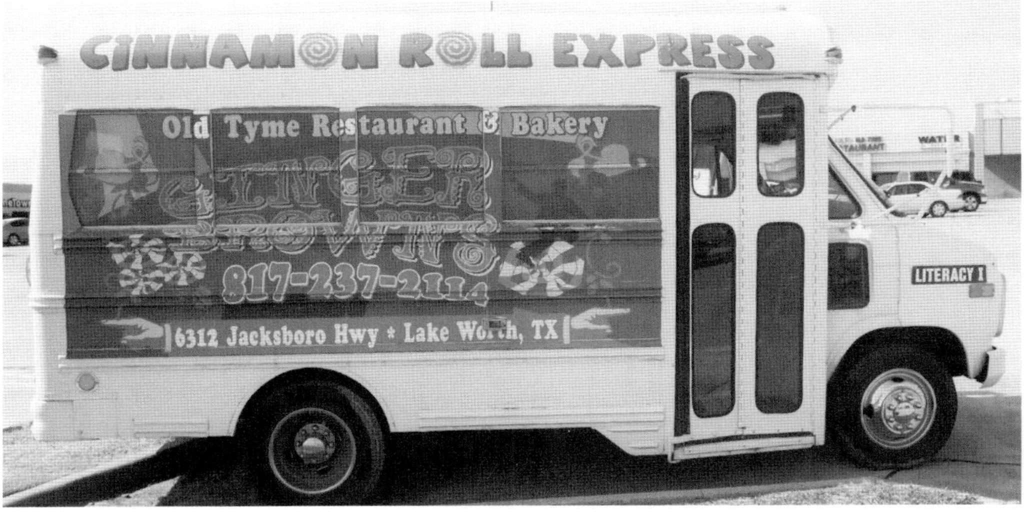

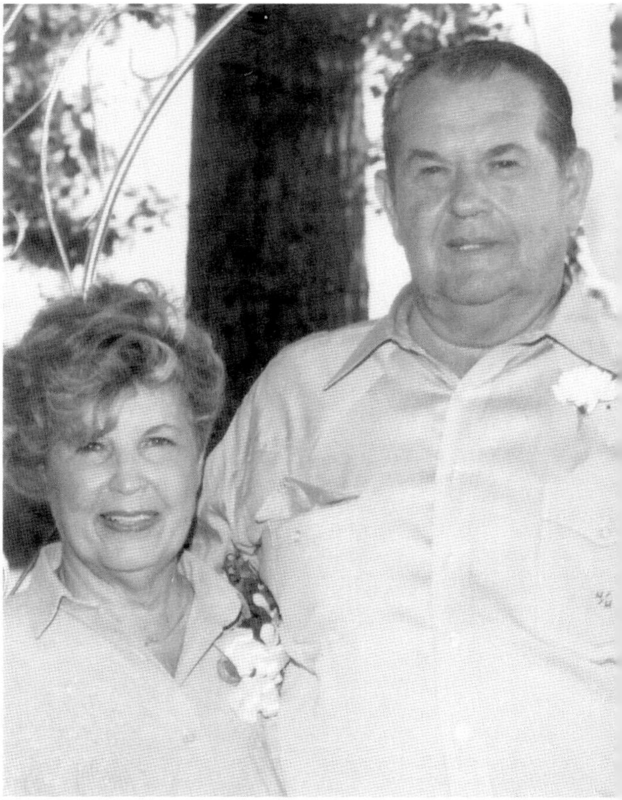

Billye Sue and Wayne Wright
Billye Sue and Wayne Wright married in West Texas in 1944. The day they married, the groom had only $17 in his pocket. After the couple exchanged vows, the bride took the money and spent it on a sweater and perfume. Even so, the marriage survived, and they lived in several places among the West Texas oil fields before settling in Lake Worth in 1956. She opened one of the first real estate offices in the area. He built homes. He died in 1998, and she died in 2012. (Courtesy Carol Wright Baskin.)

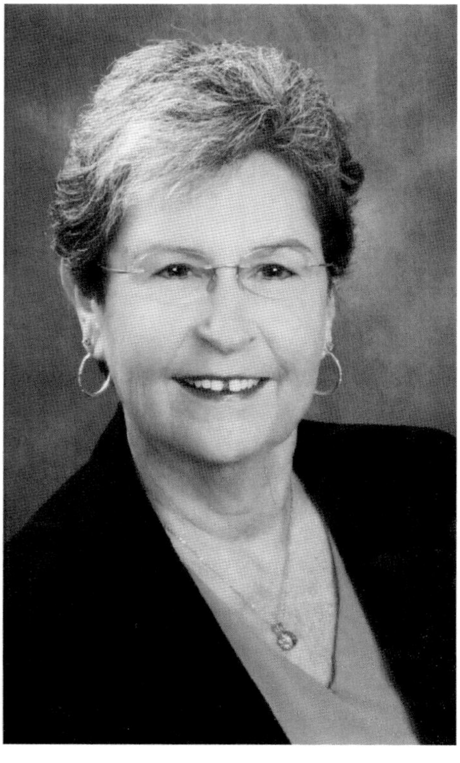

Carol Wright Baskin
Carol Wright Baskin graduated from Lake Worth High School in 1963. She participated in school as a cheerleader and became homecoming queen her senior year. She earned her real estate license in 1973 and worked as a realtor with her mother, Billye Wright, until Wright's retirement. In 1995, Baskin began selling real estate for Pierce Properties. For the past 10 years, she has been a partner in this company. As a member of the Northwest Chamber of Commerce, the Lake Worth Area Historical Society, and the Lake Worth Boat and Ski Club, Baskin stays involved in the community. (Courtesy Carol Wright Baskin.)

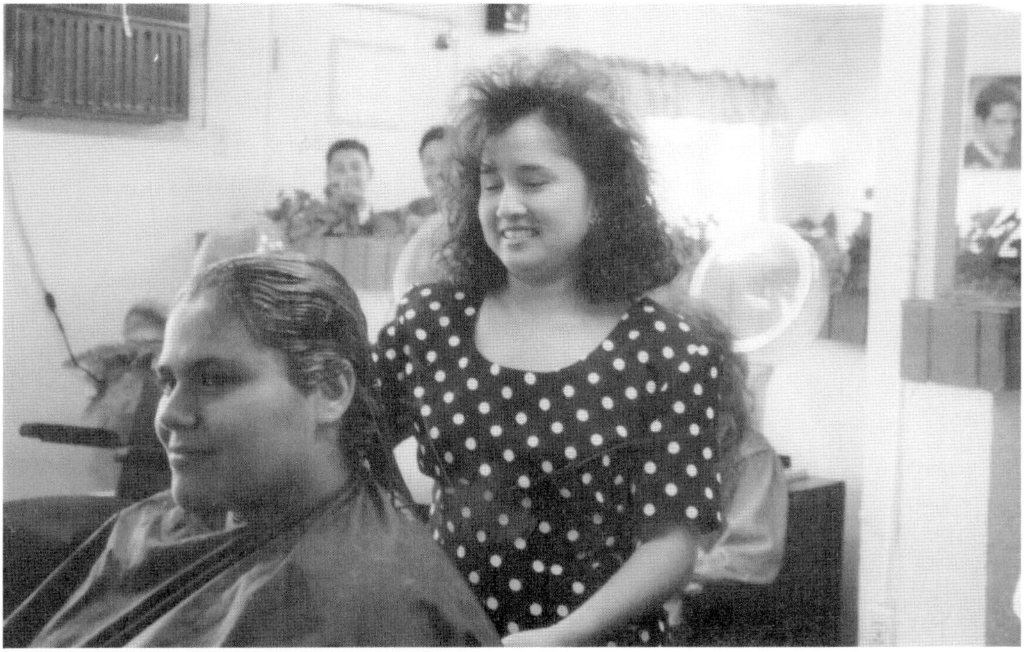

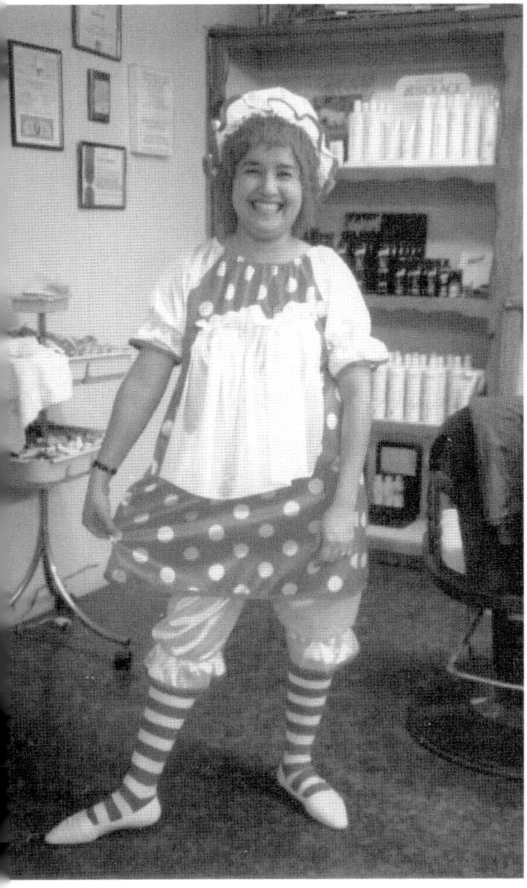

Estela Vasquez Basaldee
Estela Vasquez Basaldee, hair stylist, takes special interest in elderly clients because she misses her own mom, her inspiration and role model. With only once or twice a year visits to see her in Brownsville, Texas, Basaldee thinks about how lonely some elderly people become, sometimes compounded by health issues. She has picked them up if necessary to bring them to her salon, Estela's Hair Design, or she goes to medical facilities.

One of nine children, Basaldee's parents expected her to work. After high school cosmology classes, she has worked in various salons, opening her own at age 25. In the photograph above, she works on an unidentified customer in that salon. In the photograph at left, Basaldee's sense of humor shines as she dresses up for Halloween. Her comical yet caring disposition indicates the love of her occupation. (Courtesy Estela Basaldee.)

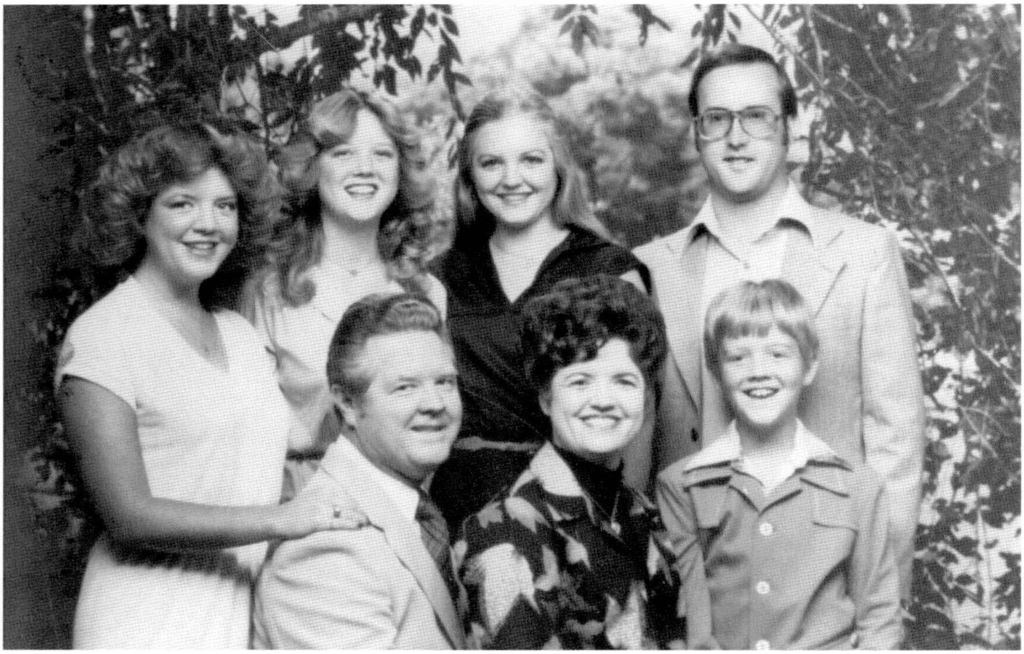

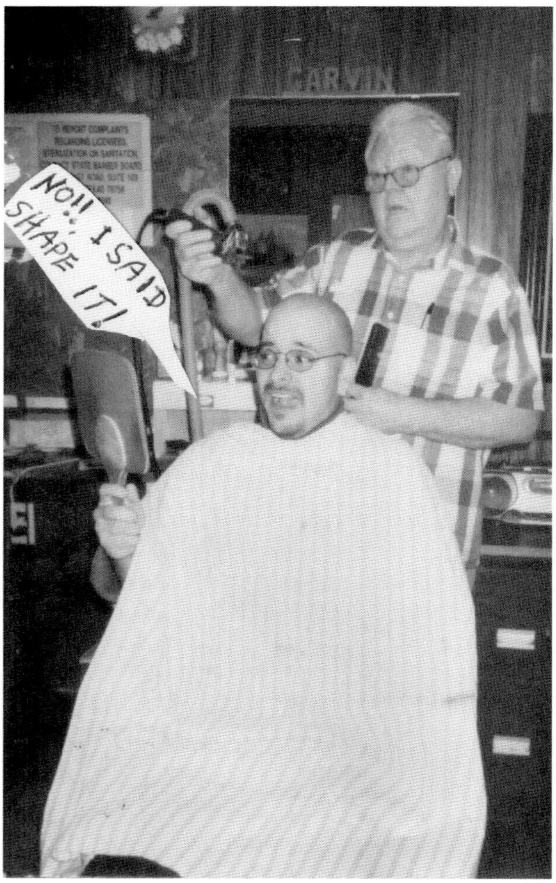

Garvin and Betty Burris

Garvin and Betty Burris, former foster parents at Christ's Haven for Children in Keller, Texas, from 1975 to 1986, at times housed 12 to 14 children at one time. While they lived there, they fostered over 100 children who sometimes needed a short stay or perhaps several years of foster care. The Burris biological family is pictured above in 1979. From left to right are (first row) Garvin Burris, Betty Burris, and son Kirk Burris; (second row) Tanya Burris, Shauni Burris, Lelani Burris Harris, and her husband, Jim Harris.

In the second image, Garvin Burris, a barber, manifests his humor as he messes with his son-in-law's haircut. At his shop, a few feet out of Lake Worth, Burris's uncanny way of having fun makes his many customers smile. (Both photographs courtesy Garvin Burris.)

Dorothy Francks and Mary Sloss

The original owner of the present-day Lake Worth Florist, Dorothy Francks had five children and started the floral business in her husband's grocery store in the 1950s to help support the family. She gave it the name, Francks' Florist. In 1960, Francks relocated her shop to Azle Avenue. After operating the shop for many years, Dorothy Francks passed away. Her family wanted one of her friends, Mary Sloss, who had grown plants at Busby Nursery for 35 years, to purchase the florist.

After accepting the offer in 1994, Sloss (pictured) renamed it Lake Worth Florist. Her daughter, son-in-law, and grandson all work there. On special holidays and events, Sloss hires extra help. Valentine's Day 2014 required 20 additional workers. The community appreciates the kind and caring employees of Lake Worth Florist. (Both photographs by Ken Brower.)

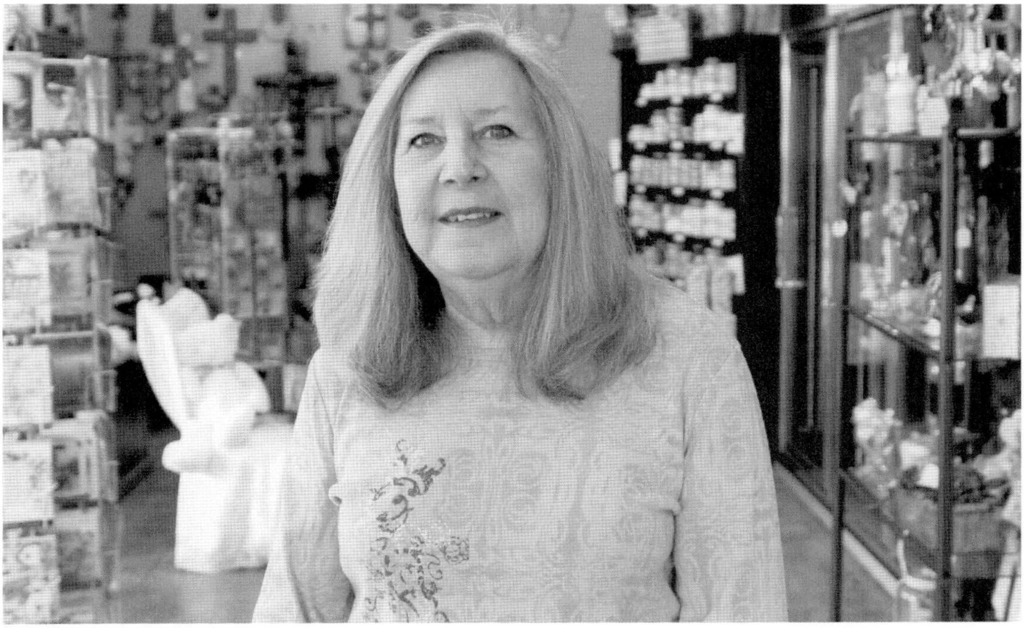

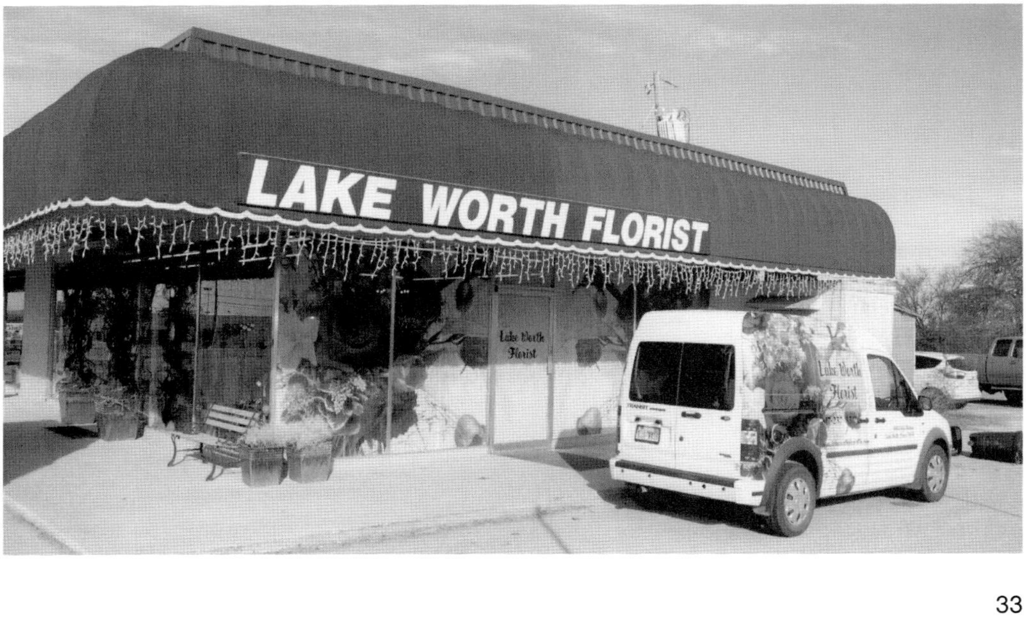

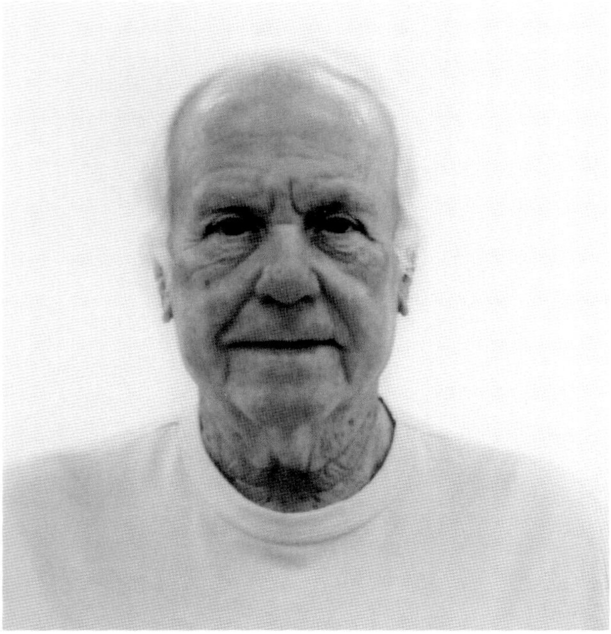

Jack Allen Burks
In 1948, Jack Burks went into business for himself, and within four years he owned 13 successful businesses. He moved to Lake Worth in 1966 and served on the Lake Worth School Board in 1970. As a hands-on dad, he enjoyed being at his children's school events. The community appreciates his irrigation-lawn services. His smiling face inspires many. (Courtesy Jack Burks.)

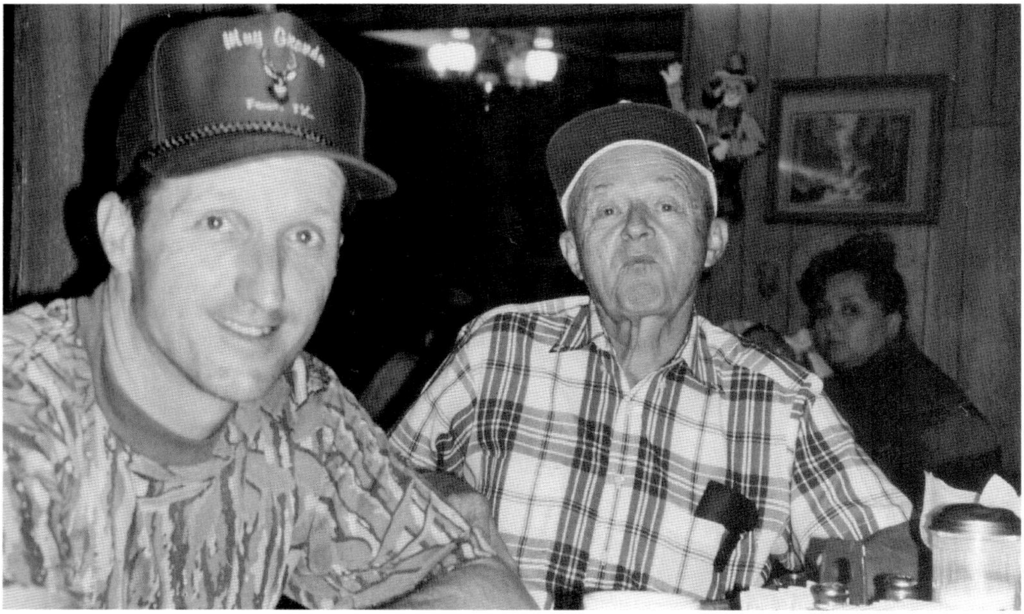

Mason Raine
Mason Raine, in the insurance business for 36 years, has been located in Lake Worth for 20 years. His grandfather sold insurance in the 1890s in various places, as did Raine's father. Years later, Mason Raine started his own agency in the Lake Worth area.

Although Raine recently retired and turned over the business to his daughter April Raine Taylor, he occasionally may work.

The new name, Raine and Taylor Insurance Agency, reflects the change. Pictured with his father, Charles Raine, right, Mason Raine, left, enjoys golfing and spending time at his ranch. (Courtesy April Raine Taylor.)

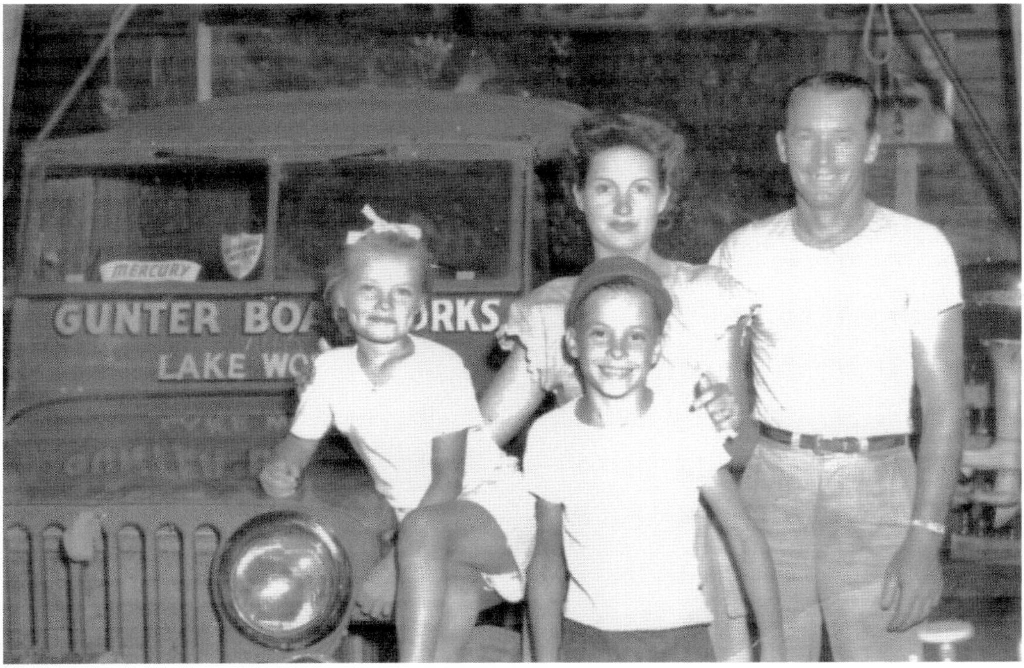

Bill Gunter
In 1942, Bill Gunter started Gunter Boat Works in Lake Worth on a slough on the southwest side of the lake near Casino Beach. Later on, he moved to another location. After his death in 1977, his wife continued to run the business until her health declined. Pictured from left to right are Sarah (daughter), Mark (son, in front), Barbara, and Bill. (Courtesy Mark Gunter.)

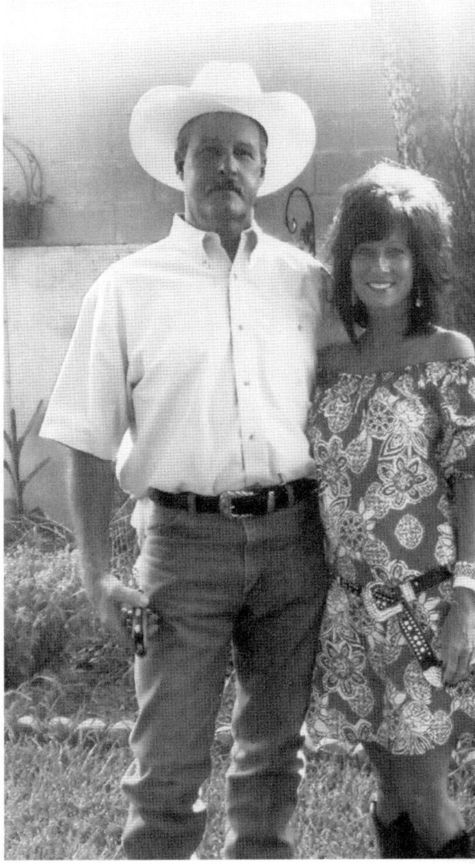

Mark Gunter
In 1982, Bill Gunter bought Gunter Boat Works from his widowed mother. At one time, the business had been located on the Lake Worth reservoir. After Mark Gunter took over the business, which his father had moved to 2243 Jacksboro Highway, he decided to change the name to Gunter Marine. This name more accurately describes his business now. Mark Gunter and wife, Sandi, are pictured here. (Courtesy Mark Gunter.)

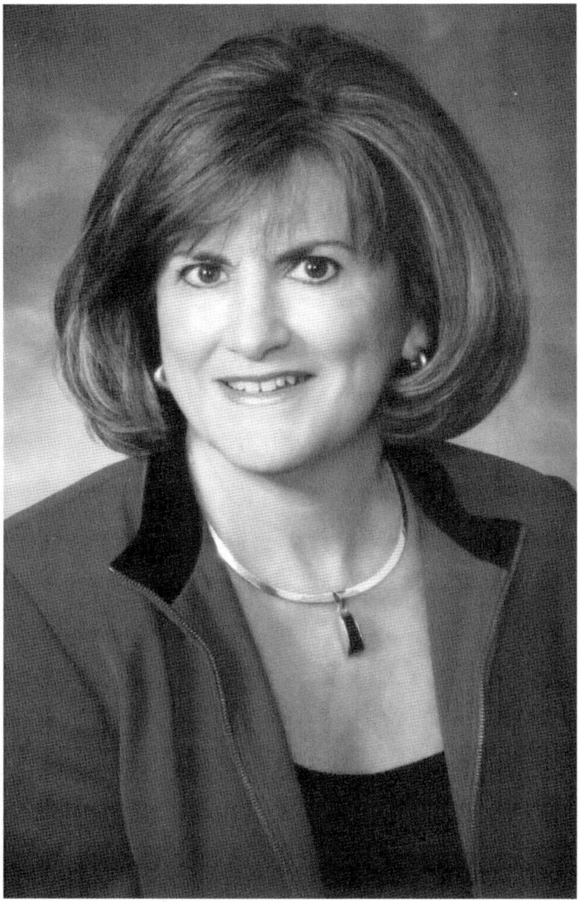

Frankie Robbins

When Frankie Robbins opened State Farm Insurance in Lake Worth., she became the first female agent for that company in the area in 1983. She found it an intriguing idea and a good way to make use of her education, talents, and abilities. She opened the office in a small frame house across from Farmer's Insurance. She later moved to the Lake Worth Center complex and then to the Star Village Commons Shopping Center. Her staff has grown from one person to six people.

Robbins grew up in Haslet and graduated as valedictorian of her class from Northwest High School. She received a bachelor's degree in education from North Texas State University in Denton. She then taught elementary school in Lubbock, Post, San Marcos, and Saginaw for a total of 17 years.

In 1981, Robbins and her family moved to Saginaw. Her older son, Jon Mark Robbins, became the first Boswell descendant to graduate from W.E. Boswell High School (named after his paternal great-grandfather). Her younger son, Jason Robbins, later became the second descendant to graduate from the school.

Civic-minded, Frankie Robbins served 11 years on the Saginaw City Council and six years as mayor of the city. She never had an opponent each time she ran for city council. As a member and past director of the Northwest Chamber of Commerce in Lake Worth, Robbins has received several awards. In 2009, she received the Good Neighbor to the Chamber Award and the Chamber Business of the Year award in 2011. In addition, as a charter member of the Northwest Tarrant Lions Club, she serves on the board of directors of Harris Northwest Hospital. Needing to accommodate her aging parents in 2006, Robbins and her husband built a new home in Lakeside, where they reside today. She has three grandsons (including twins) and two granddaughters. (Courtesy Frankie Robbins.)

B.C. Adams

In 1978, B.C. Adams opened House of Blades in Lake Worth. His inventory had well-made knives and more. In 1981, he built another store and kept roaming exotic animals. He later added Knife Alley in North Fort Worth. Adams built his dream home in the early 1990s overlooking Lake Worth. He used white pine logs, which were also used to build the present House of Blades. (Photograph by Kenny Graff.)

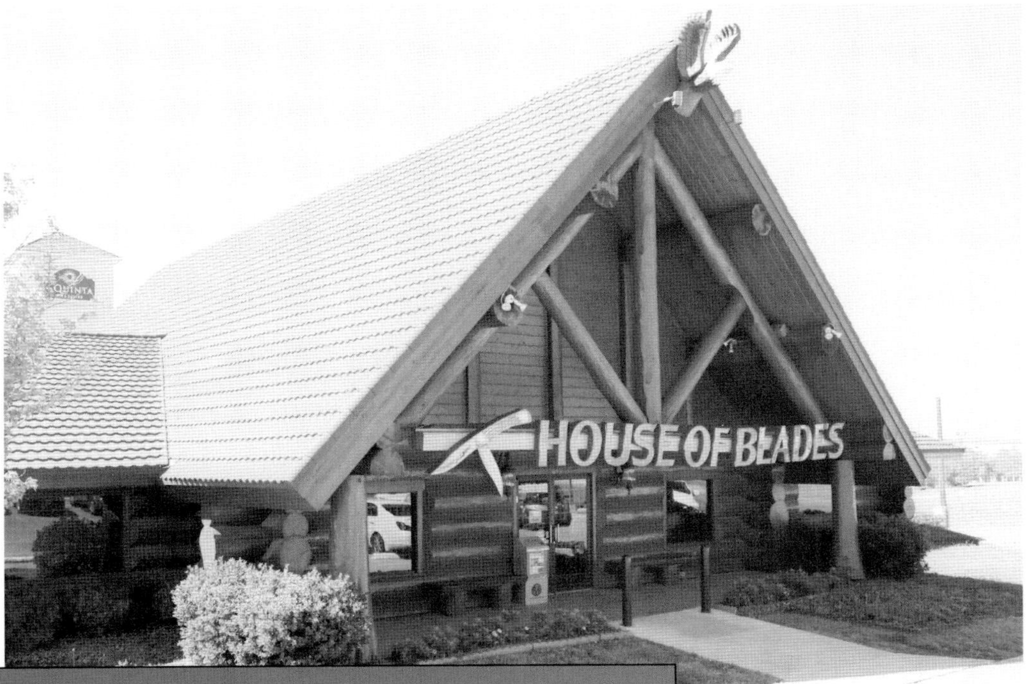

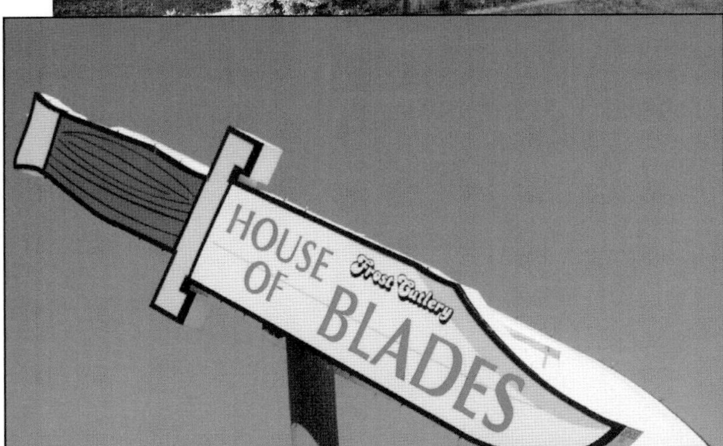

Big Knife

The House of Blades special advertising involves a facsimile of a huge knife atop a large pole reaching high into the air outside their business. Easily seen far from the building, the knife depicts the stores specialty. Inside are well-made knives and other related and interesting inventory items. The store's origin has a rich and legendary history created by the original owner, B.C. Adams. (Photograph by Kenny Graff.)

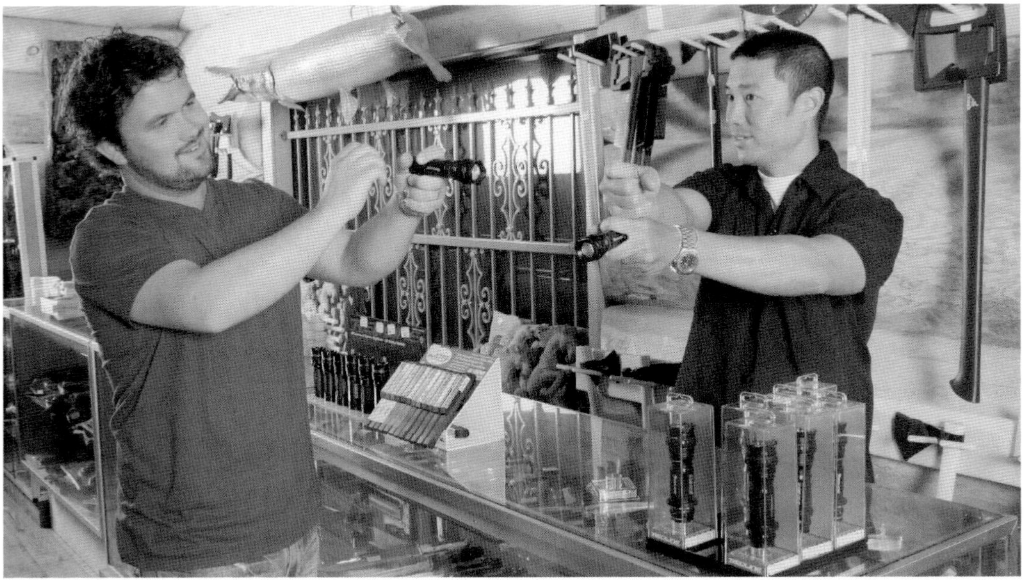

Kenny Graff
Kenny Graff, B.C. Adams's stepson, became part owner of House of Blades after Adams's death. Graff learned the business while he was young.

With one year of junior college, Graff's stepfather told him, "The only school you need is HOB [House of Blades School]."

After Graff married his high school sweetheart Jo Marie Stapleton, they had two children, Bryson and Macy. Graff hopes the business always stays in the family. (Photograph by Kenny Graff.)

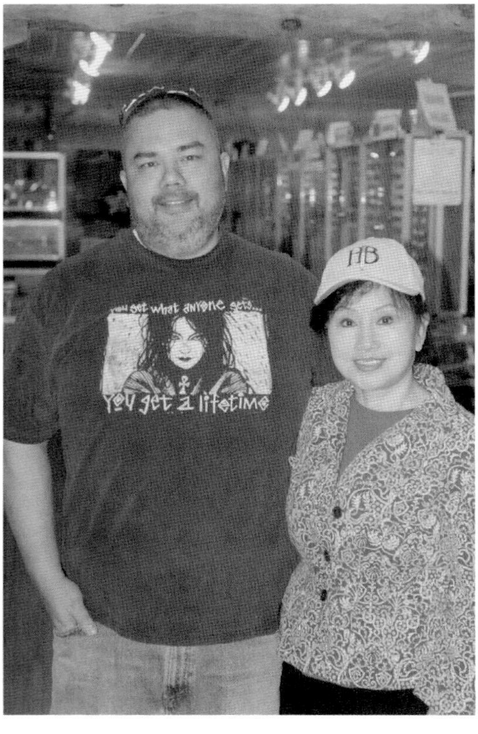

Chris Graff and Mother
The older of two sons, Chris Graff shares ownership of the House of Blades with his brother Kenny who taught him about knives. Chris has worked at the store for seven years. He and his mother, Su Lee Adams, paused for a photograph. Originally from Thailand, she has exhibited House of Blades wares at the Fort Worth Stock Show and Rodeo for 27 years. (Photograph by Ken Brower.)

CHAPTER THREE

Religious Leaders and Educators

Just as a community must have businesses for economic growth, churches and schools provide spiritual and academic growth. Without these last two, a community likely would see moral decline and illiteracy overshadowing their comfort and growth.

Many times, churches offer counseling in various areas as well as providing spiritual growth and necessities for its members and others. Murray Richey, a longtime minister, has seen to these needs for many years at Knox Presbyterian Church. He felt his calling early in life and prepared himself to fulfill his destiny.

Another pastor in this chapter, Eldon Pritchard, ministered in a number of churches in various places, worked as a substitute teacher, and served the Lake Worth community in other capacities. His wife, Linda, also worked for the school system. George Dixon ministered at First Baptist Church of Lake Worth for many years. His wife, Mildred, taught school in Lake Worth. All of these pastors have become legendary while a present-day young woman, Debra Camp, has already started her own legacy with her singing ministries.

Educators fill a number of roles as principals, teachers, librarians, counselors, sponsors, and more. The innovative methods of educators to keep students interest often go beyond the regular classroom's curriculum as will be explained within the chapter. Rip Collins taught in the classroom before becoming an assistant principal, then later was promoted to a principal's position. Jerry Welch, a former educator in the Fort Worth Independent School district, now serves in another capacity for Lake Worth Schools. His deceased wife, Karen, became an educator and left a legacy of being compassionate for students unwed and finding themselves pregnant. His current wife, Brenda, also shows warmth and love to their community by sharing in keeping an important tradition alive in the neighborhood.

Brenda Ornelas teaches special-needs students and stays connected in their lives even after graduation. She has built a strong reputation as an excellent educator and currently strives to expand the possibilities for her graduated students. Other educators, including Billy Caldwell, have earned an impressive education of their own. He has taught science in middle school and taught at a local junior college as well as pursuing his love of geology.

Some become highly interested in serving their community in the educational realm as well as finding items necessary for everyday existence. Wayne Young, one such person, has spent many hours helping the community of Lake Worth in a variety of ways. His dedication has become legendary through longevity where he has chosen to be involved. Likewise, his wife, Lynn Young, served many years in various areas of education in Lake Worth schools. Her leadership enhanced the activities she chose to sponsor.

This chapter will spotlight the importance of these people to Lake Worth and the surrounding communities. It by no means covers everyone who has contributed to this area, but it pays tribute to a few.

Dr. Murray Earl Richey

Dr. Richey has a reputation of going the extra step to help others. He has taken members of John Knox Presbyterian Church who need to go receive medical treatments, such as dialysis, and he often visits the sick. Additionally, under his pastoral ministry, a food bank has provided over 75,000 pounds of food for the needy. An often-overlooked need, that of filling prescriptions for those who cannot afford them, has received attention from his church.

Richey's quiet demeanor and assurance of God's love has brought comfort to many in sorrowful times as well as happier moments. He attributes the deep compassion he feels for others to his mother, who raised four children as a single parent and worked as a librarian. She stressed the importance of education to her children.

Even as a teenager, Richey recognized his destiny for the ministry. He prepared well to fulfill this ambition. He earned a bachelor's degree in English and religion from the University of Tulsa, then a master's of divinity degree from Dubuque Theological Seminary in Iowa. To develop further his religious knowledge, he earned a doctorate of ministry degree from Austin Theological Seminary. He currently pastors John Knox Presbyterian Church in River Oaks, Texas, which is near the Lake Worth community.

He and Linda, his wife, have opened their home for many church-related activities and have orchestrated numerous events at the church. After serving for a period of at least 33 years in the ministry at Knox Presbyterian church, Richey plans to retire in the spring of 2014. His outstanding ministerial record of service leaves comfort for his congregation to embrace.

Richey lives on a beautiful tree-lined street in Lake Worth where his friends and neighbors appreciate him just as the congregation at his church. His exceptional service to others exemplifies that of an extraordinary person whose name has become legendary. (Courtesy Murray Richey.)

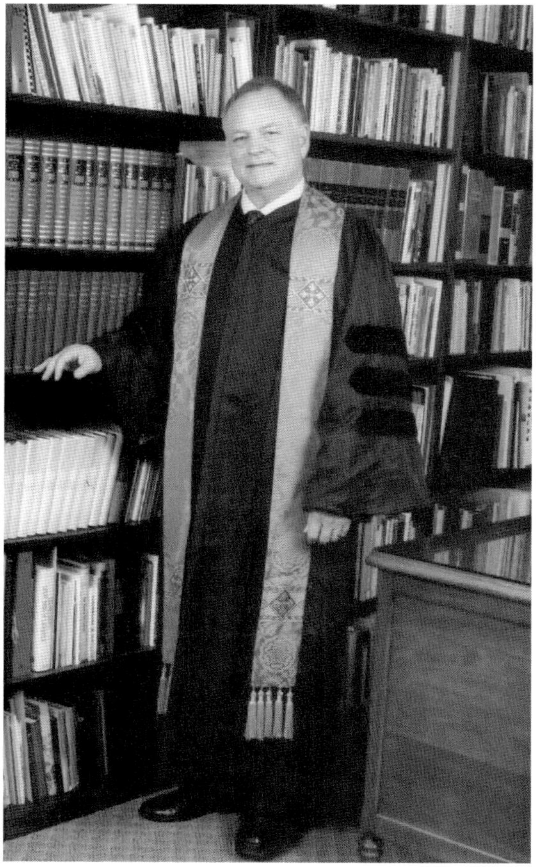

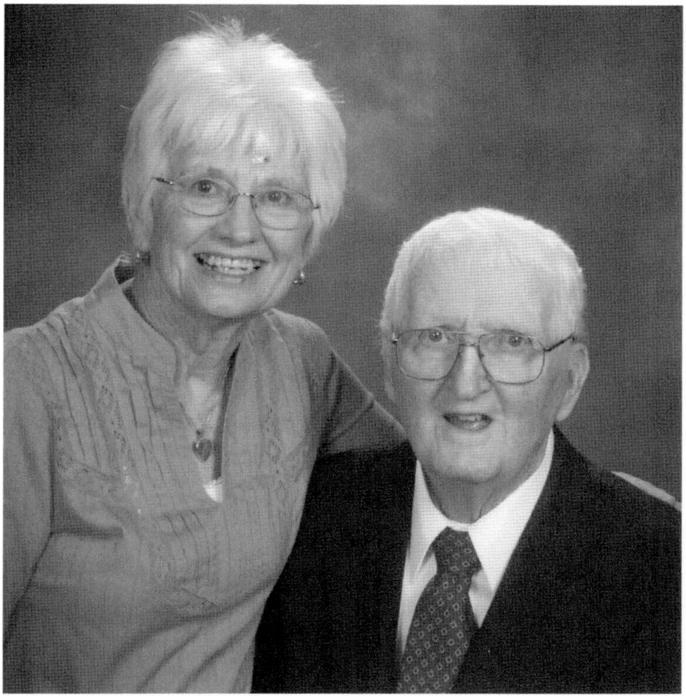

Eldon J. Pritchard and wife Linda

After graduating Southwestern Theological Seminary, Eldon Pritchard served numerous churches as a pastor, with his last church being First Baptist Church of Thorp Spring, Texas. Before this, he served on the school board of Lake Worth Independent School District. He also did substitute teaching. In addition to these aspects of his life, he took a job in sales, which required him to move to Atlanta, Georgia, with his wife and three daughters for two years. He then moved back to Lake Worth and sold insurance. He taught as a substitute in the middle school as well as substituting for pastors in various churches. He also officiated at weddings and funerals.

Pritchard, while in elementary school, moved with his parents to Lake Worth where he stayed active riding horses. He participated in Boy Scout activities and earned the rank of Eagle Scout. He later became a veteran of the Korean War.

When Pritchard grew older, his health declined and activities became limited, but he attended several luncheons in Lake Worth with his wife and friends. His death on October 14, 2013, saddened many. Linda (Caldwell) Pritchard, his caregiver and wife of over 50 years, recalls many interesting and usually happy times.

Linda Pritchard, at three years of age, moved with her parents to the developing village called Lake Worth where she started school. During her second grade, the school burned, and she had to go to nearby Castleberry to finish out the second grade. She remembers the teacher discussing discipline rules and showed the students a large paddle with holes in it. She said this made a lasting impression on her little second-grade mind. As a young girl, Linda Pritchard attended Indian Oaks Baptist Church where she stayed active in choir and youth groups. In high school, she also sang in choir and became a cheerleader.

After her marriage, and after her husband's discharge from the Army, she came back to Lake Worth and accepted employment with the school district as a secretary for the middle school. After 23 years, she retired and moved with her husband, Eldon, to Granbury for him to pastor the First Baptist Church of Thorp Spring. She also served as secretary. They made many friends and enjoyed life. This lovely lady enjoys her family, including six grandchildren and one great-grandchild, just as her late husband did. (Courtesy Linda Pritchard.)

Young Eldon Pritchard and His Sweetheart, Linda Caldwell

The young couple pictured here enjoyed attending Lake Worth schools and enjoyed each other's company. Both stayed involved in various endeavors while in high school. Photographed in front of Pritchard's father's drug store as teenagers, they later married and had three daughters. Pritchard spent much of his life in the ministry. (Courtesy Linda Pritchard.)

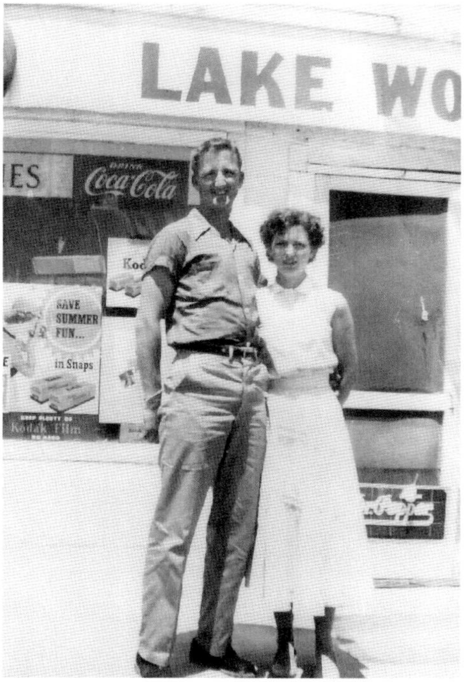

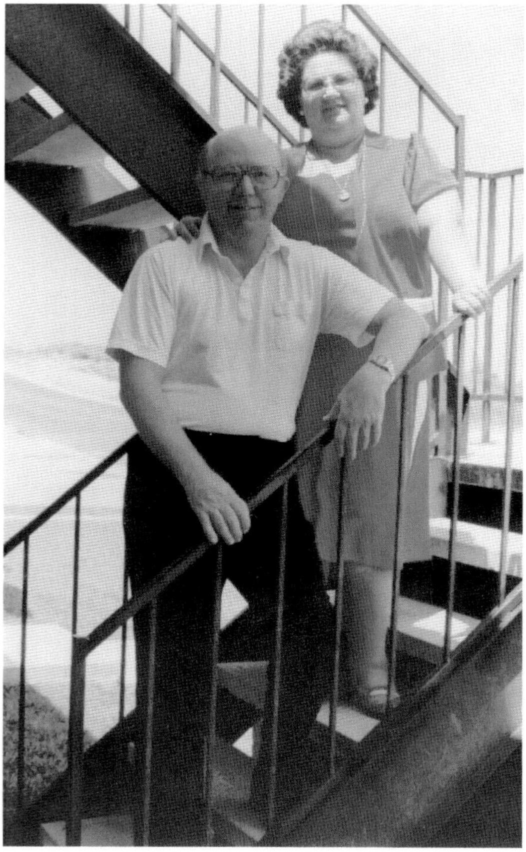

George and Mildred Dixon

George Dixon, a Korean War veteran and college graduate with two degrees, ministered in West Texas for eight years. He then came to Lake Worth to accept the ministry of First Baptist Church of Lake Worth where he preached and officiated weddings and funerals for 13 and a half years.

In addition, his wife was a schoolteacher in Lake Worth for 16 years. The couple recalls fond memories of Lake Worth. (Courtesy George W. Dixon)

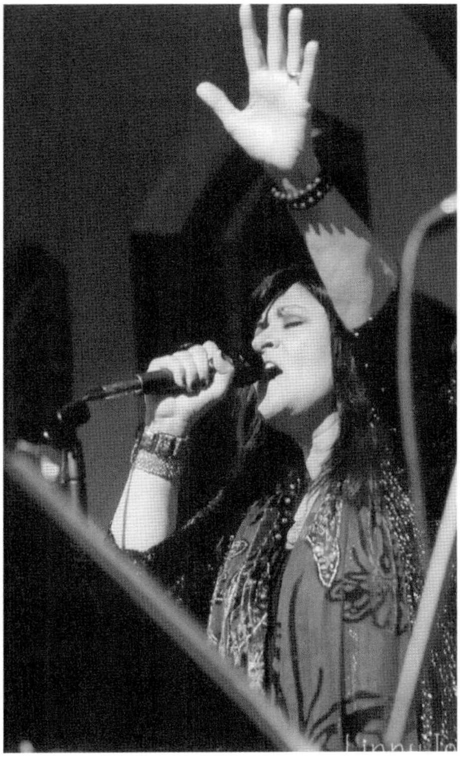

Debra Lyn Shirley Camp

Debra Camp played the piano for her first church service while in the seventh grade. By her junior year in high school, she became the church organist for First Baptist Church of Lake Worth. Camp enjoyed growing up in Lake Worth and enjoys singing and writing songs. She has founded or worked in several ministries, and she serves as the artist in residence at Grace Community Fellowship.

In addition, Camp—as founder and president of Debra Camp Ministries—uses the ministry to take worship to the world and to help bring healing to those in need. After recording two albums and a single on iTunes, she recently released her third album. She is married with two children. She is pictured at left singing and is sitting at her piano as a child in the image below. (Both photographs courtesy Debra Camp.)

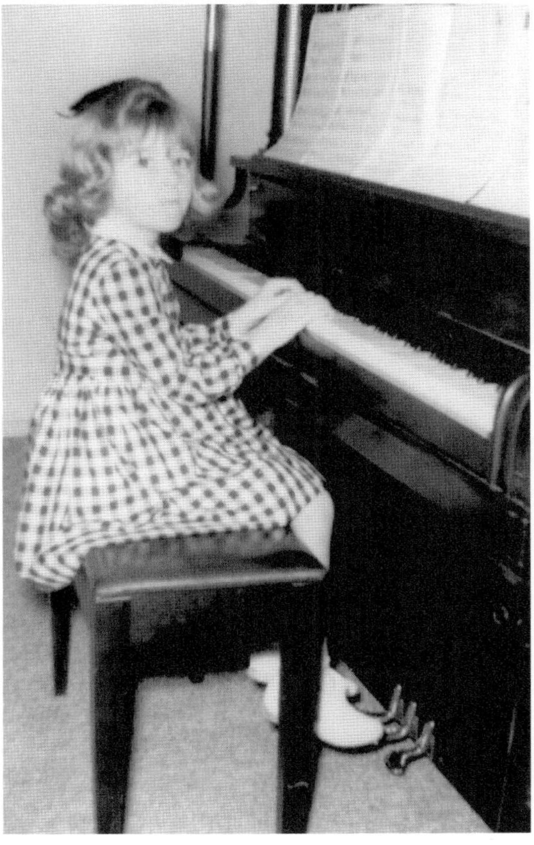

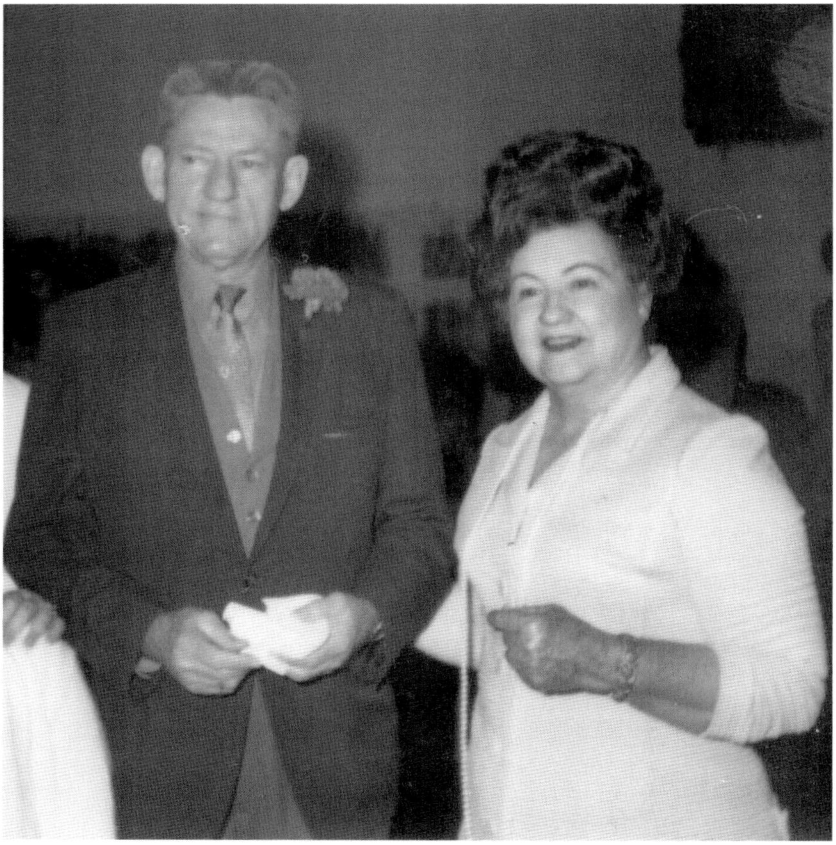

Rip and Lucyle Collins

In 1959, Rip and Lucyle Collins realized better things than rural life in West Texas awaited them, so Rip moved to Lake Worth to sell insurance. Lucyle Collins and daughter Kaye followed in 1960. That same year, Rip and Lucyle began teaching in the Lake Worth Independent School District. That began more than 30 years of their impact on many students.

W.L. "Rip" Collins grew up in Mississippi. As a youth, he rode atop railroad cars to nearby towns for fun. A train ride to Texas in 1931 landed him in College Station, where he enrolled in Texas A&M. After graduation, Collins worked as a county agricultural agent in Decatur and in Benjamin.

Lucyle Corley grew up in Rochester, the youngest of 10 children. After high school, she attended North Texas State College for two years, then returned to Rochester to help her family through the Great Depression.

Rip Collins met Lucyle Corley in 1936, and they married in 1937. During the 1950s, they settled in Knox City to rear a son, Rip Jr., and a daughter, Kaye. By 1960, the couple moved to Lake Worth and began teaching in Lake Worth schools. Rip Collins taught eighth grade English for six years. He became an elementary school assistant principal in 1966 and principal in 1970. Lucyle Collins taught first grade for eight years. She taught distributive education in high school for 20 years, and she worked as a substitute teacher for three years after she retired. The couple also served in the Lake Worth Parent-Teacher Association and held membership in the Texas State Teachers Association. Lucyle Collins served as PTA president and as president of the Delta Kappa Gamma teaching sorority.

Rip Collins worked as a substitute teacher after retirement. He substituted for the last time the day before he died in 1976. In February 1979, to honor him, an athletic facility became known as the Rip Collins Gymnasium. Lucyle Collins died in 1998. In November 2006, a school honored her by declaring its name as Lucyle Collins Middle School. (Courtesy Joe McDaniel.)

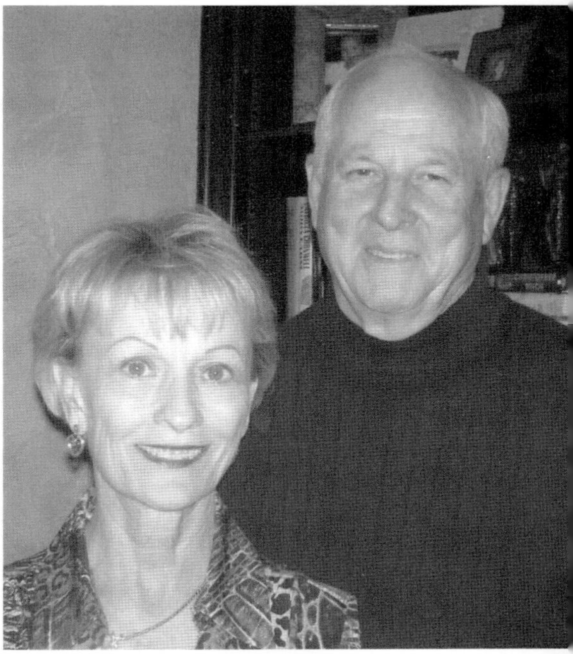

Jerry Welch

Jerry Welch and Karen Cox married in 1962 and had two sons, Russ and Rob. Welch taught in the Fort Worth Independent School District and serves on the Lake Worth School Board. Karen Welch, pictured below, taught at Lake Worth High School and Technical High School in Fort Worth. She became a vital part of the Pregnancy, Education, and Parenting Students Program of Fort Worth Independent School District. The Welch family and friends began hosting a party for Boat Club Estates residents in 1997. Unfortunately, Karen Welch died suddenly in 2003.

In 2007, Jerry Welch married Brenda Ingram, featured in first photograph. They continue to host the party on beautiful grounds near their new home in Lake Worth, located a few lots down from Welch's original home. It now belongs to his son. (Both photographs courtesy Jerry Welch.)

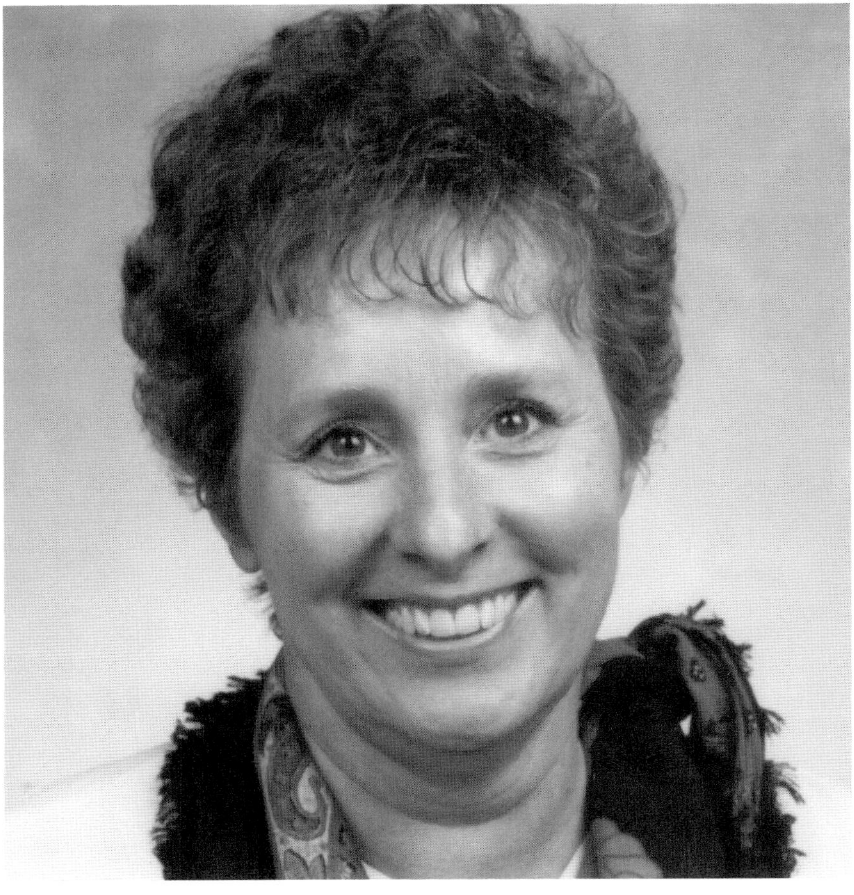

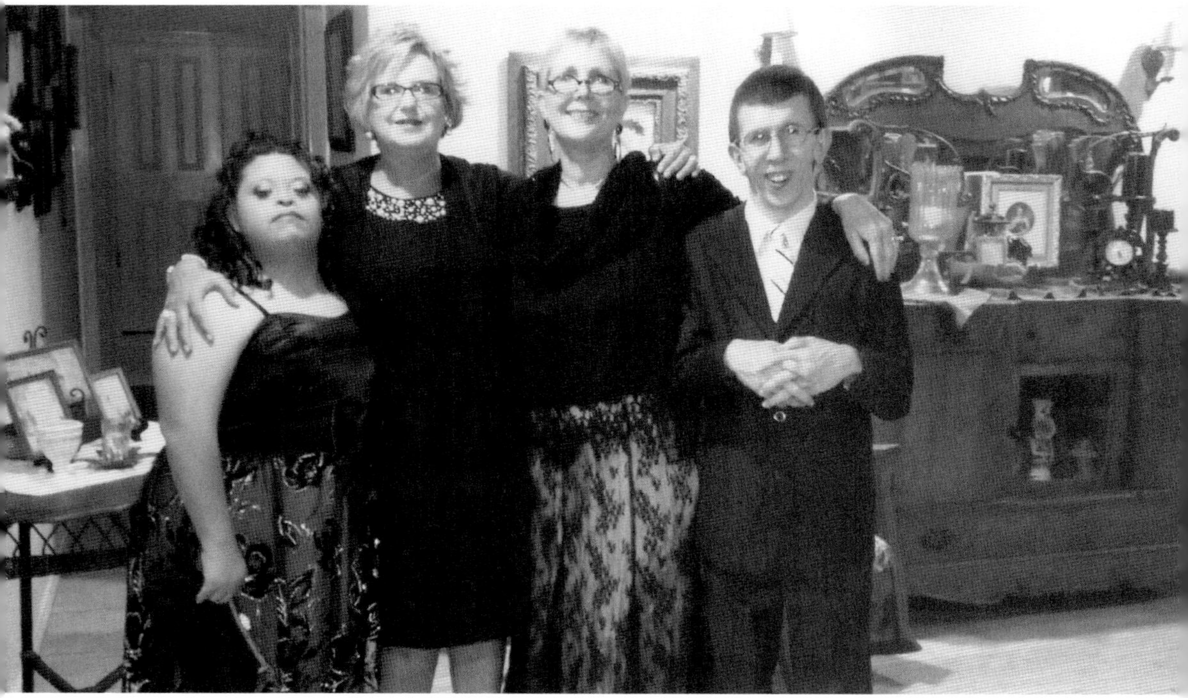

Brenda Ornelas

After earning her degree in business administration and working many years in the banking industry, Brenda Ornelas earned her special education teaching credentials and taught nine years before coming to Lake Worth High School. She said the first day she walked into the high school and interviewed for a position, she fell in love with the students and people of Lake Worth. She taught resource classes a number of years before asking for the job of teaching life skills to special-needs students. Thankfully, she got the position with a self-contained setting in which to teach students with a variety of special needs. She never left it.

Ornelas's empathy for special-needs children began as a teenager after the birth of a cousin with Down syndrome. Impressed by how love and effort of the family impacted this child's life, she carried this wisdom with her into the classroom. Students from 14 years of age until 21 years old gain enrichment while learning necessary daily living skills from Ornelas, called "Mrs. O." From time to time, because of some students' home situations, she takes special-needs students into her own home. She and others have provided meals and Christmas gifts for students.

Ten years ago, Ornelas and her friends started having an annual recognition for the students and the community that has helped them. A good friend and school board member, Sonja Norman, has a daughter in Ornelas's class. The Normans formed The Friends of Special Frogs to help with the feeding, clothing, providing field trips, and assisting with the recognition banquet (the bullfrog is the official mascot of Lake Worth High School).

After much consideration and prayer, Ornelas bought a historic building, the first transmission site for WBAP Radio Station in Fort Worth that later became a meeting hall for The Rebekah Lodge. At present, her graduated students, a generous minister, and others, engage in renovating the building and grounds. This project addresses the need of having some place for activities after graduation for these students. Ornelas says after completion of the renovation, the students can cook breakfast, have a garden, play basketball, and do projects. There will be adult supervision at all times.

Heather Soto, a former student, is standing next to Brenda Ornelas. Next to Ornelas, her co-teacher Margaret Rejtmar stands with Nick Johnson, another former student, on the end. (Courtesy Brenda Ornelas.)

Billy Caldwell

Billy Caldwell has spent more than half his life cultivating his love of geology. Born in Louisiana in 1932, he and his family later moved to Lake Worth. He graduated from Lake Worth High School in 1949. He then attended Texas Christian University, where he earned a bachelor's degree in geology in 1954.

After graduation, he worked as a geologist for the Geological Engineering Service Company in Fort Worth. For five years, he worked wells throughout Texas, New Mexico, and Colorado.

In 1960, Caldwell returned to Lake Worth High School as a science teacher. He left there to teach science at Handley Junior High School until 1963. The next year he began a six-year stint as manager for Outdoor Living. In 1970, he returned to the classroom as a student to earn a master's degree from Texas Christian University.

Caldwell then yearned to share his knowledge with businesses and college students. In 1971, he became an independent geology consultant and part-time geology teacher at Tarrant County College. In 2004, he earned a doctorate degree from Cambridge Graduate School. This ambitious man has earned recognition in *Marquis Who's Who* editions including South and Southwest, America, the World, Science and Technology, and Finance and Industry. Also, Caldwell has earned membership and certification in the American Institute of Professional Geologists and the American Association of Petroleum Geologists. In addition, he earned a license as a Texas Professional Geoscientist. He became a member of the Fort Worth Geological Society and the Geological Society of America.

Caldwell has writings published and unpublished about his favorite subject. He wrote *Geological Investigations in Environmental Studies* in 1991, an unpublished manuscript of *Barnett Shale Production Potentials* in 2000, *Geology in the Bible* in 2005, and *The History of the Fort Worth Basin* in 2012. Married to his wife, Carolyn, he served as chairman of the City of Fort Worth's Environmental Advisory Committee and as a director of the Fort Worth Jaycees. (Courtesy Billy Caldwell.)

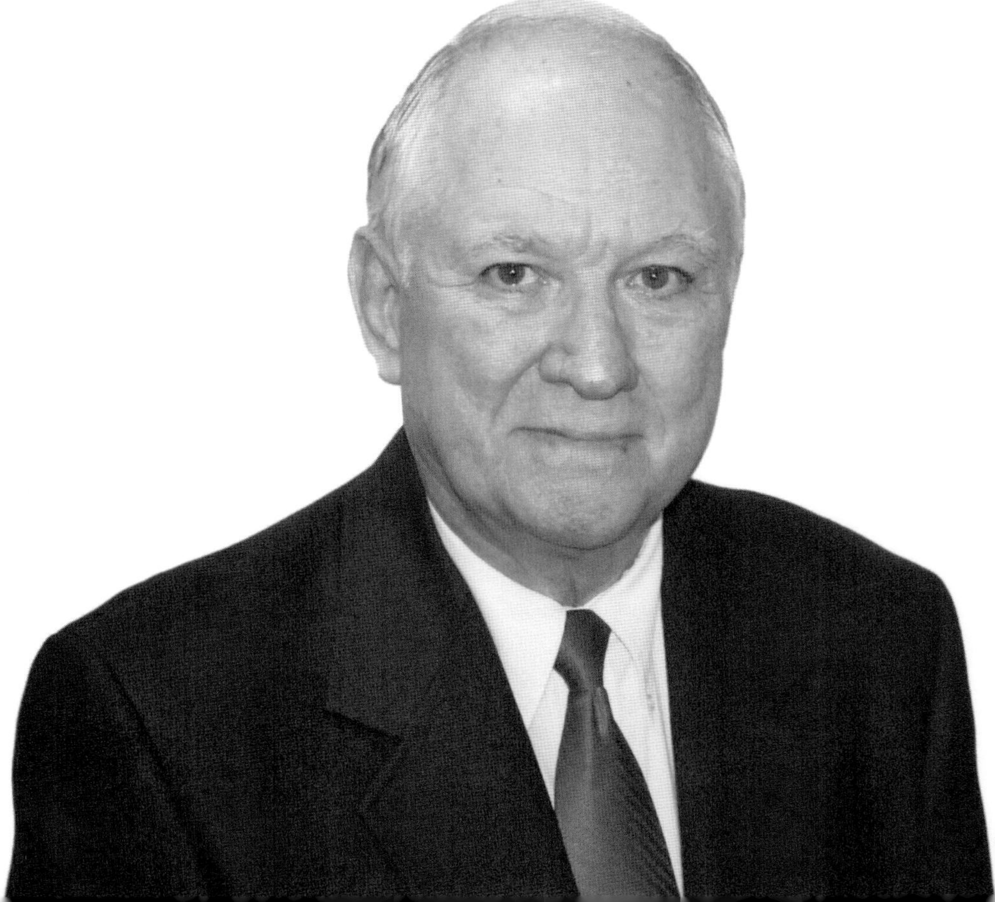

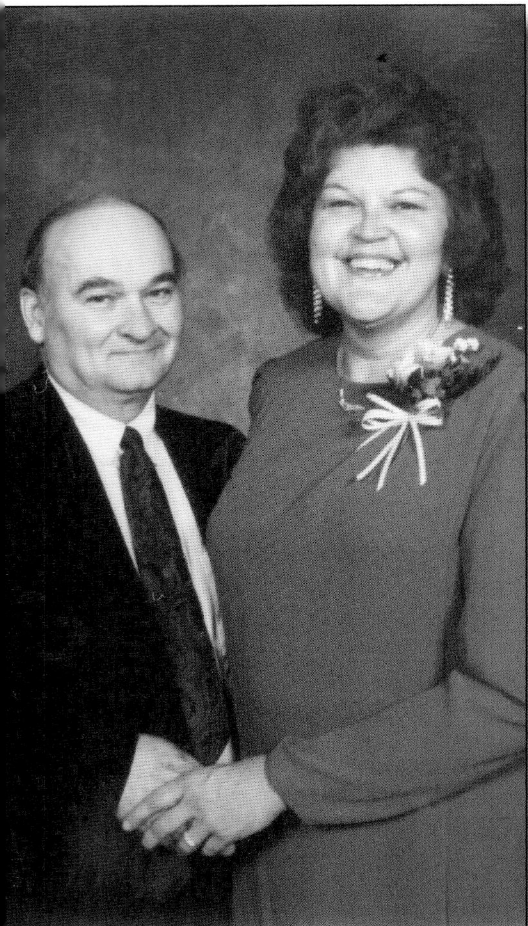

Wayne and Lynn Young

Wayne Young, active in the Kiwanis organization as president, secretary, and treasurer, has been greatly involved for many years with the annual Christmas Express, a program of the Kiwanis Club to assist needy and less-fortunate children of the Lake Worth area. In addition, Young collects goodie bags for an annual luncheon for new teachers and has participated in past classroom projects. Young received the Hero for Children Award from the State Board of Education on January 16, 1998, for his volunteer work as an advocate for education service on behalf of Texas schoolchildren. Pictured below, he and his wife, Lynn, attend the Kiwanis Convention on the ship *Ecstasy* in 2006. In education at Lake Worth High School for 31 years, Lynn taught math for two years, world history for one year, and then became the school librarian for 28 years. As sponsor for the freshmen cheerleaders, the senior class, the junior class, Future Teachers of America, National Honor Society, Future Educators of America, and the student council, Young coordinated or assisted in a host of student activities. Featured in the photograph with her husband, Wayne, she helped obtain endowments from the Meadows Foundation for Community Service. Northwest Chamber of Commerce recognized her dedication to her profession and the community by naming her Educator of the Year in 1982. (Both courtesy Wayne and Lynn Young.)

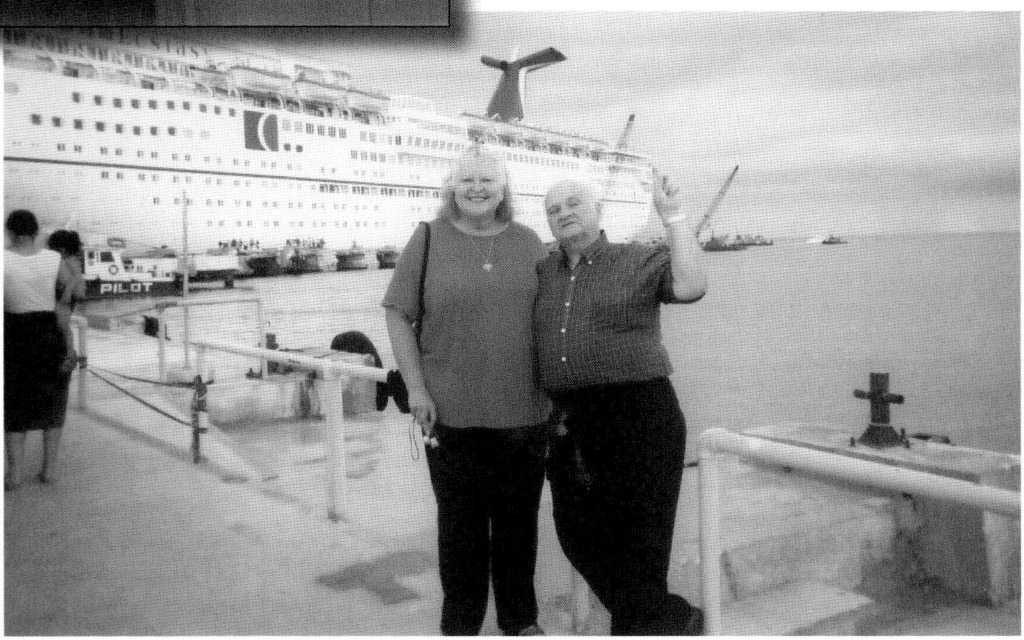

CHAPTER FOUR

Medical Personnel, Bankers, and Lawyers

Because of the times in which we live with population explosion and a number of things affecting the health of everyone, there exists a demand for highly trained professionals to care for their medical needs. Equally important, the economic world demands education and expertise from those operating financial institutions. Additionally, within many situations of everyday life, lawyers help their clients negotiate their legal matters.

This chapter presents a number of those in the professional world who fulfill the aforementioned needs of a community. All have ties to the Lake Worth area, either by former residency or by presently being located there in a professional setting.

Much like layering on one coat of paint after another to acquire a desirable finished product, the professional world of each includes building their own future step by step as they acquire the necessary credentials to obtain their professional goals. After that, their reputations trail after each person's life that they touched as a professional or as a volunteer.

The Lake Worth area is fortunate to have individuals like Dr. William Seger, whose practice has a large patient enrollment. His friendly manner eases the discomfort for many in addition to his prescribed instructions to gain improved health. His concern with youth activities also benefited many in the area.

Dr. Michael McCullough grew up in Lake Worth without his father, who died early on in McCullough's life. Despite the lack of financial security and the loving support of a father, McCullough went on to become a well-known medical doctor, practicing in Dallas. When Dr. Dwayne Beeler moved his practice to Lake Worth, he did not have much competition. As time moved ahead other dentists arrived, but Beeler's practice remains healthy, and he stays involved in community affairs.

The Giles family featured in this chapter has contributed to society by becoming doctors, educators, and one had a career in the computer world. They all grew up in Lake Worth, and some practiced their profession there. One member, Dr. Duane Giles, had an extensive medical career overlapping his military life and may be found in chapter 5.

Dr. Gary Sanders and Dr. Gene Lott became chiropractors serving a wide area, which includes Lake Worth. Cindy Bozart, a nurse, has an interesting life in serving as a registered nurse working in both a hospital setting and as a church parish nurse. A scary story involves veterinarian Dr. Steve Whitaker. His association in Lake Worth has served many.

Bankers Bill Davenport, Russ Richardson, Steve Parker, and Steve Siebenthall have served in various capacities in several banks, especially in Lake Worth.

George Shaw II and his son Brad Shaw, both lawyers, brought their services to this small community and shared offices in Lake Worth. Each one discussed in this chapter has become legendary in one way or another.

Dr. William Seger

Born in Victoria, Texas, in 1957 to parents Dr. Forrest Seger and Dr. Eva Seger, William Seger's love for science in school made his professional choice easy. One of seven children, Seger attended undergraduate school at the University of Austin and medical school at Texas Tech University. He married his wife, Cyndi, in 1988, and they have three boys and two girls.

Seger's involvement with his children includes coaching basketball and baseball. He is a past board member of the YMCA and has been medical director for the Eagle Mountain Volunteer Fire Department for 18 years. In addition, he has served on the Pastoral Committee for Harris Hospital in Fort Worth. His contributions and happy demeanor are assets to all. Pictured below are Seger, his wife, and his children. (Both photographs courtesy William Seger.)

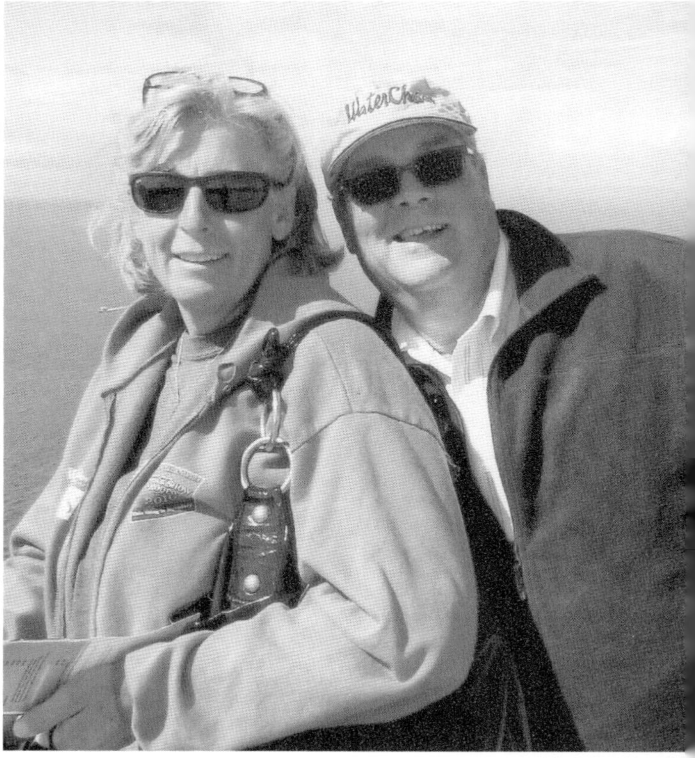

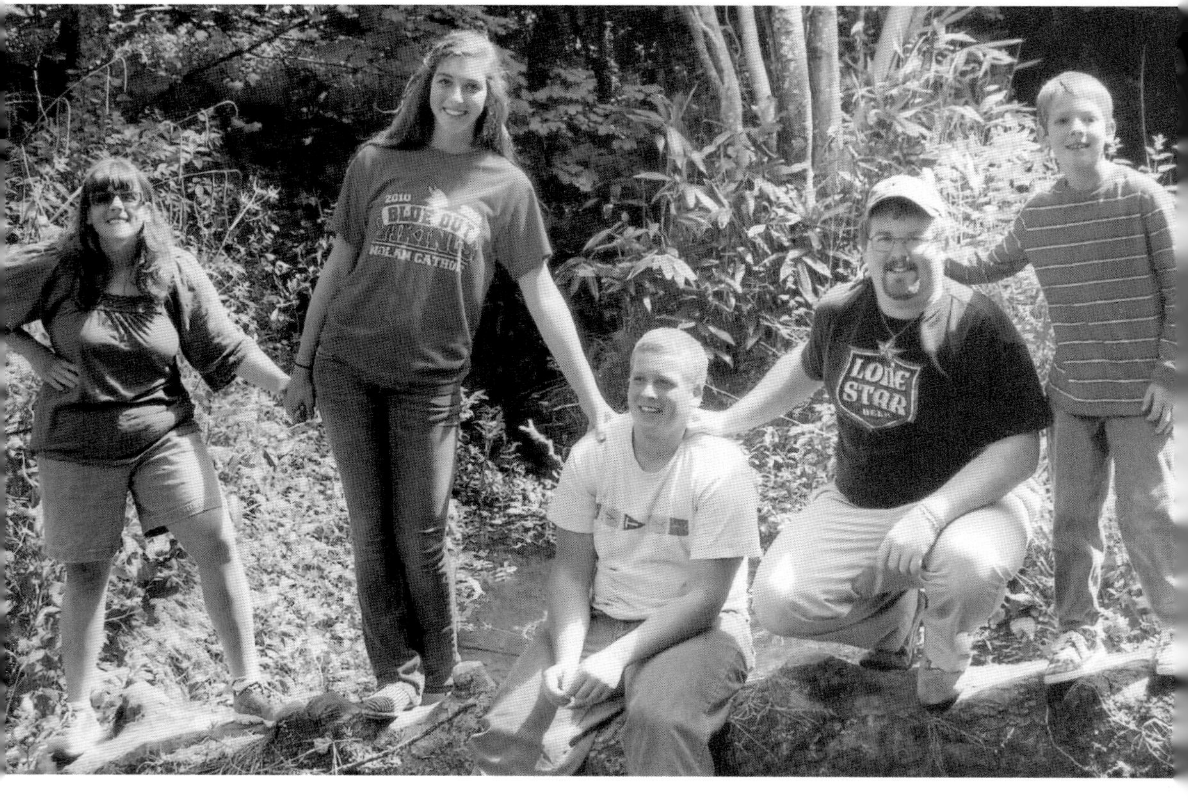

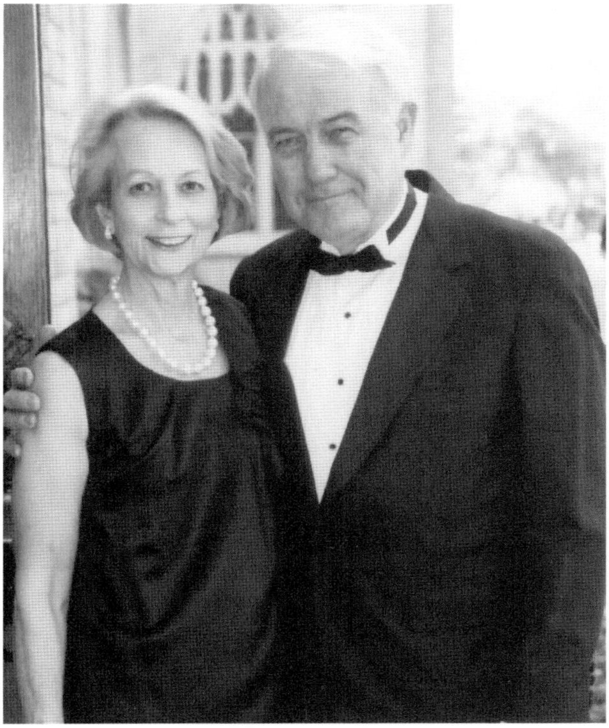

Dr. Michael L. McCullough

Michael L. "Mike" McCullough, born in Mineral Wells, Texas, in 1938, grew up mostly in Lake Worth, Texas. When Mike was six years old, his father died and his family struggled with emotional and financial difficulties. A popular and well-respected coach, Frank Kring, lived next door to him and gave him guidance. Kring inspired McCullough to accept personal responsibility, to do his share of team effort, and to prepare for the future through hard work.

McCullough remembers a comical incident when he was younger and trying to keep the school bully from knowing that he took piano lessons. Years later, while in high school, the bully and he discovered they each worried about the same thing. The bully tried to hide the fact that he also took piano lessons and worried that McCullough might find out. In retrospect, another involvement resulted in a learning experience. McCullough, a high school junior at the time, forced by the seniors, hauled buckets of paint up a ladder in the middle of the night to paint the town tower with words "Senior Class of 55." Of course the police chief hauled them all to city hall that evening and sentenced them to do a weekend of hard labor on some project. McCullough said it was embarrassing, but a good learning experience.

In 1963, McCullough married Joanne Colwell and earned a medical degree from the University of Texas Southwestern Medical School. He did his internship at the University of Arkansas's school of medicine from 1963 to 1964. The next two years, he completed a residency program at Parkland Memorial Hospital, University of Texas Southwestern Medical School.

He served in many professional organizations, such as Texas Society of Internal Medicine, the American Society of Internal Medicine, and the American Hospital Association Management Counsel. In addition, as a captain in the US Air Force, he served as chief of medicine for 439th USAF Hospital in Japan from 1967 to 1969.

McCullough has a vast amount of experience in the medical world in private practice as an internal medicine doctor and as a member of advisory boards as well as serving as the director of several health-related organizations. One of McCullough's most pleasurable hobbies is reading, which he attributes to his favorite teacher, Mrs. Leota Nations, who also loved literature and poetry. (Courtesy Dr. Mike McCullough.)

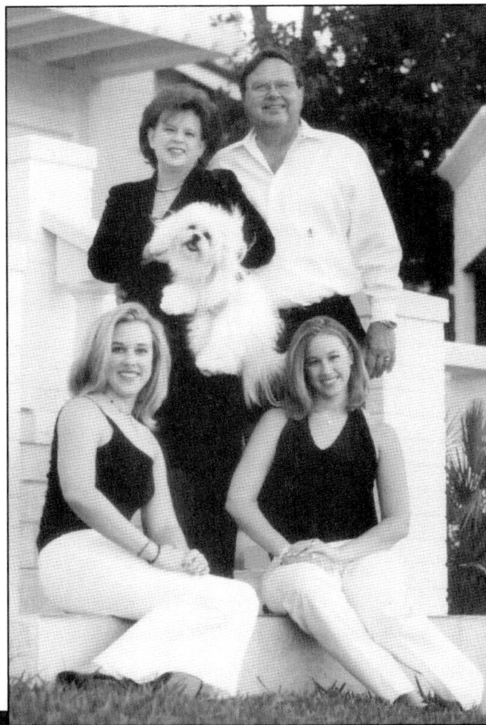

The Beeler Family

Dr. Dwayne Beeler met his wife, Sharon, in 1973 in a singles Sunday School Class at the First United Methodist Church in downtown Fort Worth. They have been married for 35 years. They have two daughters, Tara (front left) and Reagan (front right). They are visible here with their parents and pet, Bailey.

Beeler has an extensive dental practice, but his father insisted he learn to be a barber before dental college. Beeler used the trade through his college days. In 1984, he served as a member of the Tarrant County Forensics Team and helped identify victims from the Delta 1141 crash and the Mount Carmel, David Koresh disaster. Beeler has numerous awards and belongs to a host of associations. He has served as president five times in the Lake Worth Kiwanis. His assistant Jennifer Sellars posed as a patient for the photograph. (Both photographs courtesy Dwayne Beeler.)

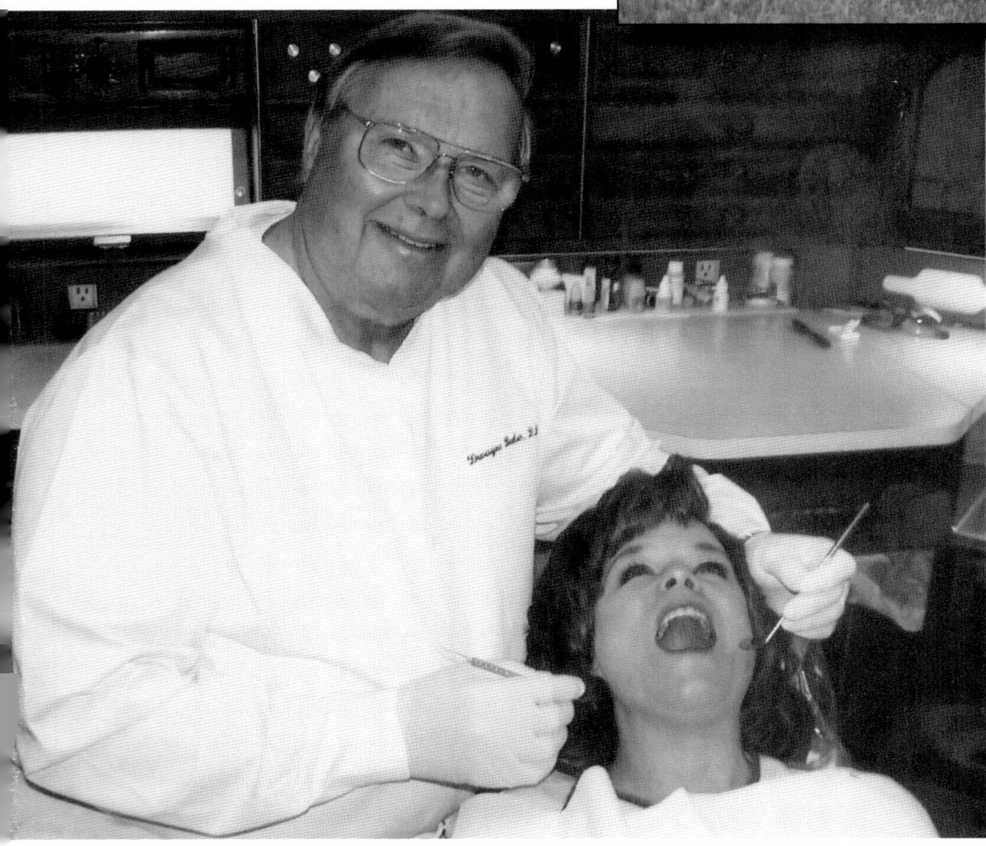

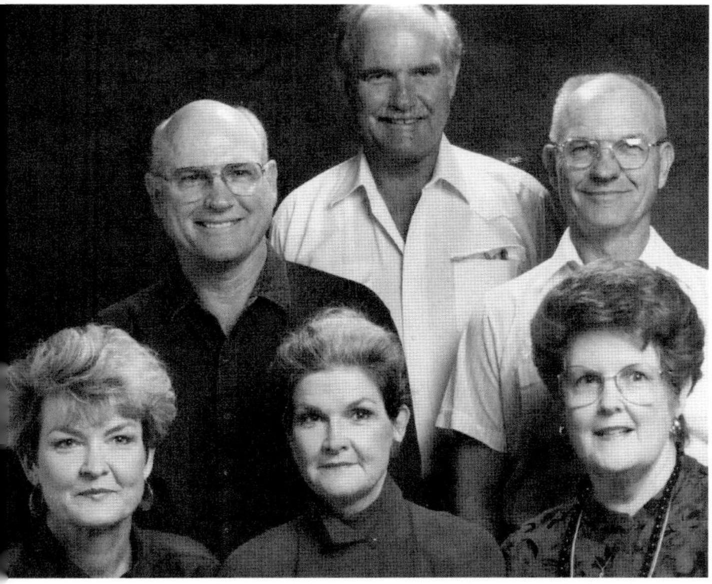

Giles Family

With three doctors, two schoolteachers, and one into the computer world, the children of Forest and Margaret Giles pushed ahead to help others. All graduated from Lake Worth schools.

Dr. Nancy Faigan, center, has a private practice. She taught over 20 years as an assistant professor at Osteopathic College of Medicine. Joanne Giles, right, became a teacher while her other sister Sara McKenzie, left, became an administrator in education.

The second row features, from left to right, Monty Giles, computer guru; Dr. Tommy Giles; and Duane Giles. (Courtesy Giles family.)

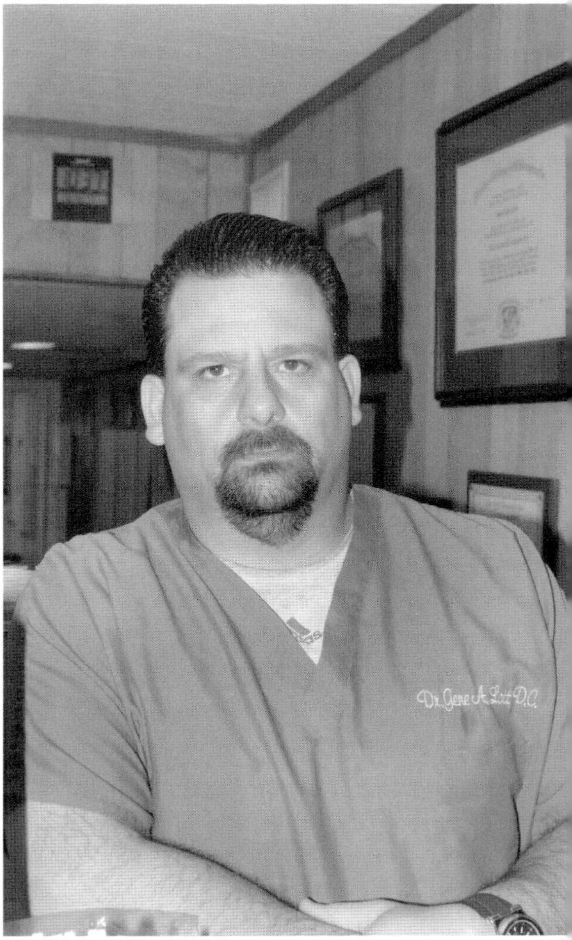

Dr. Gene Lott

Dr. Lott attended Medical School at Parker College of Chiropractic Dallas, Texas. His specialties include family and sports care, and he offers drug testing and much more. His practice in experience/clinical settings includes areas such as specialization in biomechanics and neuromuscular disorders. He has his office in Lake Worth. A member of Northwest Chamber of Commerce, Lott also served as Kiwanis Club president in 2004. He has participated in Christmas Express and Meals on Wheels. In 1985, Lott belonged to the Lake Worth Roller Hockey team that won a gold medal in the USA Junior Class. He enjoys reading, golf, and the companionship of his two Labradors. (Photograph by Ken Brower.)

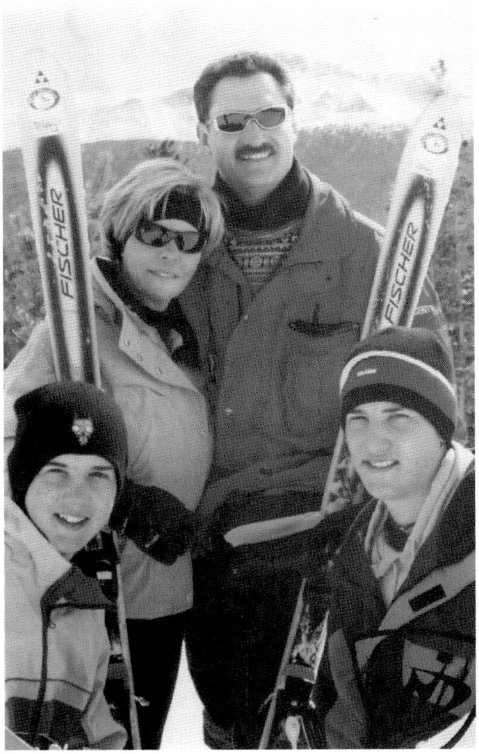

Dr. Gary Sanders and Family

Dr. Sanders once had a major skiing accident injury. After a difficult recovery, he continued skiing, as indicated here with his wife, Sandy, and their two sons Cody, on the left, and Casey, on the right, at Winter Park Colorado in 1997.

However, in 1991, vacations looked like moments of the past when he and his family returned from a vacation in Puerto Vallarta, Mexico. His wife felt extremely tired. He did chiropractic testing, ran blood tests, and then sent her for medical blood testing, which revealed nothing.

Sanders went away for a relicensing seminar, and his wife fell unconscious and went into a coma. Soon, a gastroenterologist ran blood tests again, which came back positive for liver failure, and she was sent on an emergency-care flight to Baylor Hospital in Dallas. When Sanders arrived, he learned of her liver dying, and she survived only because of the life support system.

She had maybe three days to live unless she had a liver transplant, a new kind of surgery in 1991. The surgical team worked quickly to find a match. This young mother, declared as a deathly emergency with young sons, ages two and four, became number one on the western hemisphere list. Within 48 hours, the team found a match.

Because of a grieving family's merciful decision, Sandy Sanders received her liver transplant in November of 1991. At first, her body appeared to reject the new liver, but her surgeon discovered a stopped up bile tube. After removing it, she quickly improved. Tremendous spiritual support came from people all over the United States praying for her recovery. Sanders used his chiropractic skills and nourishment knowledge to aid the medical doctors in her recovery.

As a young man, Sanders also had a challenge when he received an injury while playing baseball. A chiropractor helped him recover and encouraged him to become a chiropractor also. Sanders's decision at age 28 to sell all he owned to go to the required pre-medical school before acceptance in to chiropractic school later had a positive impact on his wife's recovery.

A large volume of patients visit Dr. Sanders's office, located a few yards outside of Lake Worth, and they likely agree about how his skills make their lives healthier. (Courtesy Sandy Sanders.)

Dr. Steve Whitaker

In 1977 and 1978 respectively, Dr. Steve Whitaker and his wife, Dr. Kathy Whitaker, graduated from veterinary school. After working in local clinics, they opened their own veterinary clinic in 1982 named Lake Worth Animal Clinic. With the vast improvements for Highway 199 came many new businesses and residents located near the clinic. The great need for such an establishment brought the clinic much success. Animals of many species and sizes received the loving care of this animal clinic.

Unfortunately, on December 6, 2000, Dr. Whitaker stepped out of the room after placing a muzzle on an animal, a pit bull, and upon return found the muzzle off. Without any provocation, the animal suddenly attacked the owner's mother, who had accompanied them. Dr. Whitaker tried to pull the dog off the woman, but the animal turned on him. Thankfully, an unknown person called the police.

Officer Benningfield arrived, but he could not get off a clear shot without hitting someone. The woman and Whitaker received injuries from the dog that also killed a resident cat. Benningfield finally had to release a can of pepper spray to suspend the animal's behavior before it could be euthanized. An ambulance rushed Whitaker to Harris Southwest Hospital. He sustained serious bites and lacerations to his arms and legs but returned to work the week after Christmas.

Over the years, the Whitakers have given excellent care to their clients' animals. They have taken home a number of animals that sometimes became their own. Lake Worth Animal Clinic now belongs to Dr. Mariena Smith, who continues excellent and compassionate care. Dr. Kathy Whitaker retired after 33 years of service, but Steve Whitaker still goes in on a limited schedule. A resident cat rests in Dr. Whitaker's arms in this photograph. The photograph was taken by Ken Brower. (Courtesy Ken Brower.)

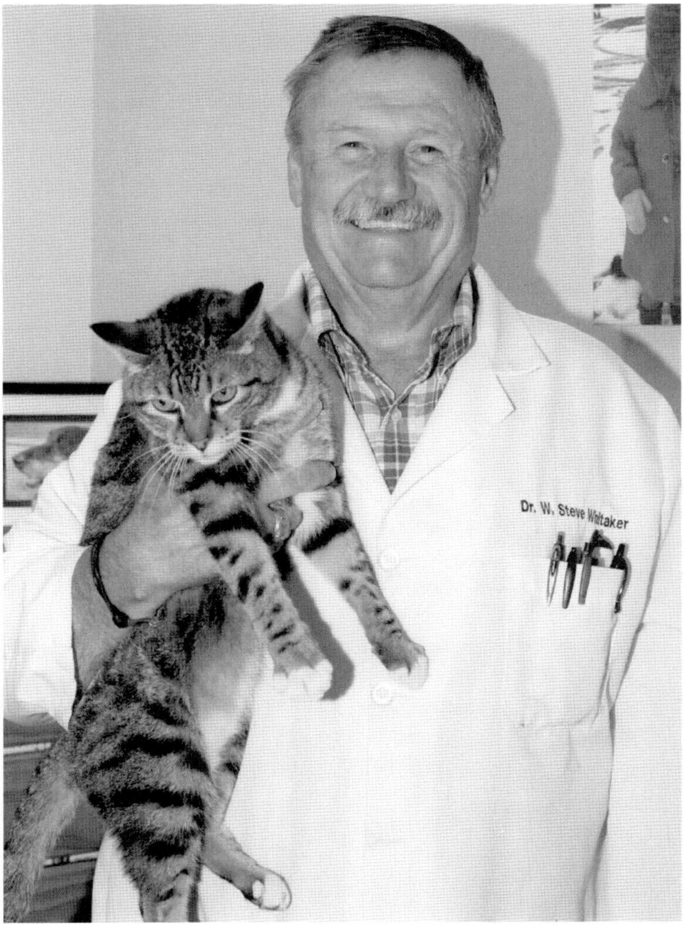

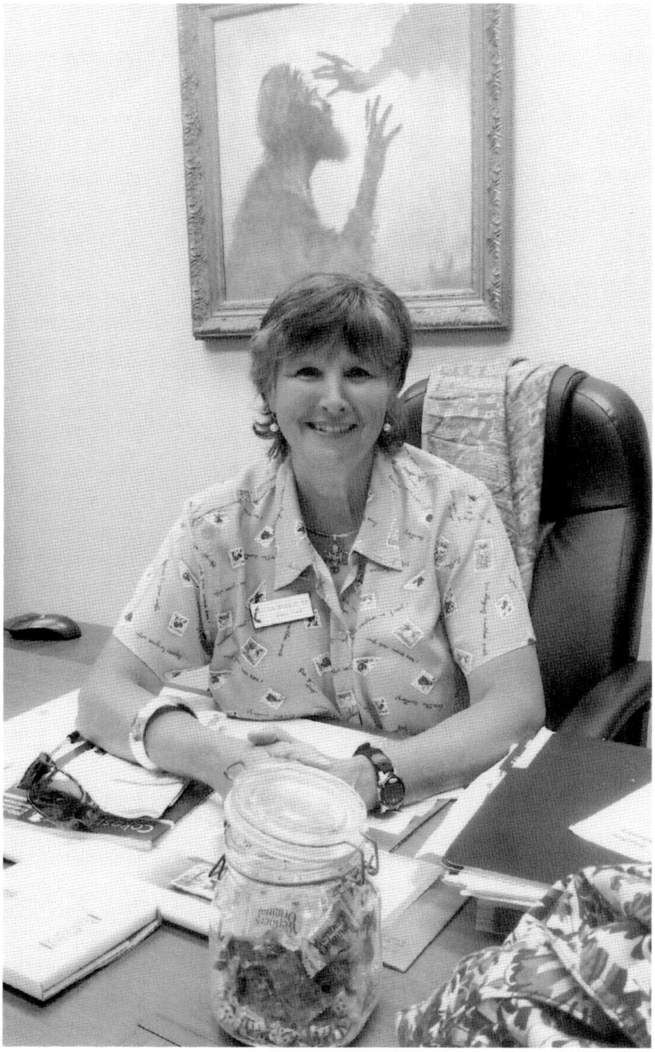

Cindy Bozart

Cindy Bozart worked as a nurse at All Saints Episcopal Hospital from 1977 to 1996, mostly in the intensive care unit. One day she learned of Parish Nursing, which combines faith and health. Bozart became aware of the possibility of ministering to church members of the former Lake Worth United Methodist Church, now called Lighthouse Fellowship Church, where she attends. Soon she split her time between nursing at Harris Methodist Hospital Fort Worth in the recovery room and church nursing duties, administering health programs. She takes blood pressures, gives referrals, and administers home and hospital visits.

When Cindy Bozart graduated from the University of Oklahoma in 1977, she came back with two of her friends and moved into the vacant home on Lake Worth where her grandparents, the James E. Parkers, had lived. Sometimes the girls late-night skinny-dipped in the lake. They were surprised to learn that a neighbor had been spying on them with his binoculars. She said, "It was a good thing there were no dock lights back then."

Bozart also loves remembering things about her grandfather, nicknamed "Coley," and his days as a wildcatter during in the West Texas oil boom of the 1930s and 1940s. He often wore clean, but stained, white starched shirts. "The splattered oil on his shirts meant good luck to him, so he kept right on wearing them," Bozart said. (Courtesy Cindy Bozart.)

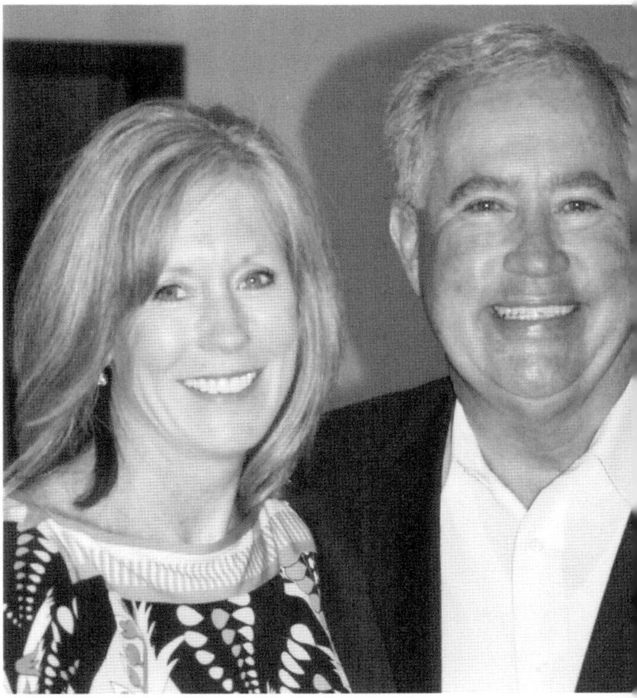

Bill Davenport

Bill Davenport worked in various banks, and after finishing graduate school for banking, worked for the former Shady Oaks National Bank in Lake Worth. In 1998, he and Russ Richardson opened Star Bank of Texas in Lake Worth. Davenport serves as president of this bank, the Star Bank of Texas in White Settlement, and Star Bank of Texas in Burleson.

Additionally, Davenport, an active member of Northwest Chamber of Commerce in Lake Worth, once coached a girl's softball team for seven years. He served on the Education Foundation Board at Boswell High School and has served in numerous organizations.

He and his wife, LeAnn, appear in this photograph. She appears on the front cover also. (Courtesy Bill Davenport.)

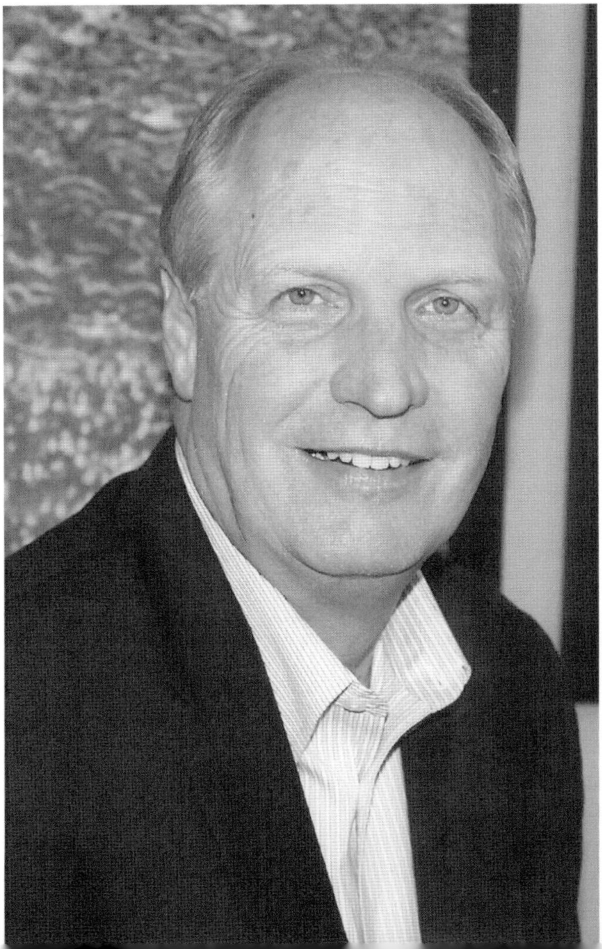

Steve Parker

Steve Parker, as vice president of Lake Worth National Bank, came to Lake Worth in 1984. In 1985, he became senior vice president and married Lee Ann Hardy. Parker became involved in numerous organizations. An active member of his church, he also served on Lake Worth City Council from 1987 to 1991. Named as 1987 Lake Worth Citizen of the year, he also served as president of Lake Worth Chamber of Commerce. He currently holds the position of president of Pinnacle National Bank in Azle. (Courtesy Steve Parker.)

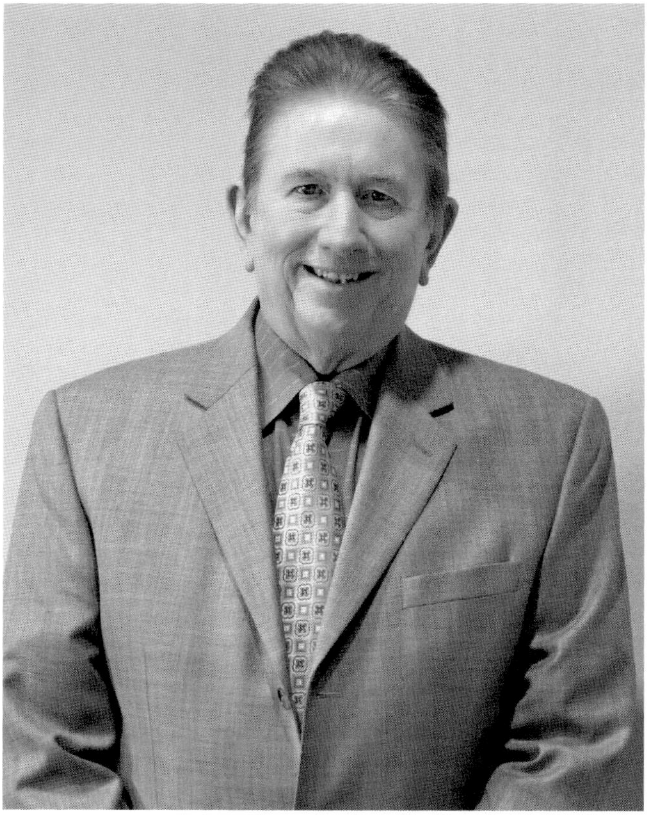

Russ Richardson

Russ Richardson began a lifelong passion for helping others when he became a banker after leaving the Air Force in 1971. He went into banking as a teller at Cleburne National Bank, then moved to Burleson in 1972 and went to work for Burleson State Bank. The next several years, he learned bank operations from chairman of the board Bill Allen. Richardson furthered his education, graduating from Southwestern Graduate School of Banking at Southern Methodist University in 1978. He eventually became director of Burleson State Bank. In 1980, he married Jeannie Gail Martin who worked as a banker at First State Bank of Grandview.

Soon, they left for West Texas to be involved in new bank charters in Midland and Odessa. He became president and CEO of Midland American Bank. She became a senior officer at Odessa Industrial Bank. In 1984, the couple returned to the Fort Worth area to be involved again in the new charter process. Russ Richardson helped open Shady Oaks National Bank in Lake Worth as their chairman and president on April 2, 1984. Jeannie Gail Richardson became a senior officer at Landmark Bank in downtown Fort Worth.

The Richardsons had a son in 1986 named Ryan, and—years later—he too become a banker. Joining up with several investors in 1997, Russ Richardson sought a charter to start another bank, Star Bank of Texas in Lake Worth. It opened on February 23, 1998, on Boat Club Road with Richardson as its chairman and president. In October 2006, Richardson earned a master's of banking degree from Louisiana State University. He became director of Independent Bankers Association of Texas from 1993 to 1999 and of the Texas Bankers Association from 2005 to 2008. He served on the Burleson City Council from 1992 to 1997. Currently as a trustee at Hallmark Baptist Church, he also serves as director of the Burleson Chamber of Commerce.

Additionally, as CEO of the three Star Banks of Texas, Richardson's leadership has left a positive impression within the Lake Worth, White Settlement, and Burleson communities. (Courtesy Russ Richardson.)

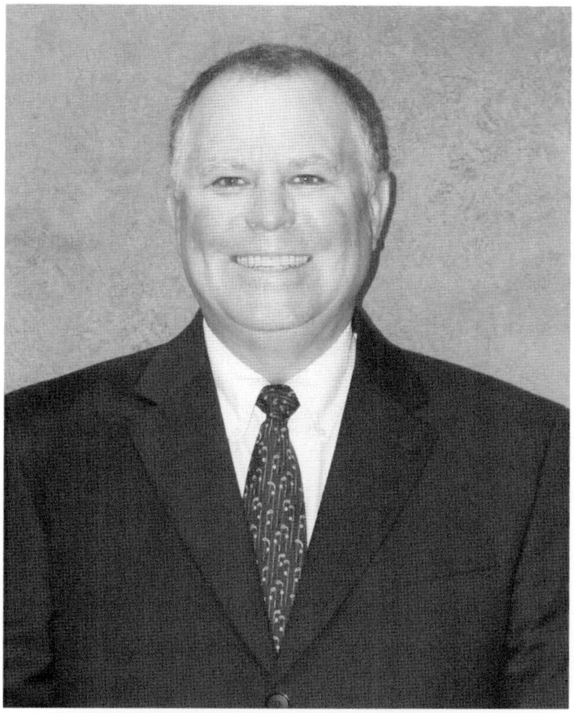

Steve Siebenthall
Steve Siebenthall started his career as a loan officer at Lake Worth National Bank in 1980. In 1983, he moved on to become vice president of Security State Bank in River Oaks until 1986. He then served as vice president of Burleson State Bank for 10 years.

He returned to Lake Worth in 1997 as vice president of Shady Oaks National Bank becoming branch president in 1999. In 2002, he left there to join Star Bank of Texas, now serving as executive vice president and board member. Siebenthall has served as past president of the Lake Worth Kiwanis Club, past president and board member of the Northwest Chamber of Commerce, and past president and board member of the White Settlement Area Chamber of Commerce. (Courtesy Steve Siebenthall.)

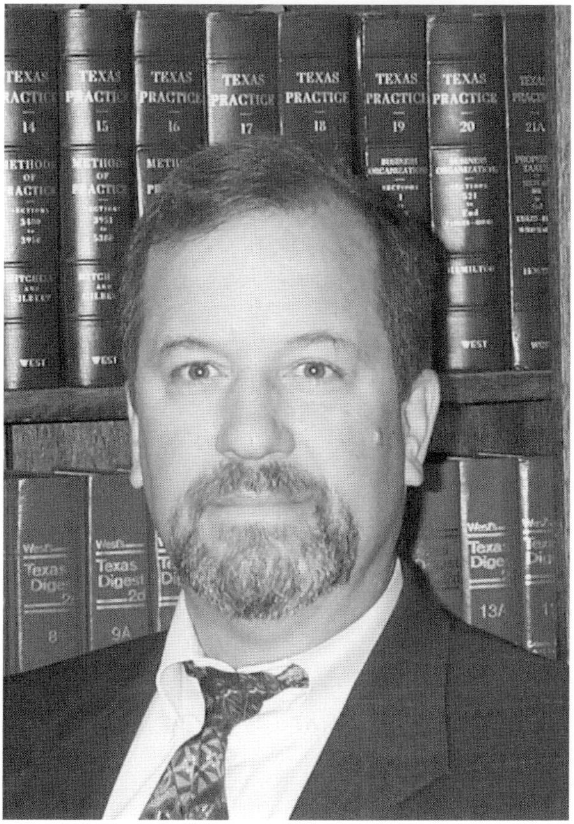

Brad Shaw
Brad Shaw's involvement with Lake Worth came after he received a bachelor of arts degree in political science in 1985 and a juris doctorate in 1988, both from Baylor University. In 1989, Shaw joined George Shaw's practice in Lake Worth.

As a member of the State Bar of Texas, Brad Shaw holds licenses from the Supreme Court of Texas, the US District Court, the Texas Criminal Defense Lawyers Association, the Tarrant County Bar Association, and other important groups. His area of practice varies, including family law matters, criminal defense, real estate, probate, personal injury, and general litigation. As a member of the Lake Worth Kiwanis, he has served as president three times. (Courtesy Brad Shaw.)

George Shaw II

George Shaw prepared himself well for his profession. He graduated from Texas A&M in 1959 with a degree in mathematics and then attended Baylor Law School. He held membership in the Delta Theta Phi Law Fraternity. He graduated in May 1962 and received his license in September 1962. He also obtained licenses from the Supreme Court of Texas, the US District Court, the Northern District, and the US Claims Court.

After college, Shaw worked for the Texas Highway Department in the land acquisition department. He later worked in the Tarrant County Criminal District Attorney's Office for several years as an assistant district attorney. In the 1960s, he went into private practice and later moved his office to Lake Worth in 1970. Shaw covered a wide range of cases including criminal, family, probate, and real estate. In 2012, he received recognition by the Tarrant County Bar Association for having his license for 50 years.

With a love of traveling, he and Gail, his wife of 53 years, saw much of the world. Shaw took his children to see all 50 states and their capitals. Other interests included a passion for reading history, collecting coins, and historical autographs. He belonged to the Lake Worth Kiwanis Club and participated in activities until his failing health necessitated a leg amputation. In addition, his short-term memory loss began to have its effect on his life, but his son stated that in spite of this problem, he never forgot his wedding day when he married Gail Wolfkill, the love of his life. Shaw's love of family and friends left an indelible imprint on their lives. (Courtesy Brad Shaw.)

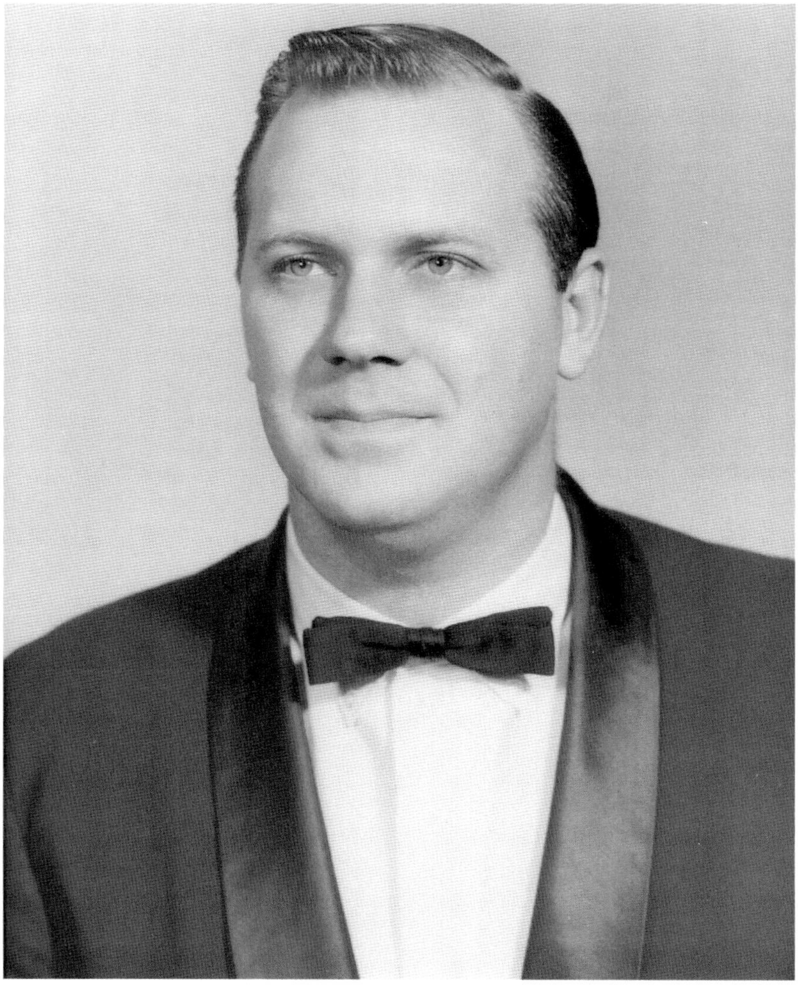

CHAPTER FIVE

Military, Police Officers, and Firefighters

Many Lake Worth citizens have answered the call to duty as military personnel, police officers, or firefighters. Some have worked in military civilian-related jobs. Those featured in this chapter have brought honor to their home community through dedicated service.

A few who served in the military lost their lives in homeland accidents. Dan Giles, an aviator in the Marine Corps and a flight instructor perished in a mid-air collision. More recently, Antonio Ferrara served 10 years in the Army before he died in a motorcycle accident. Others did extensive training without seeing combat, while some survived actual warfare to return to Lake Worth and other places to excel in various professions.

Lt. Col. Kenneth Brower experienced several dangerous situations and sustained injuries parachuting from his burning B-26 airplane in World War II. Members of the French underground service saved Brower. He and others serving in France recently received meritorious recognition from the French government during a ceremony at the Naval Air Station Fort Worth (NAS/FW), formerly Carswell Air Force Base.

V.T. McKay endured dangerous combat in the Army's 101st Airborne Division in World War II. After the war, he also guarded some of German Nazi leader Adolf Hitler's belongings. Harold Kermit Smith served as an Army fighter pilot in World War II. He and his wife moved to Lake Worth in 1945. Smith once served as Lake Worth's city attorney. Dr. Duane Giles, the father of Dan Giles, served as a local physician and received many awards for medical military service. He rose to the rank of colonel. Paul Harmon, Ferrara's grandfather-in-law, served in the Army and received advanced training in several areas. He later devoted himself to the service to Lake Worth.

One couple has done civil service work with the military. Bob Crow worked in civil service with the Air Force. His wife, Jennifer Crow, worked as a civilian personnel officer at NAS/FW. Both worked extensively on plans for Lake Worth's centennial celebration. The couple also serves in their neighborhood association.

Lake Worth's local police officers and firefighters have served and protected citizens well. The city has grown from having self-appointed law enforcement and volunteer firefighting to having fully staffed police and fire departments. In the late 1950s, Virgil Wallace became one of Lake Worth's first police officers when modern-day radar and other law-enforcement tools did not exist. Now, police chief David Tatsak has modern-day technology to aid in his work. Tatsak also proudly shares his faith and trust in God. Prior to becoming city manager, Brett McGuire worked his way through the ranks and preceded Tatsak as police chief.

Firefighters and police officers in Lake Worth hold friendly chili cook-offs each year. Fire chief Michael Christenson, Capt. Michael Voorhies, and other firefighters' photographs appear as they display their trophy won in 2013.

The military, police officers, and firefighters in this chapter have served honorably at home and abroad.

Lt. Col. Kenneth A. Brower

In January 1938, Kenneth A. Brower enlisted in the Oklahoma National Guard. After the Pearl Harbor attack, the call went out by the Army Air Corps for aviation cadet applicants. Staff Sergeant Brower applied, and after being accepted and commissioned, went to Hondo, Texas, completing navigator training in March 1943.

Lieutenant Brower shipped out for the European Theater of Operations in August 1943 and began flying combat missions in January 1944. Brower recalled their first flight on D-Day as lead crew navigator in his B-26 Marauder. He watched the battleship *Texas* firing its big guns and visually followed the shells from the ship to targets on shore. On his 46th bombing mission, July 8, 1944, flying at night, a German Messerschmitt ME410 attacked forcing the crew to parachute out from their flaming aircraft. Unable to walk because of two sprained ankles, Brower caught the attention of a passing French boy. His intervention, along with the aid of the French Underground in the village of Bettencourt-Saint-Quen, saved his life. They hid him for three months until their liberation by the English in mid-October. Repatriated 10 days later, following several days of debriefing, Brower, along with 16 other evaders and a plane of V-mail, took the long flight stateside to LaGuardia Airport in New York, aboard a US Navy PB2Y2.

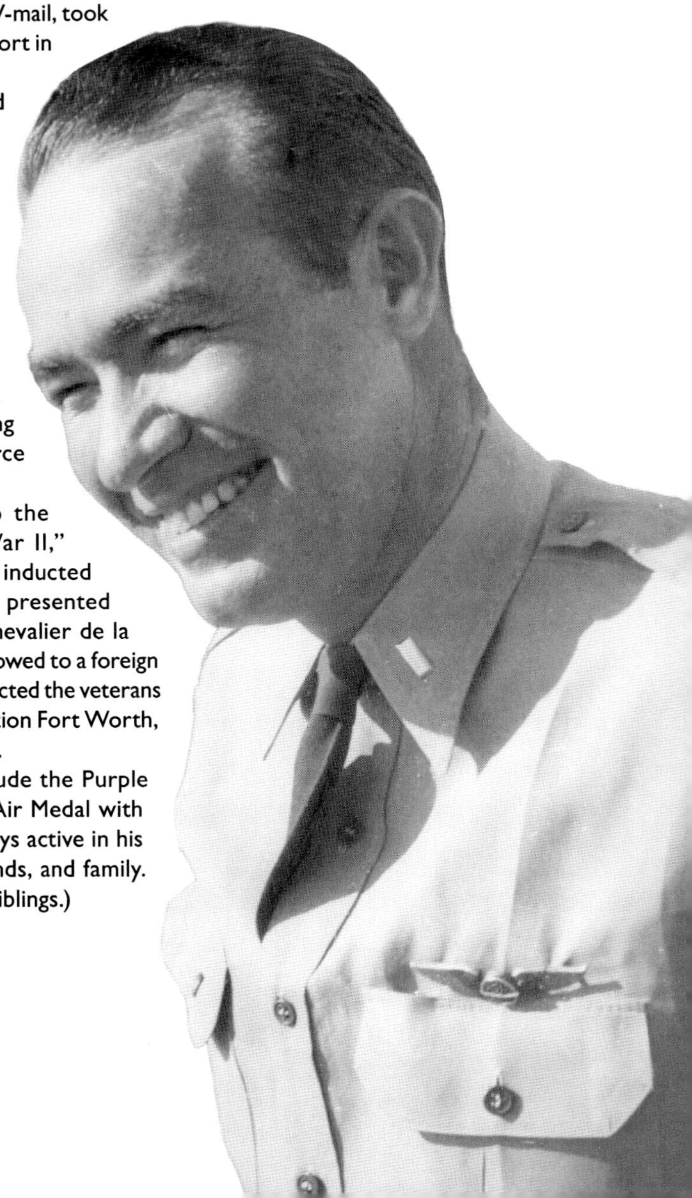

He served in the reserve until recalled to active duty in 1951. He flew 29 combat missions from Japan and Okinawa into North Korea. Returning to America, he elected to remain on active duty in the US Air Force. He served in the Strategic Air Command during the Cold War, flying nuclear training missions in the B-58 Hustler from Carswell Air Force Base, Amarillo Air Force Base, Texas, and Bunker Hill Air Force Base, Indiana. In 1967, he went to Southeast Asia, flying combat missions from U Tapao Air Force Base, Thailand into Vietnam.

"For Exceptional Contributions to the Liberation of France during World War II," Brower and three other veterans were inducted to the rank of chevalier, or knight, and presented the French Legion of Honor Award (Chevalier de la Légion d'Honneur), the highest medal bestowed to a foreign military. The Consul General of France inducted the veterans in a moving ceremony at the Naval Air Station Fort Worth, formerly named Carswell Air Force Base.

Brower's other personal medals include the Purple Heart, Distinguished Flying Cross, and Air Medal with eight clusters. He retired in 1968 and stays active in his community with neighbors, veteran friends, and family. (Courtesy Maj. Kenneth R. Brower and siblings.)

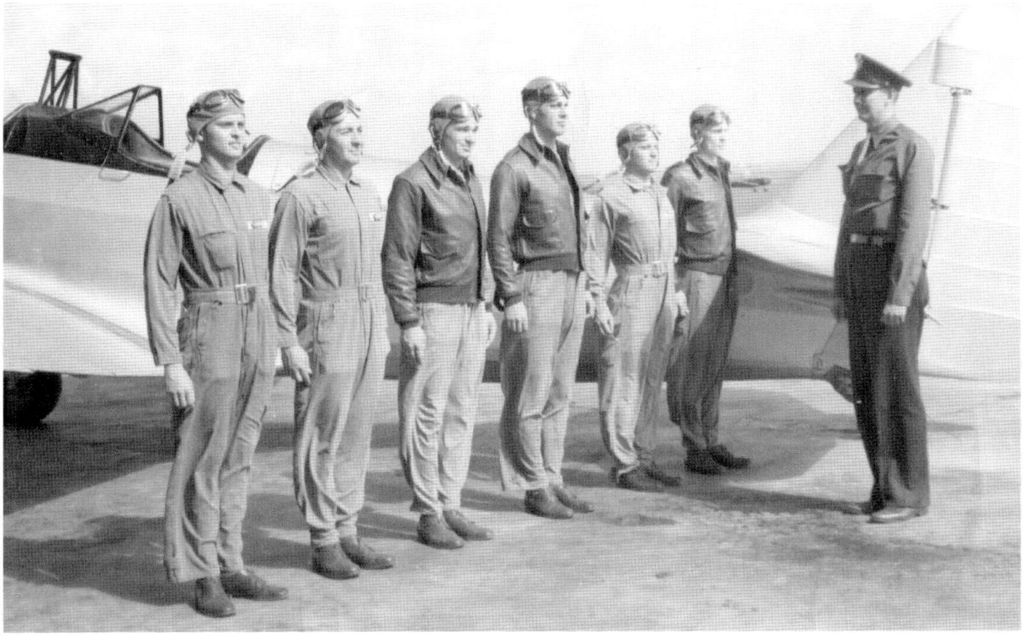

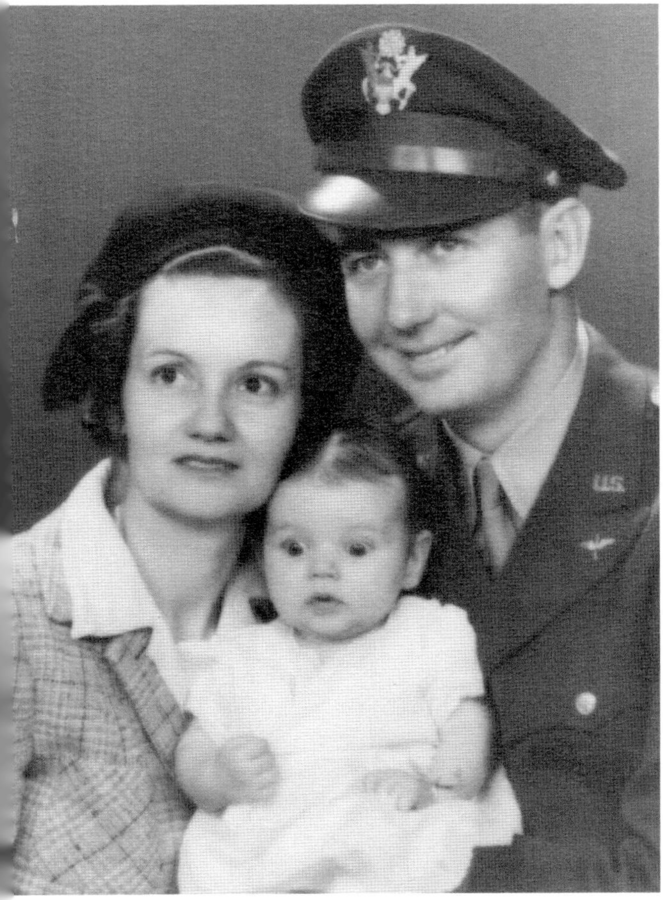

Harold Kermit Smith

Harold Kermit Smith, World War II veteran, pictured above with some of his crew, served as a fighter pilot in the Army Air Corps. He and his wife, Lula Estelle Todd Smith, are pictured at left with their first child, Harold Kermit Jr., moved to Lake Worth in 1945. Their second son, named James Robert Smith, is shown elsewhere in this book. Harold Kermit Smith Sr., a practicing attorney in the oil and gas industry, served as attorney for the Lake Worth Independent School District for many years. (Courtesy James Smith.)

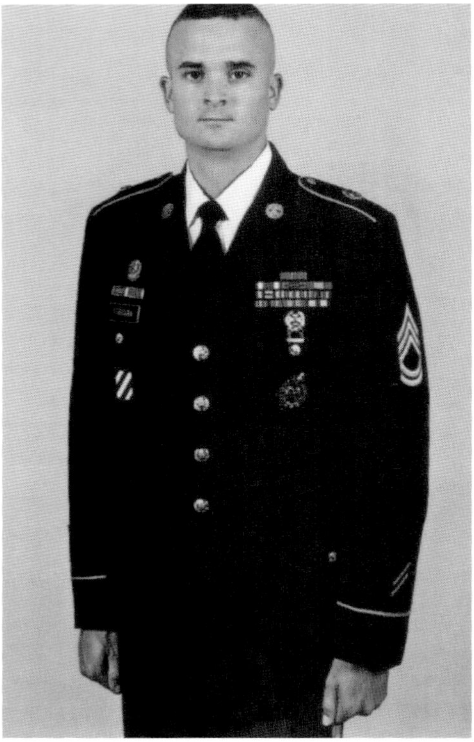

Antonio Ferrara

Sergeant First Class Antonio Ferrara graduated from Lake Worth High School in 2001. He served 10 years in the military with three tours of duty in Iraq and one in Afghanistan in support of Operation Enduring Freedom. He received many medals, including the Meritorious Service Award (twice), the Bronze Star, the Good Conduct Medal, the Army Achievement Medal, and a Recruiters Gold Badge. In November 2013 Ferrara reenlisted. This young hero made it safely through those tours of duty on foreign soil, but lost his life in a motorcycle accident in his homeland just a few days before his 31st birthday. Ferrara leaves behind two young sons and his wife, Jhodi Harmon Farrara. (Courtesy Paul Harmon.)

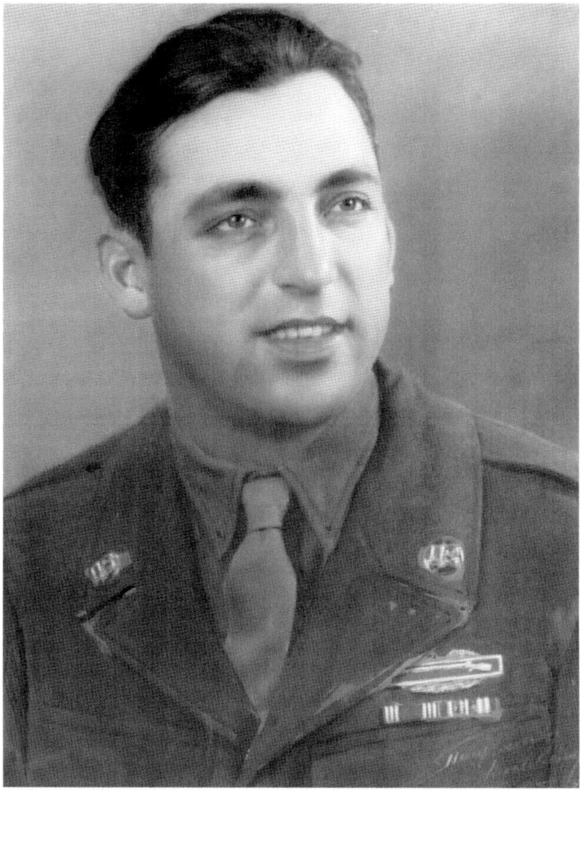

Paul Harmon

Paul Harmon served in the US Army from 1957 to 1961. He belonged to E Company, 506th Regiment, 101st Airborne Division. Harmon received advanced infantry training at Fort Carson in Colorado Springs, Colorado, and later attended jump school elsewhere. His company eventually linked up with the 82nd Airborne Division for further training, each taking turns playing the role of the enemy. As part of the Care Unit in the Zone of Interior, he went to Panama Canal and Puerto Rico. Years later, Harmon served on Lake Worth's city council for 12 years and the school board for eight years. (Courtesy Paul Harmon.)

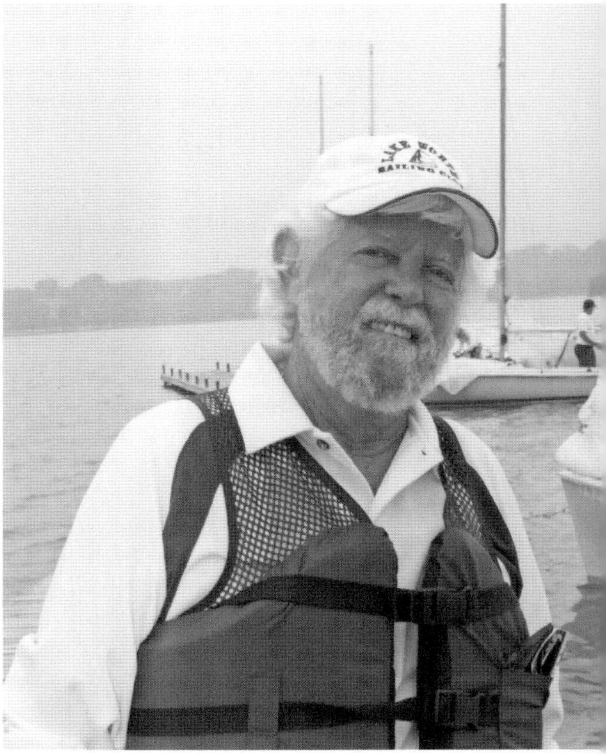

Bob Crow

Bob Crow, a civilian service employee of the US Air Force, has lived in Lake Worth since 1950. A few years ago, he tore down his old home on the shores of the lake and built an outstanding new residence. This location accommodated his love of sailing, an important part of his life for many years. He has served as Post Commodore of the Lake Worth Sail Club.

In addition, Crow worked diligently putting together the 100-year celebration of the lake's construction in 1914. The 2014 celebration includes numerous events throughout the year. (Courtesy Bob Crow.)

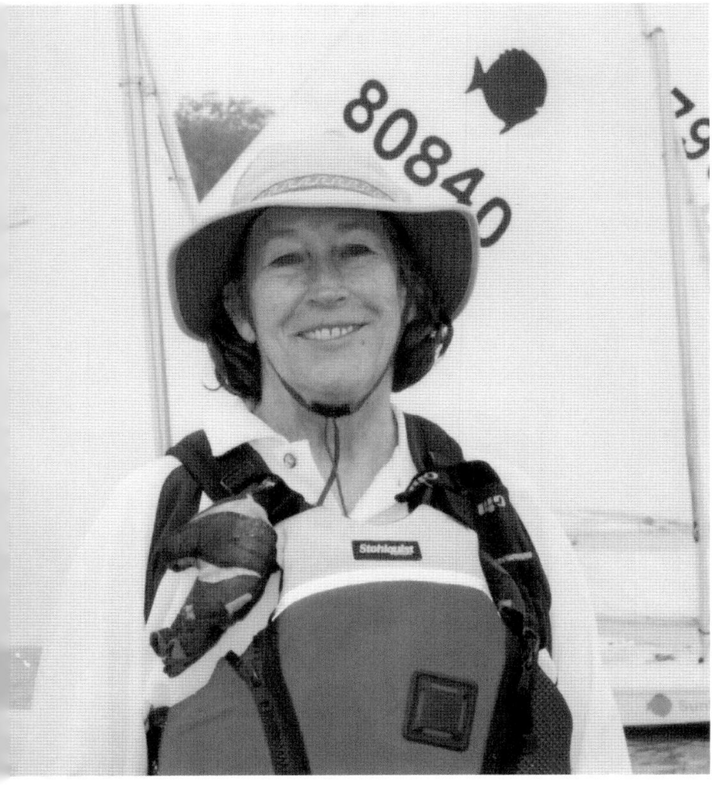

Jennifer Crow

Jennifer Crow worked at NAS/FW, as a civilian personnel officer for two and a half years. She and her husband, Bob Crow, live in a lovely home on the shores of Lake Worth. The convenient water environment provides ample encouragement for her love of sailing. She also stays involved as a member of the Neighborhood Association of South Lake Worth. She and her husband engaged in plans for the 100-year celebration of the lake's development in 2014. (Courtesy Bob Crow.)

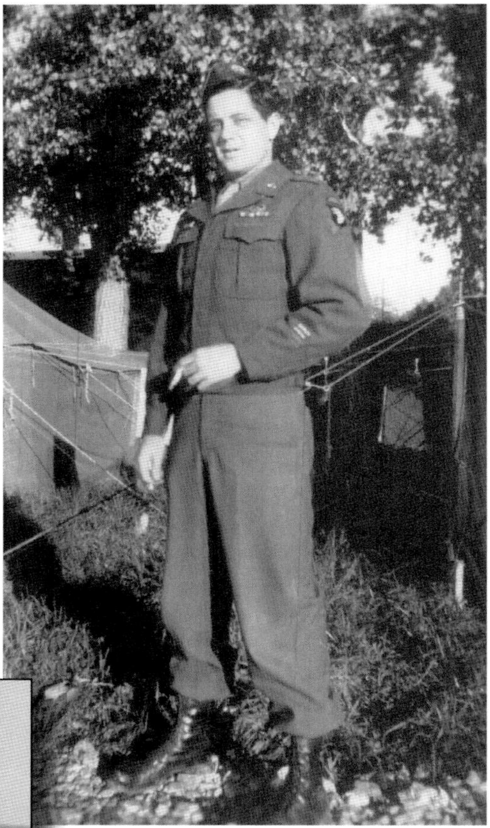

V.T. "Mac" McKay

A man of substance, having been in the 101st Airborne Division of the Army in World War II, V.T. McKay acquired the nickname of "Mac." He fought alongside others to hold off the Germans in Bastogne, Belgium, by parachuting to join friendly forces. This and other assignments proved dangerous and challenging. His division received recognition from the US War Department in name of the president when awarded the Distinguished Unit Citation, later designated the Presidential Unit Citation, for gallantry in action. Another assignment for his division occurred after the war. It involved guarding Hitler's Eagle's Nest, which had many paintings and other important stored items.

One of this brave man's hobbies included fishing. In addition to all the other abilities he possessed, it appears from the photograph below that McKay certainly knew something about this sport. (Both photographs courtesy Eddie McKay.)

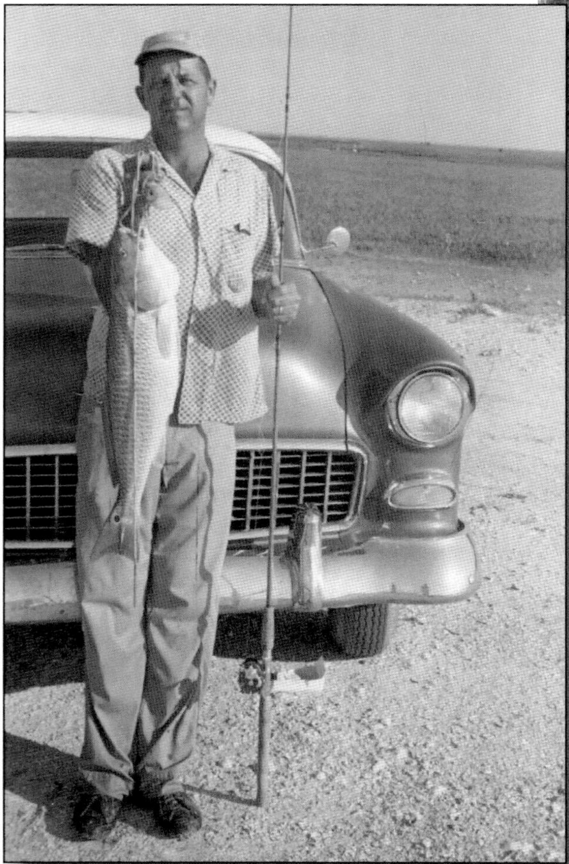

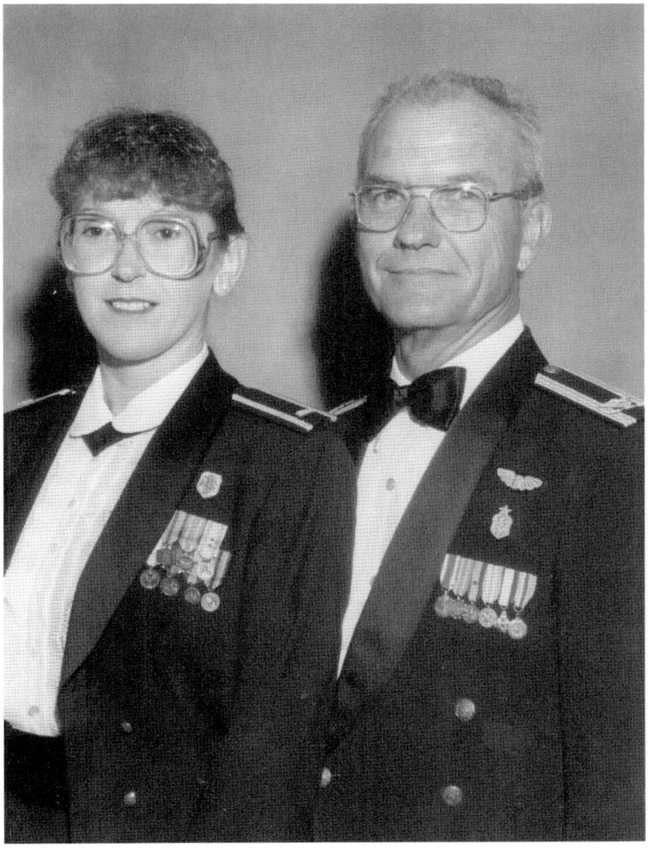

Forrest D. Giles

Forrest Duane Giles graduated from Lake Worth High School in 1949 and started college at Texas Wesleyan College. In 1951, active duty in the Air Force interrupted his education. After serving, he continued his education at Texas Wesleyan College, earning a bachelor of science degree in chemistry in 1955. During this time, he worked at Consolidated Vultee on the night shift.

He then moved to Los Angeles, California, with his first wife, June, and their two sons, Danny and Steve, to attend medical school. He earned a doctorate in osteopathic medicine, a doctorate in medicine, and later took a course in aviation medicine, and he attended Air War College via correspondence.

Still in the reserves, Giles moved back to practice medicine in Lake Worth, Texas, from 1961 until 1987 when he returned to active duty as Air Force Reserve Surgeon General at Carswell Air Force Base. Since that time, Dr. Giles has served in a variety of assignments at base, group, and Air Force levels and attained the promotion to colonel in April 1983.

Giles received a number of awards and decorations while in service, including the Meritorious Service Medal with two oak leaf clusters, the Air Force Commendations Medal, and the Air Force Outstanding Unit Award with four oak leaf clusters. In addition, he received the Air Force Organizational Excellence Award, the National Defense Service Medal with one device (Bronze Star), and Air Force Longevity Ribbon with four oak leaf clusters. Other awards include the Air Force Reserve Medal, an Air Force Training Ribbon, and several other achievement ratings.

At present, this energetic doctor and his wife, Nancy, live on a small pecan and fruit orchard in Northeast Parker County, adjacent to Tarrant County. Nancy Giles also served in the military as a nurse.

With an avid fondness for aviation, Giles practices aviation medicine and still loves to fly as well as build and repair airplanes. In addition, he and his wife belong to the Lake Worth Area Historical Society, located not far from his childhood home in Lake Worth, Texas. (Courtesy Duane Giles.)

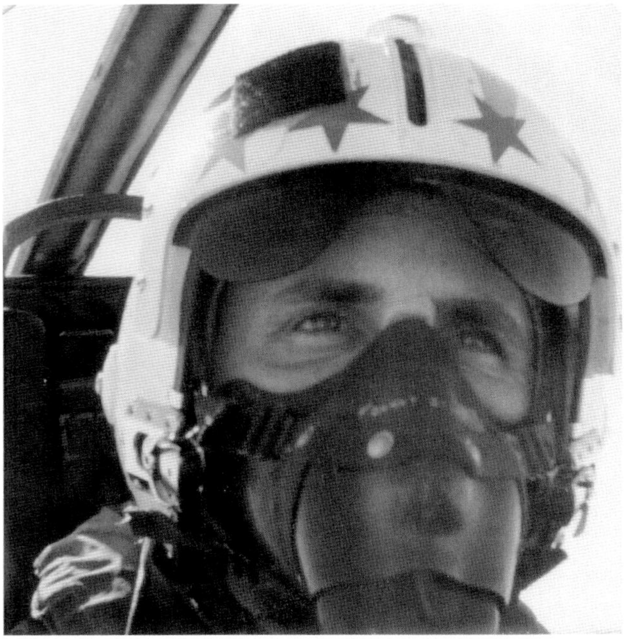

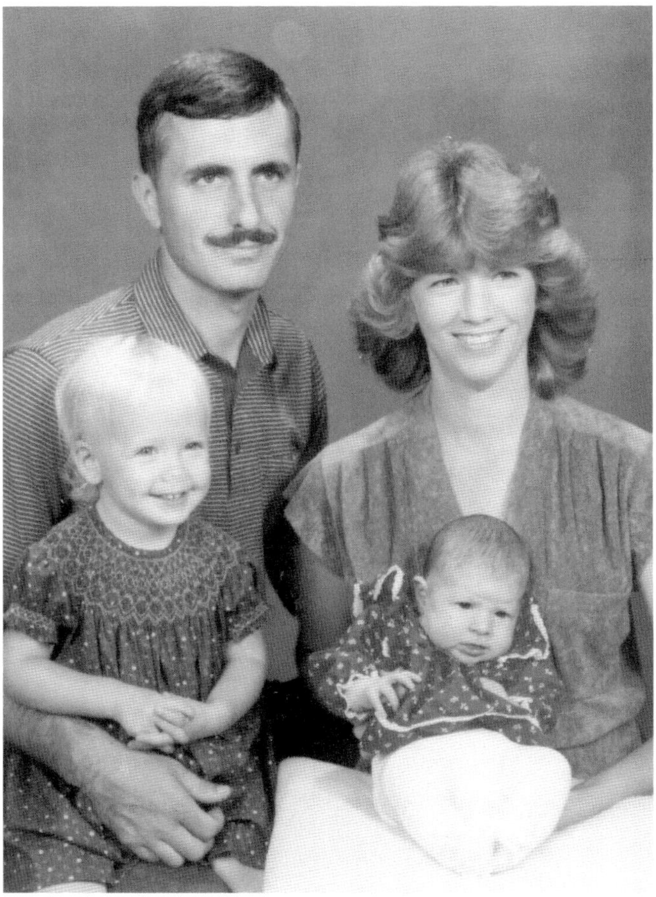

Dan Giles
Capt. Dan Giles, an aviator in the US Marine Corps, and a flight instructor, shown here in his flying gear, flew the Douglas A-4M. One of two children of his parents, Dr. Duane and June Giles, he acquired the nickname "Danny." He graduated from Lake Worth High School in 1972 and from North Texas State University in 1978. He married a woman named Nancy, and interestingly, his stepmother and sister also have that name. Giles, his wife, and children Kelly (the oldest) and Stacey (the youngest) appear in the photograph at right, taken while he served at Marine Corps Air Station Cherry Point, North Carolina. Unfortunately, Giles later lost his life in a mid-air collision in 1985. (Courtesy Duane Giles.)

David Tatsak

David Tatsak, a man who walks in faith, believes that grace received from his savior Jesus Christ, has brought him to the present-day position, the police chief of Lake Worth. His civilian education included L.D. Bell High School in Hurst, Texas, St. Anthony's Seminary in San Antonio, Texas, Tarrant County College in Hurst, Texas, and Criswell Bible Institute in Dallas, Texas.

His education in law enforcement includes a number of specialized trainings starting with the Advanced Police Academy in 1985 in Tarrant County, Dallas Special Weapons and Tactical School, Drug Abuse Resistance Education Officer Training in Kerrville, Texas, and Leadership Command College in 2005. This consisted of training at Texas A&M University at College Station, Texas, and Texas Woman's University at Denton, Texas. The last training before receiving his Master Peace Officer's Certificate involved study at Sam Houston State University at Huntsville, Texas.

Tatsak has served as reserve officer, full-time patrol officer, corporal, tactical officer, sergeant, detective, administrative lieutenant, administrative captain/assistant police chief, and then chief of police.

Ironically, Tatsak's first encounter with Lake Worth's law enforcement happened when being stopped for speeding by Officer Ed Crowdis, who is now chief of police in Springtown, Texas. Tatsak unknowingly sped down a hill doing 47 miles per hour in a 30 miles-per-hour speed zone. The two men talked and Crowdis learned that Tatsak had once been a reserve police officer for six years prior in Pantego, Texas. He told Tatsak that Lake Worth could use some good reserve officers. With that said, Crowdis gave him a warning and in Tatsak's words, "The rest is history." He said he sometimes tells others, "I am in my 29th year of doing assigned community service in Lake Worth for a speeding violation on Boat Club Road."

David Tatsak, a great attribute to the law enforcement in Lake Worth, also serves at Marine Creek Church where he ministers in several capacities. He enjoys playing bagpipes, traveling, bicycling, and working out. (Courtesy Dave Tatsak.)

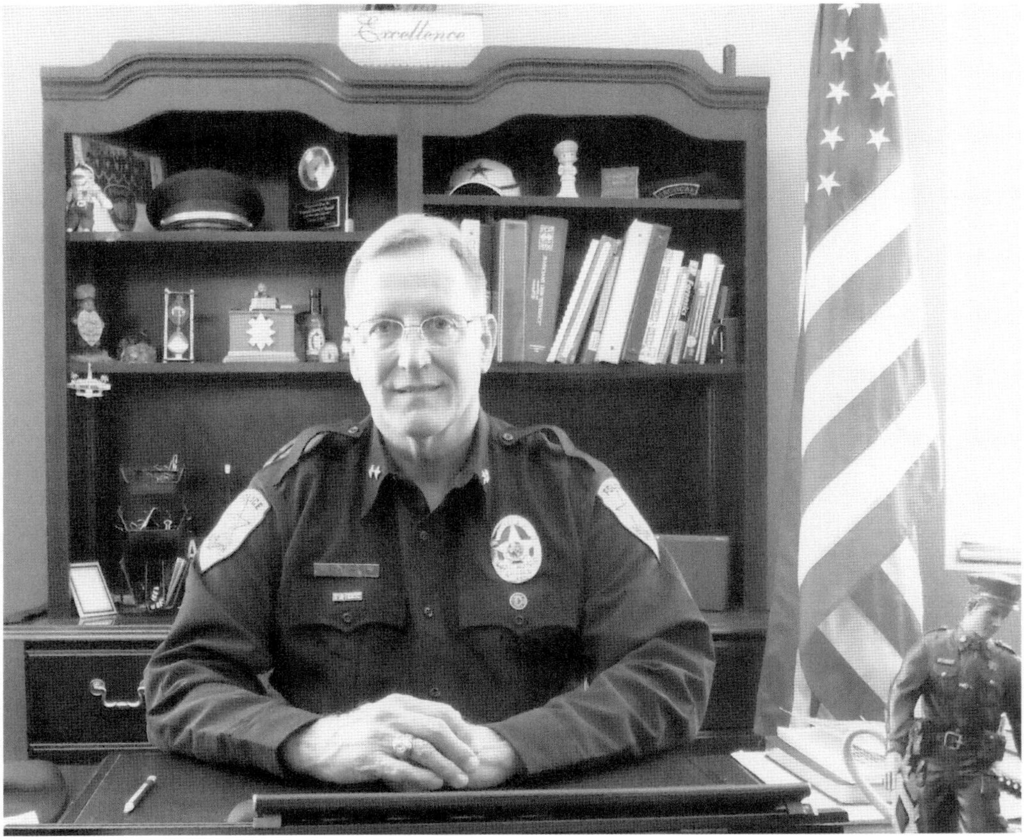

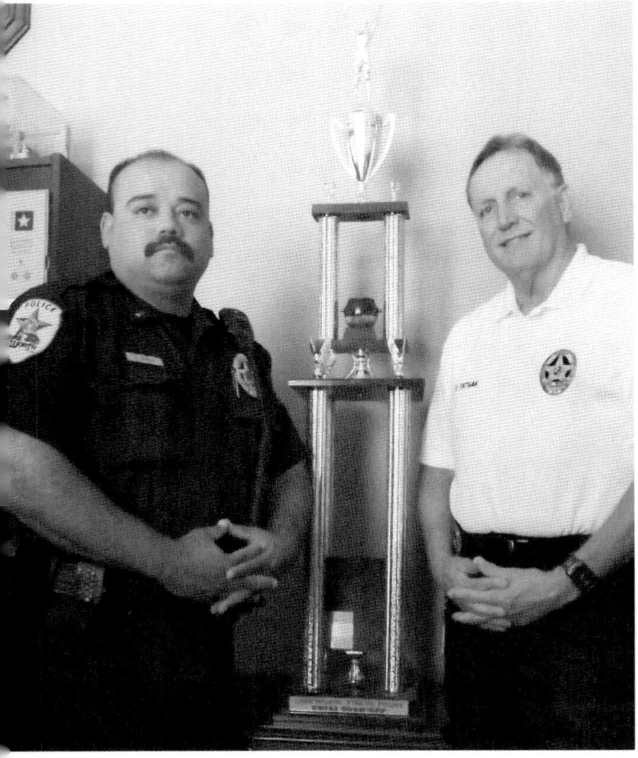

Lake Worth's Chili Cook-Off

The annual chili cook-off between the Lake Worth Police Department and Lake Worth Fire Department makes for a yummy competition for the community to enjoy. Each group provides a number of chili recipes to sample. Only the judges know which is which. The tasters write down their choices as first, second, and third.

Lake Worth's Police Department won this large trophy in the first image in 2009 for the best tasting chili. Police chief Dave Tatsak and Lt. Sammy Garcia are pictured at left.

In 2013, the firefighters won out against the police officers and took away the trophy for the Lake Worth Chili Cook-Off. Standing proudly with the trophy, pictured from left to right are firefighters Mike Christenson, Joe Hamilton, Shannon Stephens, Alan Cunningham, Andrew Ailara, and Mike Voorhies. (Left, courtesy of Dave Tatsak; below, photograph by Ken Brower.)

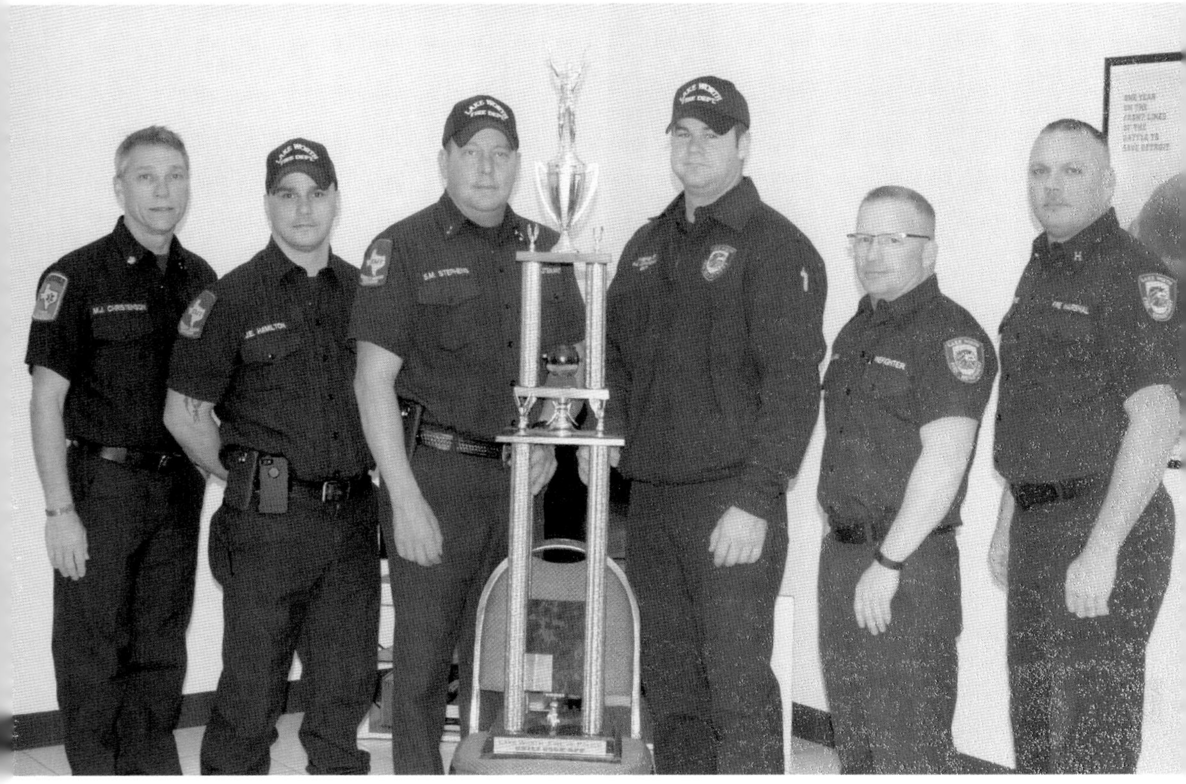

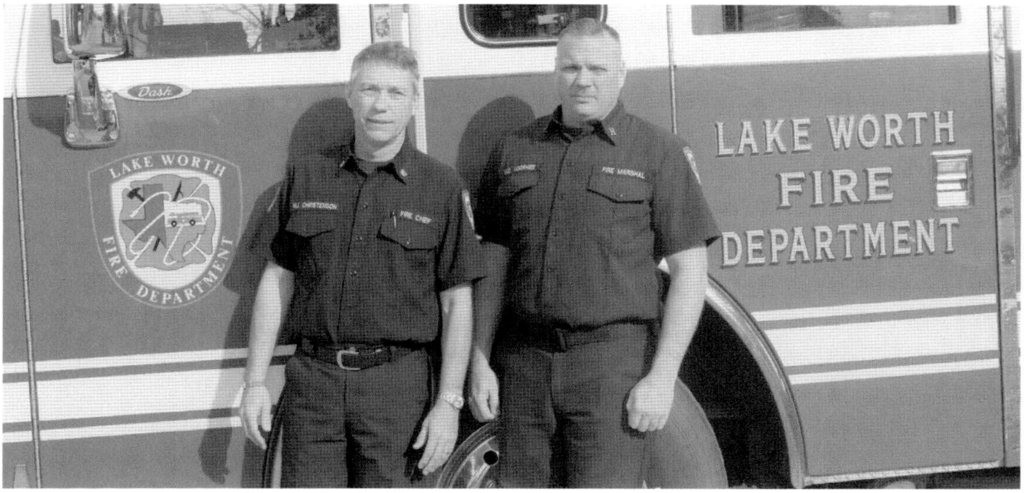

Michael Christenson and Mike Voorhies

Fire Chief Michael Christenson of Lake Worth Fire Department served as a firefighter for 26 years in Euless, Texas. In 2007, he became a shift lieutenant with the Lake Worth Fire Department and earned promotion to chief in 2011. Working on a bachelor's degree, Christenson already holds an associate degree.

Lake Worth Fire Marshal Michael Voorhies joined the US Army in 1987 and later became a police officer. He has worked as an emergency medical technician, firefighter, and arson investigator. He joined the Lake Worth Fire Department in 1999. Voorhies, an Air Force reservist, completed his associate degree. He continues working toward his bachelor's degree.

Christenson, left, and Voorhies, right, are pictured above. (Photograph by Ken Brower.)

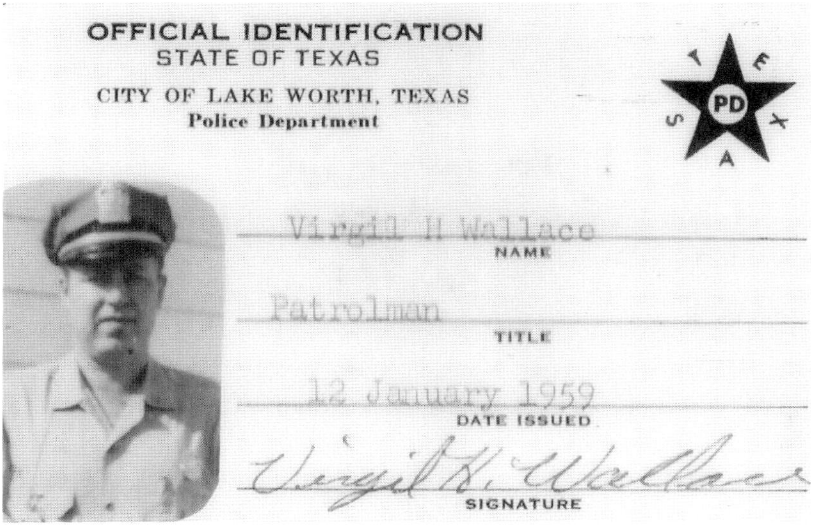
OFFICIAL IDENTIFICATION
STATE OF TEXAS
CITY OF LAKE WORTH, TEXAS
Police Department

TEXAS PD

Virgil H Wallace
NAME

Patrolman
TITLE

12 January 1959
DATE ISSUED

Virgil H. Wallace
SIGNATURE

Virgil Wallace

On the morning of January 12, 1959, Virgil Wallace learned of his layoff at General Dynamics Aircraft Plant. Fortunately, Lake Worth police chief George Campbell hired him as a full-time police officer that afternoon, making him legendary as one of the first officers in Lake Worth. Wallace had previously served as a reserve officer under Campbell while working at General Dynamics. Wallace, a Lake Worth officer for only eight months, took the opportunity offered him to become a Fort Worth policeman. An officer there until 1963, he left to work for Bell Helicopter. (Courtesy Virgil Wallace.)

Brett E. McGuire

From firefighter and paramedic in Washington State, to reserve police officer in 1993 in Lake Worth, to full-time patrol officer in 1995, Brett McGuire advanced even further. He had promotions from sergeant in 1997, to lieutenant in 2000, to captain/assistant chief of police in 2002, and finally to chief of police in 2003. McGuire's interest in public safety has driven him to serve communities diligently wherever he has involvement.

As lieutenant, McGuire had charge of the entire patrol division. The position also included command of the K-9 officer and the drug interdiction officer. Chosen, he attended the Leadership and Command College at Sam Houston State University Law Enforcement Management Institute of Texas. He successfully graduated as part of Class No. 50. With his vast knowledge of management, his appointment as the police department's representative for plans for building a new police department and jail facility currently in use, proved a wise choice.

McGuire believes in allowing responsible others, such as the sergeants and officers working in the field, to make decisions without going through a chain of command. He attributes the success of this decision to the professionalism and the street smarts of those on duty.

Promoted to captain/assistant chief of police in 2002 by Chief Ron Wadkins, McGuire's duties continued in the aforementioned venues, but now included taking charge of telecommunications, property/evidence, and records divisions of the department. Deciding to have more than an enforcement-only model in place, a community-based and citizen-related avenue became more evident with a public-spirited approach.

After the retirement of Chief Wadkins in late 2002, McGuire acted as interim chief. In 2003, he received an appointment as chief of police. He implemented a number of ideas that he said could not have been possible without listening to others on his staff. One of the thoughts included writing a proposal for a crime control and prevention district. This proposal allowed one-fourth of a cent from sales tax to be put into a special fund that could only be used by the police department for anticrime initiatives within the city. The voters approved it in 2004.

He achieved much more as police chief and later become the city manager in 2008 after handling the vacancy for a while as his police staff handled all the law enforcement duties. His expertise continues to serve the area well. (Courtesy Brett McGuire.)

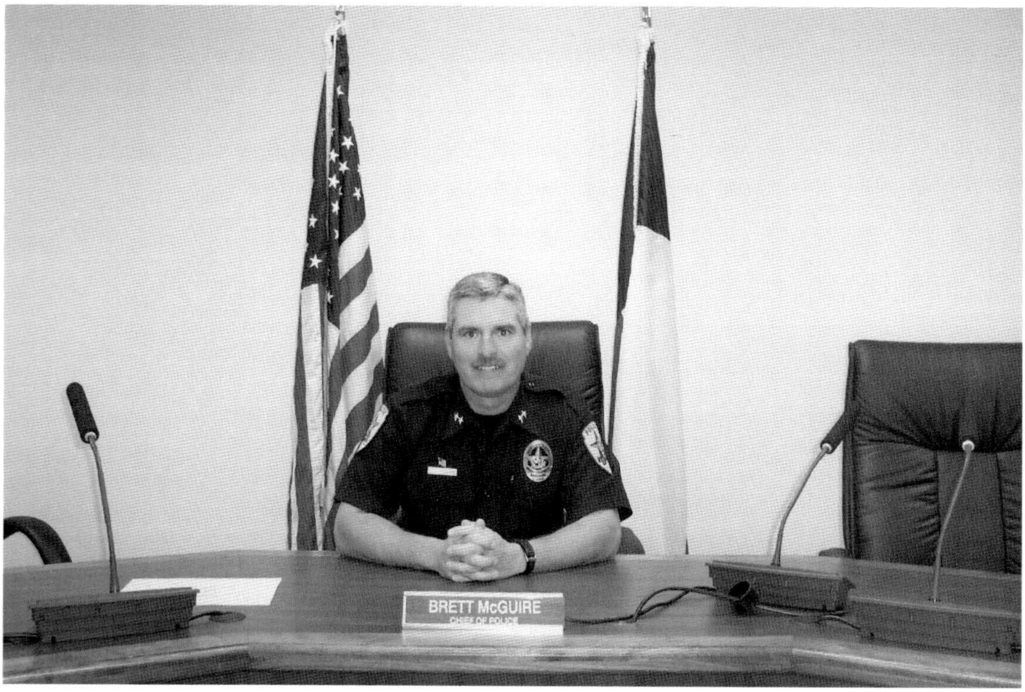

CHAPTER SIX

Authors, Artists, and Musicians

Throughout the history of mankind, the works of authors, artists, and musicians have acknowledged nature, as well as other moments in time in their own unique ways. Whether their works include actual events or fantasies, society looks in their direction for acquiring knowledge or stirring their imagination.

Within this chapter, a few authors and artists, as well as several musicians, have provided an interesting array of information for readers to enjoy. In some instances, the entries in this chapter have had an overlapping career, such as teaching. One such person, Dr. J'Nell Pate, taught history for a number of years at a local junior college. As a speaker and writer, her expertise in this field extends to others. She became one of the original members of a past writing club in Lake Worth and generously shared her writing knowledge. Another author, Jan Peck, writes children's books. Often, her own childhood provided her with experiences she used to create imaginative characterizations. Her books entertain and educate children.

David Davis writes and sometimes does illustrations as well. Like Jan Peck, he has a host of childhood memories. Time spent with his grandfather as a child and other situations provide him outstanding material for his writings and illustrations. He and Jan Peck often go to elementary schools to do entertaining book reviews.

A most unusual combination of talents like those of Henrietta Milan, amaze and intrigue her followers. She creates beautiful paintings and did gymnastics. Her husband, Jerry Milan, taught school, coached teams in both football and basketball, and taught gymnastics for many years. They own an art gallery in Fort Worth and have donated many items to the Lake Worth Museum.

Chuck Ebert, featured in this chapter also, has over 25 years in professional productions in recordings of sound and music. He served in sound control for a number of years at Lighthouse Fellowship Church, formerly Lake Worth United Methodist Church. His current biography includes a number of professional relationships.

Katy Ebert, Chuck Ebert's wife, also has a professional background. She sings and plays several musical instruments. This petite young woman also served as director of music at Lighthouse Fellowship Church. Facing serious medical challenges in the past, she overcame them with her faith in God and the help of many friends.

Just as many other endeavors in life, quilting and sewing involve much work, talent and creativity. Joan Crittenden used her talents to create outstanding quilts. Some of her handiwork has won recognition by others.

Art and Joan Jones owned and operated a local newspaper for a number of years. Their newspaper provided outstanding reporting of local events in and near Lake Worth. Without a doubt, others also possess varied talents, but those presented in this chapter represent some of the finest and best in their fields.

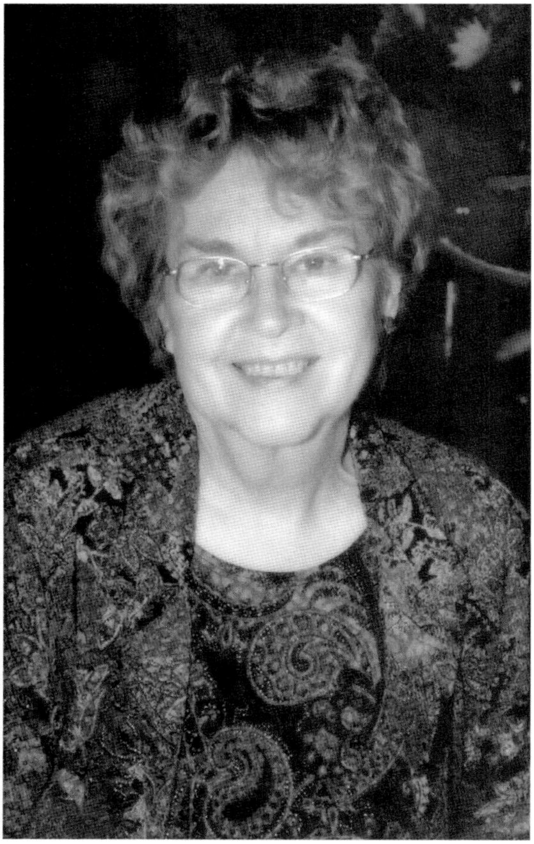

J'Nell Pate

J'Nell Pate received her doctorate in history years ago. Having written 10 books and many articles, struggling members of a new writing club welcomed Dr. Pate's expertise. She became one of the charter members of the Northwest Writers' Club of Lake Worth when it began in 2004. She joined to encourage aspiring writers because she had been fortunate enough already to have been published.

Of the 10 nonfiction books she wrote, half of them relate to Fort Worth history. In addition, she has written a column titled "Pages from Western History" for her hometown newspaper, The *Azle News*, since 1968. At that time, she and her husband, Kenneth, had moved from Fort Worth to Azle, which lies a short distance from Lake Worth.

Her favorite column, inspired by Bob Greene's work, was about his book concerning North Platte, Nebraska. The community organized the feeding of World War II troop trains that stopped daily in that town. This area also became a watering stop for the railroad. Fifty other towns participated.

In the first book, Pate wrote about the Fort Worth stockyards, and the 10th one was called *Arsenal of Defense*, which tells the entire military legacy of Fort Worth. They became her favorites of all the books she wrote. Both won awards. She also spoke to the Lake Worth Area Historical Society about the book, *Arsenal of Defense*.

Pate, born in Jacksboro, Texas, came to Fort Worth with her family at the age of four because her father took a job in the defense plant now called Lockheed Martin. She graduated from Arlington Heights High School, Texas Christian University, and earned her doctorate in history at North Texas State University in Denton. She taught social studies in the Fort Worth Independent School District for seven years, and history and government at Tarrant County College for 32 years.

Now in her retirement, Pate travels but still writes. She enjoys reading mysteries, regencies, and nonfiction history of the West. (Courtesy J'Nell Pate.)

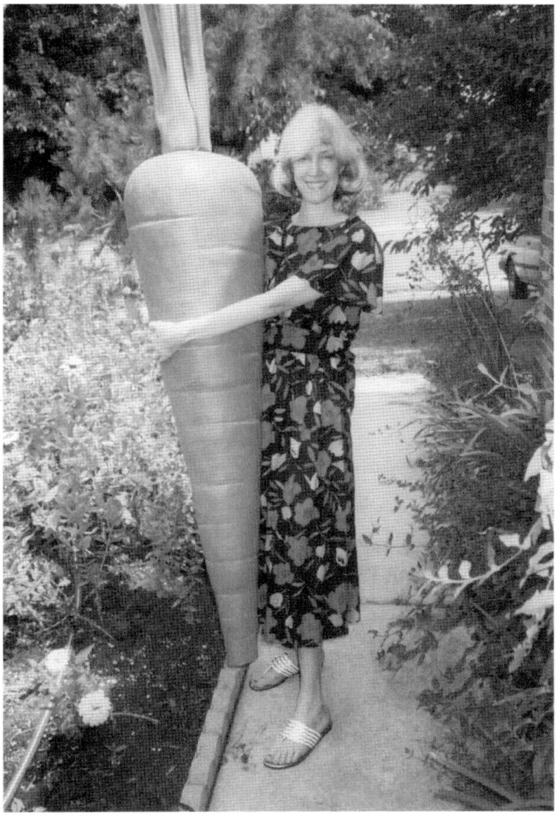

Jan Peck

Jan Peck, an award-winning author, sold her first story, *Hands Full of Worms*, based on a true happening right off Farm to Market road 1886 in Azle, Texas. Her understanding mother allowed her to keep all kinds of baby animals and taught her much about nature. Peck feels that growing up in the Texas countryside gave her a rich background of information that stirred her imagination and contributed to her being an organic gardener.

She got serious about writing at age 33 after reading to her three-year-old son. As she read and looked at picture books with him, she thought it looked easy to write them. At that time, she was attending the University of Texas at Arlington, taking analytical geometry, physics, and other science courses. She made straight As in spite of having dyslexia. This determination served her well.

Not able to stop thinking about writing children's material, she began the process. It took her three years before she sold her first story to *Highlights for Children Magazine*. Joining the Society of Children's Book Writers and Illustrators, she immersed herself in their volunteer work and became close friends with many of the members. She also learned much about writing.

She refers to one of her popular books, *The Giant Carrot*, as her first "New York" book, which received star reviews and appeared on many states' awards lists. One of her most popular books, *Way Down Deep in the Deep Blue Sea*, has been in the Scholastic book fairs and sold internationally to Australia, Japan, England, and South Korea.

In 2002, Peck teamed up with a fellow member of SCBWI, David Davis. They have traveled all over Texas performing an interactive agenda with schoolchildren, which gets the students excited about reading, writing, and art.

This writing grandmother enjoys life with her husband in a home just one block from the community of Lake Worth. Many appreciate her dedication to writing educational and entertaining books for children. (Courtesy Jan Peck.)

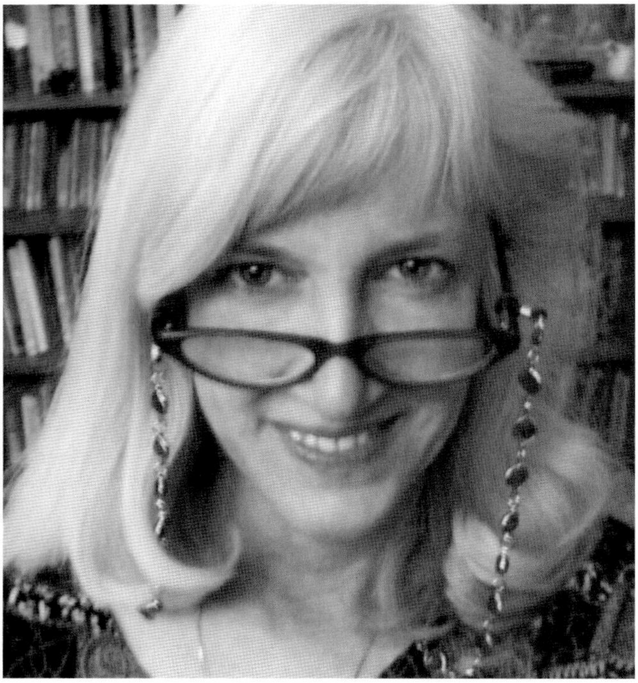

Jan Peck, Encourager

With many demands in her life, back when she wrote *The Giant Carrot*, Jan Peck took time out to visit and encourage aspiring writers of the former Northwest Writing Group located in Lake Worth, Texas.

She has written seven books and has contributed many stories and articles for various children's periodicals. In addition, she has contributed to anthologies including *Chicken Soup for the Kids' Soul*. (Courtesy Jan Peck.)

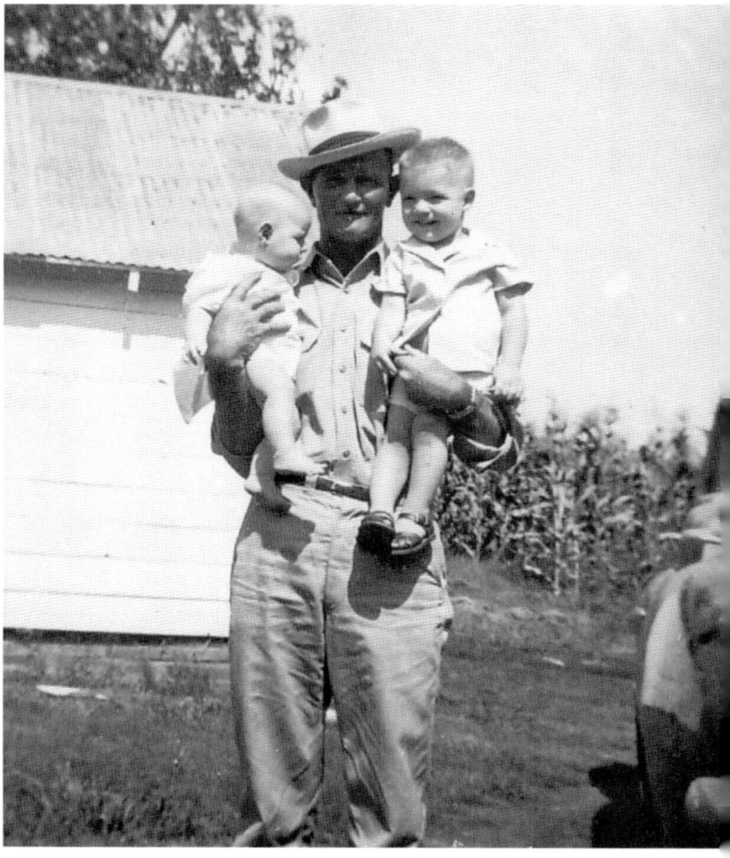

David Davis Travels with Grandpaw

One of David Davis's most delightful books, *Travels with Grandpaw*, puts to paper his Texas memoirs about growing up with his beloved grandfather Raymond Lacy.

Davis describes himself as a fifth-generation Texan. When he speaks of the love and admiration he holds for his grandfather, his face lights up. Sometimes his touching stories bring tears to the eyes of his audience.

In the photograph, David Davis, on the right, and his sister Linda, on the left, appear quite happy in the arms of their grandfather. (Courtesy David Davis.)

David Davis

David Davis, a well-known and respected humorist, writer, and cartoonist honored members of a local writing group in Lake Worth several times in the early 2000s by attending, sharing his stories, and offering his expert critiquing skills.

He has a successful background of articles and cartoons including cartoon panels that appeared in *Celebration: A Creative Worship and Christianity Today*, as well as *Sojourner's Magazine*, among others.

In the 1990s, he won an award from the Mississippi Press Association for one of his cartoons featured in the Madison County Journal. As a child, Davis often got sent to the principal's office for his cartoon drawings sometimes depicting a teacher. The vice principal might laugh, but would quickly follow with, "Three days in detention hall."

With his sense of humor as his sidekick, Davis said he has not changed much, for he still likes to spread a little mirth with his work. That charming characteristic of Davis landed him a job writing humor for *Comic Buyer's Guide*, each article accompanied by his comic art. Later, he gave a twist to a classic story by writing a satirical poem titled "Redneck Night Before Christmas." Pelican Publishing Company liked the work, and this led to publication of his first book.

Since then, he has written over 23 books, many as children's picture books, one of which he wrote with Jan Peck, another well-known children's writer. They have presented hundreds of programs for elementary schoolchildren.

Davis has received a number of prestigious awards for his various works, including his book titled *Jazz Cats*, named to the Children's Choice Top 100 List. It also became a finalist for the Texas Golden Spur Award. Much of his work, available in print and as e-books, may be located on Amazon and Smashwords.

Davis, a fifth-generation Texan coming from East Texas farming stock, grew up in San Antonio. The rich and colorful culture of the Anglo-Hispanic people has influenced his creative genius as seen in his art and writing. (Courtesy David Davis.)

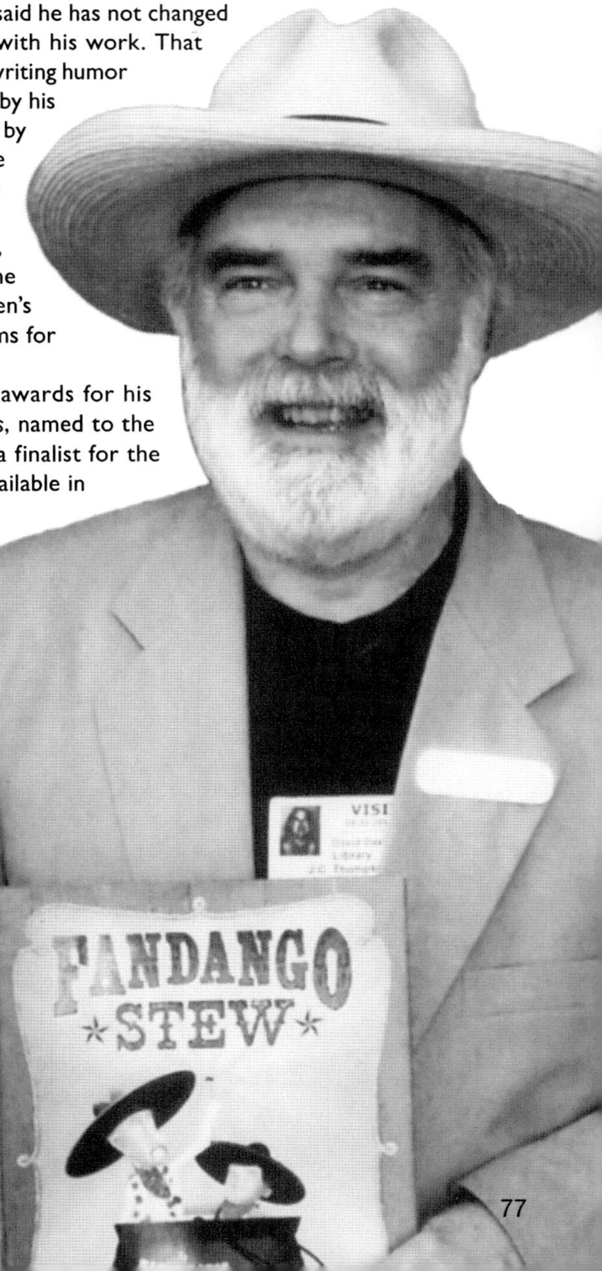

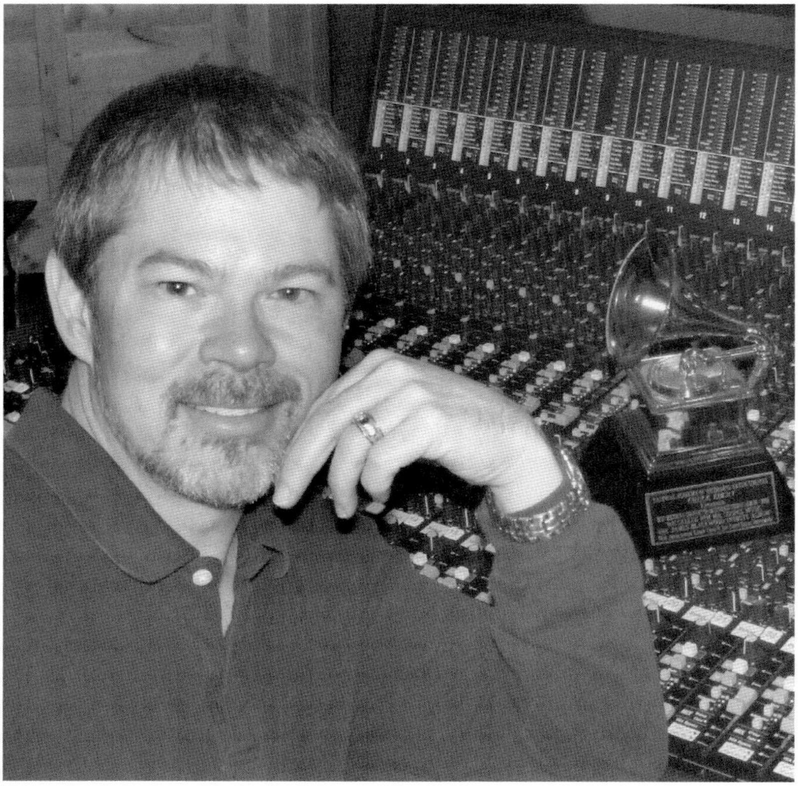

Chuck Ebert

Known as "The Sound Doctor," Chuck Ebert, president and chief executive officer of Axon Entertainment Incorporated, has over 25 years of experience in professional production involving sound and musical recordings. His talent and skills as a producer, master sound engineer, and acoustician won him a Grammy Award. In addition to having been nominated seven times for a Grammy and three times as a Dove Award Nominee, the highest honor achieved in Christian Music today, Ebert's body of work has become well known.

His ties with Lake Worth stem from having been in control of sound at the Lighthouse Fellowship Church, formerly the Lake Worth United Methodist Church. He also has a number of friends formerly from Lake Worth whom he has visited, especially George Hollis, a Lake Worth entrepreneur.

Ebert's various musical endeavors include the fact that he produced and engineered work with many artists including James Blackwood, The Light Crust Doughboys, The Jordanaires (Elvis Presley's group), Twila Paris, the Dixie Chicks, Don Henley, Kris Kristofferson, and many more. He has worked with several television channels including ESPN, HBO, and The Travel Channel. He belongs to a number of professional organizations, such as the National Academy of Recording Arts and Sciences, Audio Engineering Society, American Society of Composers and Publishers, the 2008 Heritage Who's Who, and Princeton Inductee of Business Owners. Ebert, a voting member of the Grammy Awards, sits near his own Grammy on his sound mixer in this photograph.

The latest CD project that Ebert worked on, "Making a Difference," features Denver Moore, a bestselling author. Moore wrote *Same Kind of Difference as Me*, currently in film production with Disney Studios. A short time ago, Ebert designed and built a log cabin that houses a large recording studio. *Mix Magazine* featured it as "The Cabin."

Located in Azle, Texas, a small community not far from Lake Worth, the cabin presents an outstanding example of quality architecture. Fortunate to have Chuck Ebert, the world of music lovers embraces his contributions. (Courtesy Chuck Ebert.)

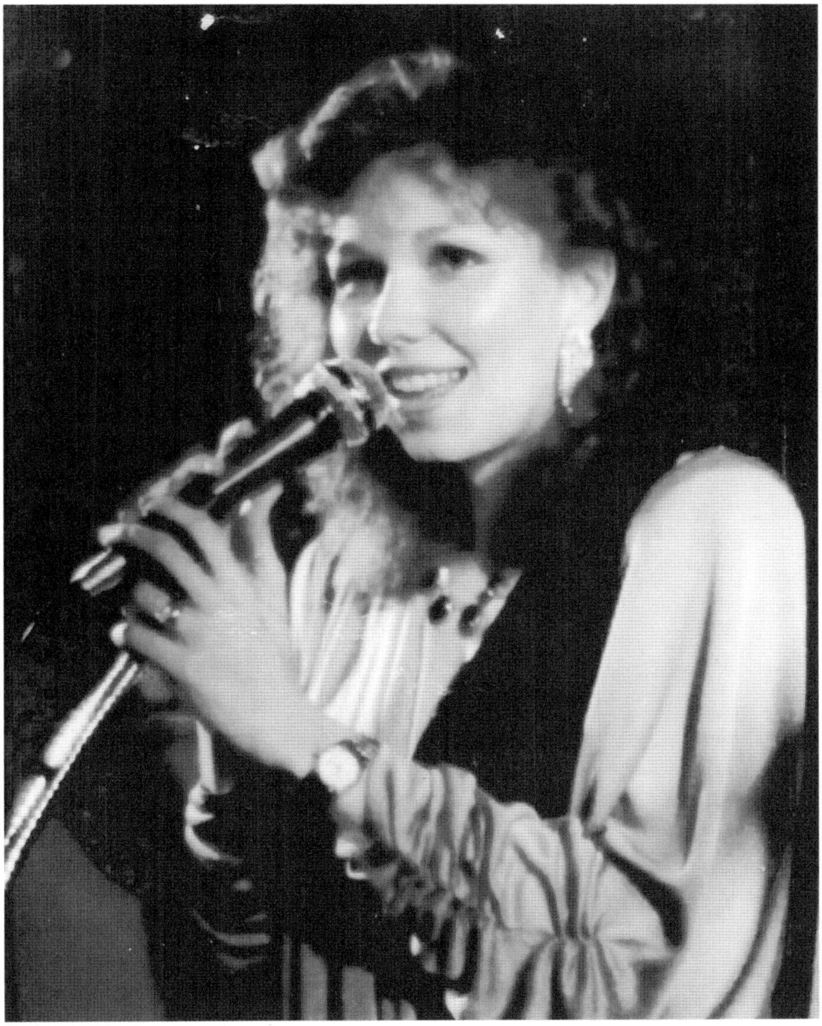

Katy Gaby Ebert
Born in Fort Worth, Texas, in 1963, Katy Ebert at age 16 began singing professionally with local bands and soon started opening acts for other musicians including Frank Sinatra and Bob Hope. She sang on demo records and jingles for Coca-Cola and the Dallas Cowboys.

Ebert has directed music in local churches, such as Lighthouse Fellowship Church, formerly Lake Worth United Methodist Church, helping them make the transition from traditional music to contemporary Christian music. She especially enjoyed leading adults in the praise band and praise choir and has worked with all age groups including teaching music to pre-kindergarten and kindergarten students.

This highly talented woman's music career was interrupted by rheumatoid arthritis–associated interstitial lung disease and a rare autoimmune disease known as dermatomyositis. After many medical treatments, including chemotherapy in the United States, her church family at Lighthouse Fellowship helped her go to Germany to receive specialized medicine formulated for her body. When she returned to America with her new medicine, she took it for a year, and then blood test results showed normal with no trace found of scarring on her lungs. Her health became much improved.

Ebert says that her strong faith in God helps her with health problems, and He gives her happiness and as the conductor of her life, strengthens her prayers lifted up to His name. Today, this inspiring female continues to sing and play the violin with the Fort Worth Civic Orchestra. (Courtesy Katy Ebert.)

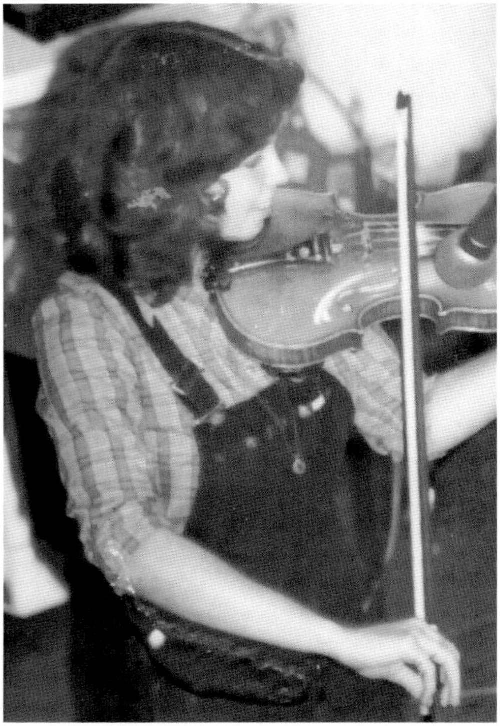

Young Katy Gaby Ebert

A native Texan and raised by her grandparents, Katy Ebert learned to play the piano, guitar, organ, mandolin, flute, recorder, accordion, and violin. As a teenager, she especially enjoyed playing her fiddle. She won numerous contests for her age division. At age 13, she began performing at the Grapevine Opry and other local opries before going on to her professional career.

At age 20, Ebert began directing music in local churches. She wrote a successful children's musical about the disciples titled *We're Gonna Follow Jesus*. She has taught pre-kindergarten and kindergarten children as well as directing bands for high school–age students. (Courtesy Katy Ebert.)

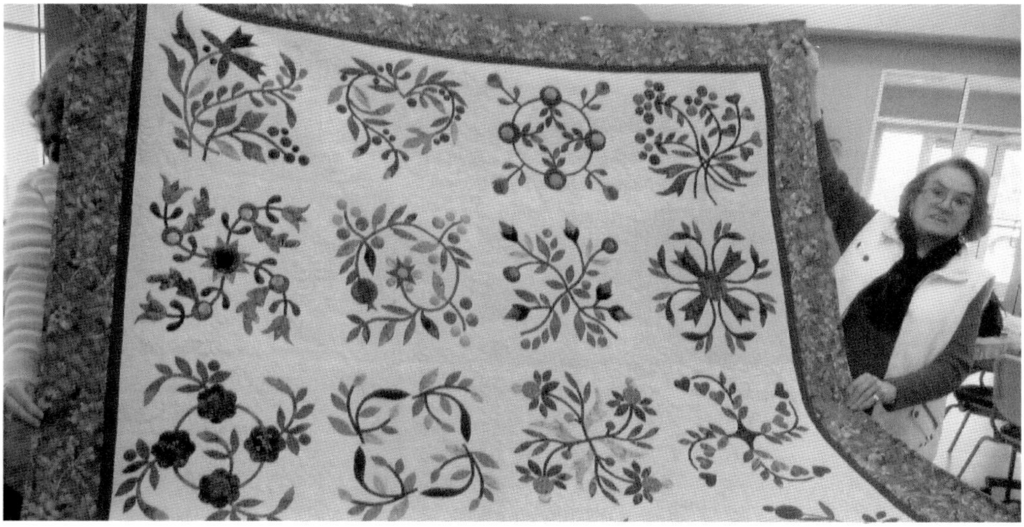

Joan Crittenden

Joan Crittenden's two passions in life include quilting and her genealogy research. Crittenden has attended quilting sessions at the L.O. "Bud" Irby Senior Citizen Complex in Lake Worth. Having quilted since age 11, she helped her grandmother make her first two quilts with the Dutch doll pattern on one and the butterfly pattern on the other. Her grandmother supplied the feed sacks and Crittenden did the appliqué stitch with her grandmother doing the quilting and binding.

In 1985, Crittenden won two ribbons for two of her three quilts entered in the Trinity Valley Quilt show. She says that quilting allows her to express herself. Fortunately, she enjoys helping others quilt. (Courtesy Joan Crittenden.)

Henrietta and Jerry Milan

Henrietta Banfi Milan, a well-known artist with paintings sold internationally, never took an art lesson outside of what she learned in high school. Not only a renowned artist, but also a national gymnastics champion in 1959, she sometimes enjoys attending the Olympics.

In 1960 while in Rome, she could not attend as she gave birth that day to a son. In honor of where and when he was born, she named him Rome. The following Olympics schedule, held in Japan in 1964, would require a good deal of money for those wishing to attend. Milan wanted to go, so she painted her way there. All of this work spearheaded opening the Milan Gallery where Milan's and others' art hangs. Her son Tal runs the gallery. Her son Ron and his wife, Pauline, run Sokol of Fort Worth, which is part of a national organization called American Sokol. Its Czech heritage dates back to 1913.

One of Milan's creations, the beautifully inspired book, *Quiet Contentment*, portrays her rendition of Monet's restored gardens, which she has visited. She also has other pieces of art done in her impressionist style. Each year, Henrietta Milan donates pieces of her art for a fundraising auction for breast cancer.

Jerry Milan taught gymnastics to many, including his wife, Henrietta. He taught 20 years in the Hurst-Euless-Bedford Independent School District. Milan, a past director of the HEB Age Group Gymnastics Program from 1959 to 1988, received induction into the Sports Hall of Fame in 2003.

Prior to teaching in HEB, he taught 10 years in the Castleberry ISD, where he served as a teacher and coach in football and basketball. He has vast experience in working with youth connected associations including Young Men's Christian Association in Fort Worth, Texas. He has served as president of Sokol and taught gymnastics there as well as workshops and clinics throughout the world. He has been director of programs and served as coordinator to many programs internationally and also co-owns Milan Gallery in Fort Worth, Texas.

Milan belongs to numerous organizations associated with sporting events as well as Czech-related heritage organizations. He and his wife have traveled extensively, often attending the Olympics. The Milans have donated many items to the Lake Worth Museum. This highly talented family with its rich heritage has proven to be a treasure to the city of Lake Worth. (Courtesy Henrietta and Jerry Milan.)

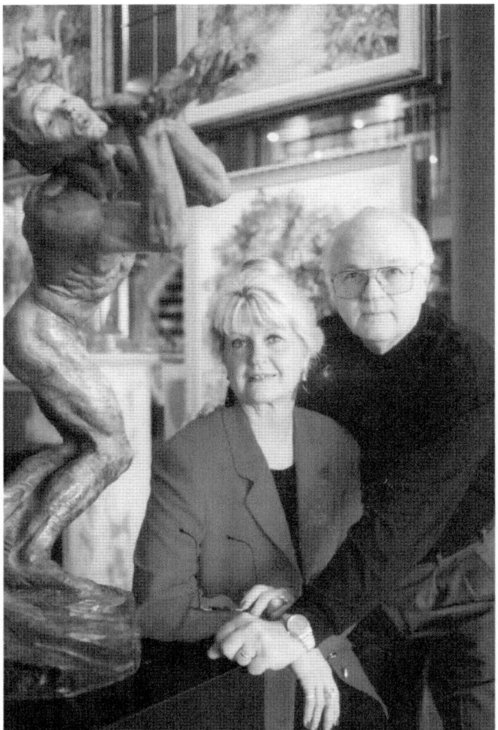

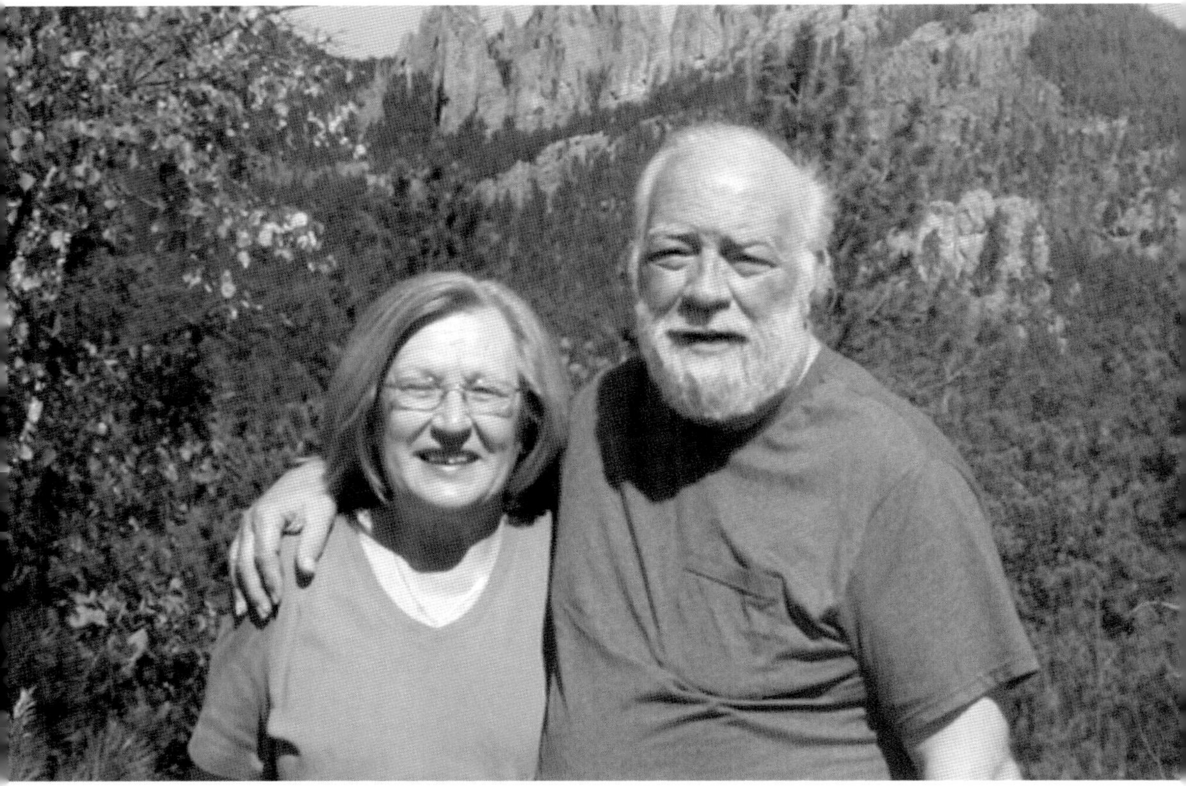

Art and Joan Jones

Art and Joan Jones acquired the *Times-Record* newspaper located in Lake Worth, Texas, in September 2001, the month he turned 60.

Writing and owning a local newspaper did not qualify as a lifelong dream for either of them; however, they each had background experience, which served them well.

Even though the paper covered an extensive area including Lake Worth, Saginaw, Blue Mound, and Lakeside, they tackled the job quite successfully.

Fresh out of high school in 1959, Art Jones began a 20-year broadcasting career, which started at KCLE Radio in Cleburne, Texas, about 40 miles south of Lake Worth. He covered many stories involving police beats, accidents, city council and school board meetings, as well as rodeos, parades, and the assassination of a president.

In 1980, he received numerous awards for creative radio and television commercials he wrote and produced while working for a Fort Worth advertising agency. Also, during the 1980s, Art Jones began writing articles for a number of trade journals and niche magazines. Later, he formed a production company where he specialized in both commercial and industrial promotional materials. His work included graphics, photography, layout, and design for such companies as Radio Shack, Champlin Petroleum, and Alcon Laboratories.

He previously had met his wife, Joan, who worked as an assistant director of a Midwest trade association. She moved back to Texas in 1977 and became marketing director for an international automotive trade association based in Fort Worth. She had the responsibility of setting up the association's annual convention and trade show.

Her people skills and editing abilities and her husband's various talents and previous employment served them well when they bought the *Times-Record*. The community embraced the fine reporting and writing from this local newspaper, and now that it does not exist, they miss it greatly. (Photograph courtesy Art and Joan Jones.)

CHAPTER SEVEN

Miscellaneous Individuals

This chapter further presents a number of various individuals who have contributed in their own way to enhance the lives of their surrounding communities, particularly in the city of Lake Worth, Texas.

For some individuals, their ability to use what they have and take it to the highest level possible not only benefits themselves, but those around them. That realm of thinking must have been what George Hollis discovered early in life.

As a young boy, he started his first business, a vegetable stand, in front of his home. In the years ahead, he continued to find ways to be productive both personally and civically.

Harold Green's entire family served society in a number of ways. Through their church and, or, through a formal education, each of the siblings have a professional career. Their parents enjoyed working in their church and school.

After losing a loved one, Helen Vallery created a foundation to help young people in recovery from drugs. This type of generosity keeps hope alive for many.

Author Joe McDaniel, invited by the original author of this book to come aboard rather late in the game, gracefully accepted and participated admirably. In addition, he serves as the current president of the Lake Worth Area Historical Society.

James Reza, a Lake Worth resident, with many skills and talents, has experienced a wide variety of involvements that make him most interesting. Other selected ones for this chapter include Charley Haddad, a waitress who loves to talk about her faith in God. Her excellent service at her place of employment has created a delightful reputation. Maria Macias, also in the food industry, loves her job as a cook in a local restaurant where she makes her customers feel special.

Another waitress and manager, Linda Ferris, known as "Lulu," inspired the owner of her restaurant to create a special bingo night named in her honor. Farris's outgoing personality and background enhances her employment.

In the beauty business for many years, Opal Beauchamp and Reba Thurman teamed up together and opened their own happy beauty salon. Their clientele received outstanding service.

Barbers, in a similar environment, can have as much enjoyment cutting hair as the beauticians. David Ford had a witty personality that entertained his customers. He also did civic service. Bill Mowell, musically inclined, provided entertainment at his business, which he called Wild Bill's Barber Shop. His singing was legendary.

Eddie McKay had a lengthy career in the insurance business and spoke to Lake Worth City Council members in 1982 about the importance of computers. She also co-led a Girl Scouts group. One of the girls in the troop went on to become a well-known personality. In selecting the entries for this chapter, the various types of employment necessitated a broad-spectrum title. Each one chosen became outstanding in whatever their work encompassed.

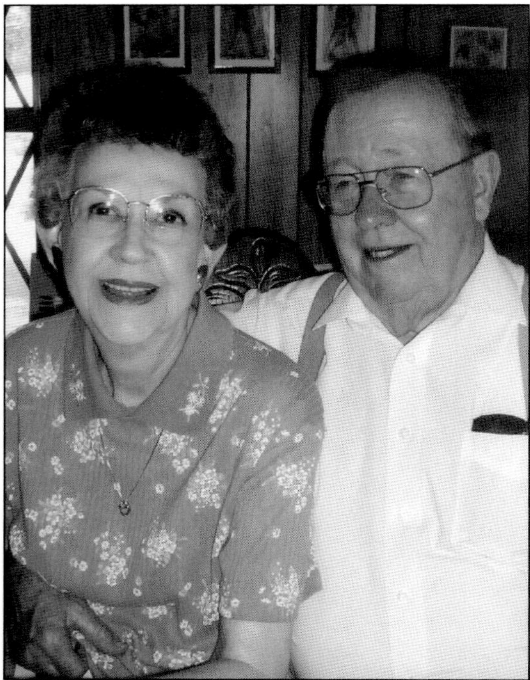

George Hollis

In 1946, George Hollis married Peggy McElvany. After his baptism, he became a member of her church. He entered college in 1947 and bought his first small home.

He served as the first appointed corporation judge for the City of Lake Worth from 1957 to 1959. Born in his grandfather's log house, his business career started at age six. He had his own produce stand in front of his home. He later saved $75 and purchased his first cow.

At 13, he started working for others in various jobs. Between his junior and senior year at Lake Worth High School, he leased and operated a service station. He later became involved in a number of business venues. He also served 12 years in the Navy. Hollis has belonged to the Lions Club, Kiwanis Club, and Northwest Chamber of Commerce. (Both photographs courtesy George Hollis.)

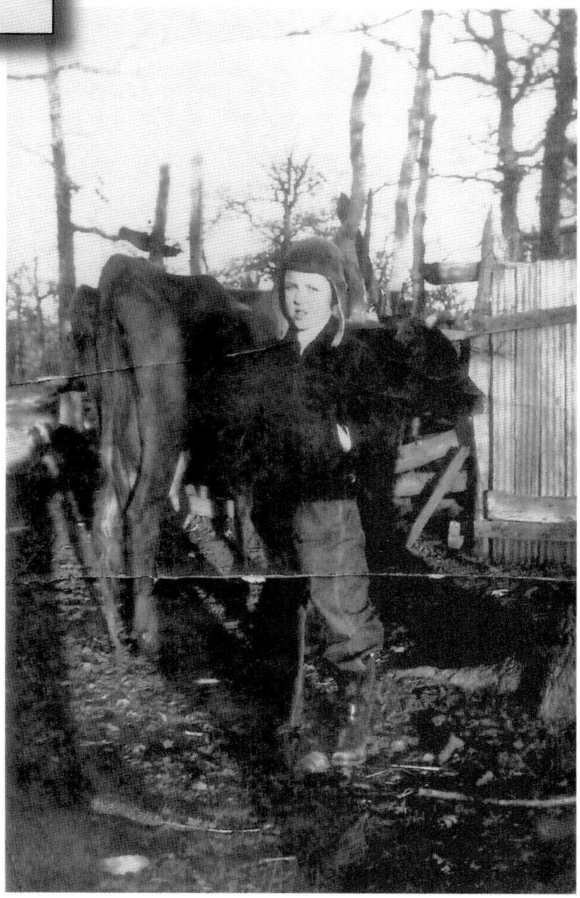

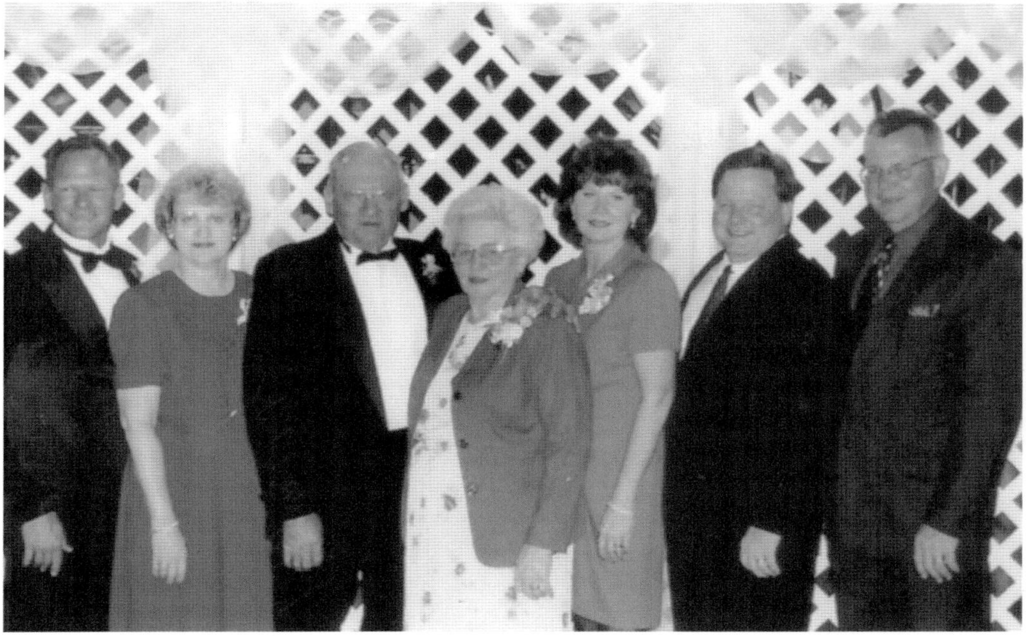

The Harold Green Family

Harold and Irene Green moved to Lake Worth in 1963 along with their five children. He worked for Bell Helicopter, and Irene worked for the Federal Aviation Administration. Their children attended Saint Thomas Catholic Church and school near the Lake Worth area. Their parents maintained involvement at church and school. They also delivered Meals on Wheels to shut-ins. They lived in Boat Club Estates in Lake Worth for many years until Irene passed away in 2009 and Harold in 2012.

The Greens' children, Donna, Gary, Elaine, Kenneth, and Alan, each contributed to society in their own way. Donna Green became involved in Future Homemakers of America in Lake Worth High School, serving as secretary in her senior year. She also married Larry Davis in her senior year and later earned her education degree. She taught school in Joshua.

Gary Green came to Lake Worth High School in his sophomore year and enjoyed playing on the basketball team. His paper route money allowed him to buy a 1953 Chevrolet in 1965. His management skills served him well as he has been a banker for 40 years. He presently serves as market president for the Liberty Bank, in Hurst, Texas.

Elaine Green moved to Lake Worth with her parents as a freshman in high school. She became a member of the High Steppers Drill Team at Lake Worth, loving the camaraderie and school spirit of bonfires and homecoming dances. After graduation, she attended the University of Texas at Arlington, earning her bachelor's degree in business administration from the School of Business.

Ken Green's fond memories of Lake Worth include learning to drive a boat at an early age. He, his siblings, and his parents spent many days swimming, water skiing, fishing, and picnicking. Green attended Lake Worth High School and has special memories of the principal, Kit Kittrell, and his paddle. He graduated from Texas Wesleyan University. A certified public accountant, he has his own firm in Colleyville, Texas.

Allan Green came to Lake Worth when very young. He remembers it as the only place he lived growing up. Like all of his family, he enjoyed water-related activities and remembers most fishing around the Fort Worth Nature Center and Greer Island, both part of the Lake Worth reservoir. After college, he also became a CPA.

Photographed left to right are Kenneth, Donna, Harold, Irene, Elaine, Alan, and Gary Green. (Courtesy Green family.)

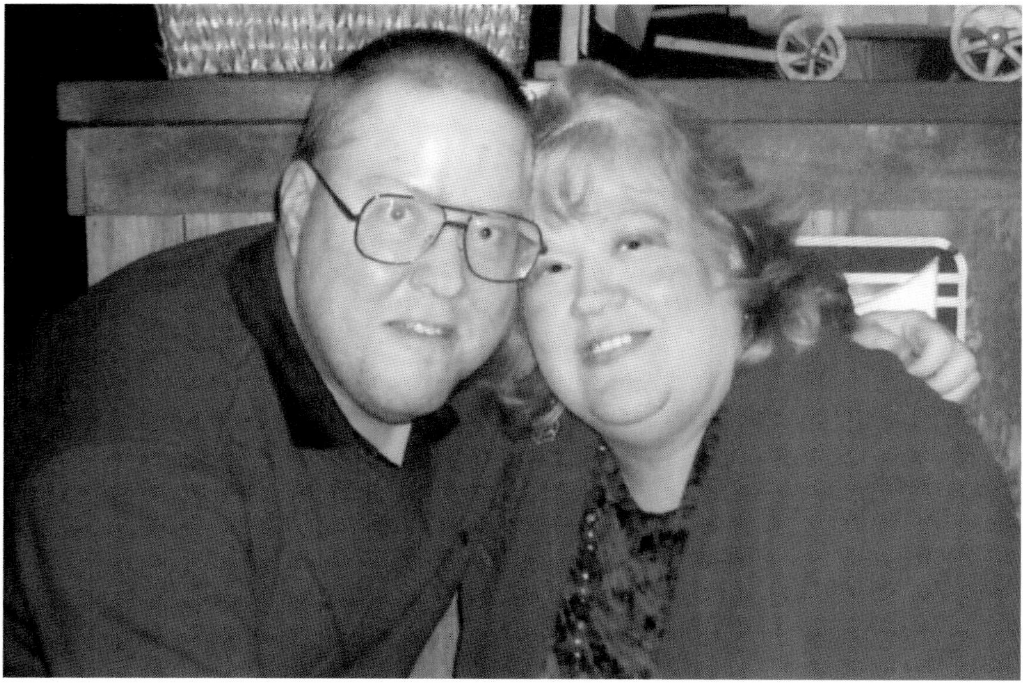

Joe McDaniel

Joe McDaniel started life with a diagnosis of spina bifida. At 32 hours old, he received surgery, but the surgeon offered no hope for him ever to walk. However, at age two, he walked without any assistance.

Since that time, McDaniel's life has been full of hard work and successes, including earning a degree in journalism from the University of North Texas in 1990. Two years later, he married Teresa Maxwell.

Throughout his life, he has used his writing skills in numerous employments. Currently employed by the Fort Worth Police Department as a civilian worker, he has been there 15 years. In addition, McDaniel has served on the City of Lake Worth's Board of Adjustment. He also serves as president of the Lake Worth Area Historical Society and enjoys writing about Lake Worth's history. (Courtesy Joe McDaniel.)

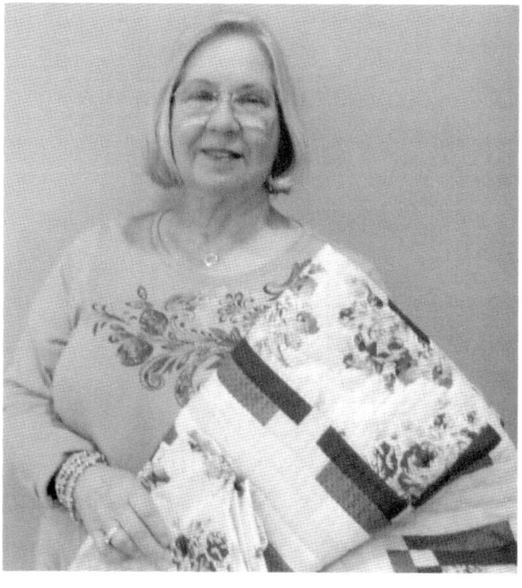

Lake Worth Senior's Foundation Gift

Kaitlyn's Promise, a foundation created to help young people in recovery, received this handmade quilt as a gift from several caring senior citizens in the Lake Worth area. The foundation offers counseling and help for those involved to get an education. It also teaches about the dangers of huffing keyboard cleaner, drugs, and alcohol.

Helen Vallery, holding the quilt, lost her granddaughter Kaitlyn in 2006 at age 16. The foundation, named after Vallery's granddaughter, offers hope for many.

Barbara Howard, Mary Ann Kozel, Marilyn Llewellyn, Anne Floyd, Joan Crittenden, and Carla Bezner, all from the Lake Worth area, made and donated the quilt. (Courtesy Helen Vallery and Carla Bezner.)

James Reza

James Reza, a native Texan born in Fort Worth in 1937, has accomplished much in life. His achievements include, but are not limited to, becoming a musician, writer, speaker, engineer, heavy equipment operator, and choir director. Everything within these parameters and more has produced a positive impact on many. Even as a young boy, Reza's intellect stood out. Recruited as an altar boy for his church, he had to learn all responses in Latin.

James was never close to his father, but his grandfather taught him that his great-grandparents came from Spain and became wealthy landowners in Mexico. After the Mexican Revolution, his grandparents moved to Thurber, Texas. Reza's grandfather later moved to North Fort Worth and lived in a house rented from the original founder of Joe T. Garcia's famous restaurant.

In high school, Reza learned the trade of linotyping and in the summer learned to build mobile homes. After seven years, he got a job as a linotype operator for Jack Jordon. When hired by Motheral Printing, he continued to work for Jack Jordon as well. Reza received honors several times for having the best ads in Fort Worth while he worked at Motheral Printing.

After 18 years with Motheral, he went to work as an engineer for General Dynamics and later worked for Commissioner J.D. Johnson for 10 years. In addition, he wrote editorials to newspapers, which landed him a job writing for the *Dallas Morning News*, *Fort Worth Star-Telegram*, and other newspapers. Due to his wide success as a writer, he often appeared on radio and television shows. Sometimes his articles created heated public discussions.

Reza also became involved with a children's guitar mass at All Saints Catholic Church, which included the choir performing outside of church. After 18 years as choir director, he formed a singing guitar group. They sang at various engagements around town. Later, his friend Johnny Cisneros opened up Los Vaqueros Restaurant and hired the singing guitar group to perform. After 30 years, Reza still enjoys singing and playing there. He has met and performed for many celebrities, including Chuck Berry, Bo and John Derek, the Gatlin Brothers, Vince Gill, and many others.

Now devoting his time to family, singing at the restaurant, and writing a Dallas blog for Tom Pauken, Reza often takes long walks in Lake Worth where he resides. (Courtesy James Reza.)

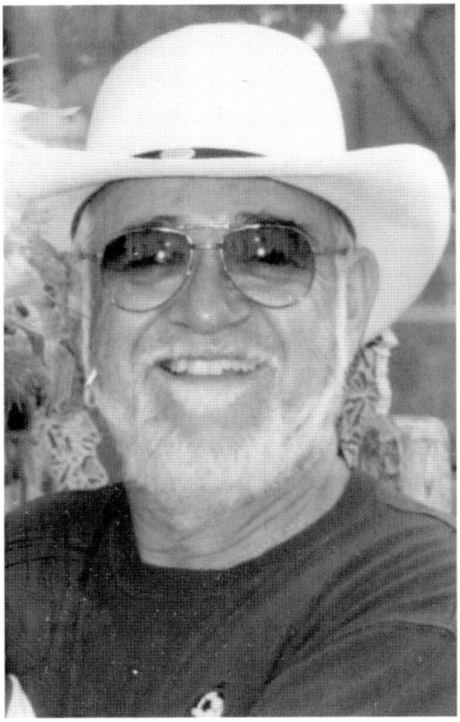

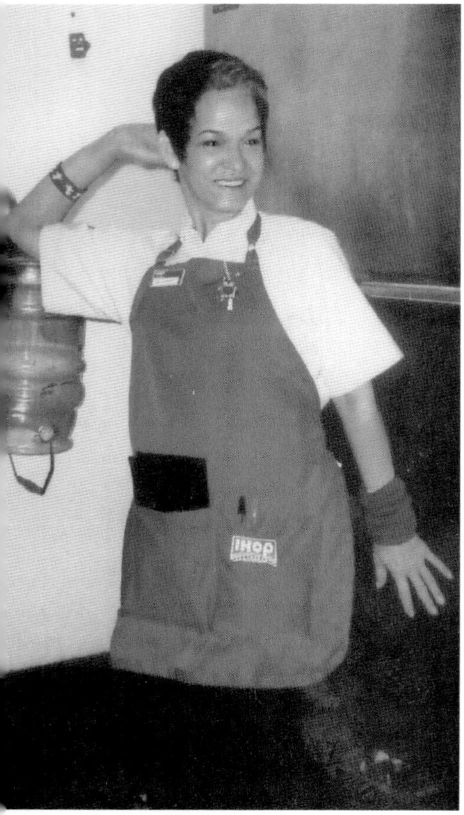

Charley Haddad

Charley Haddad, a perky waitress, has worked for a local restaurant in Lake Worth for 23 years. She describes herself as a "jabberjaw" who loves people and her job. Her conversations with customers often include her love of Jesus also shared with first-grade children in Sunday school, which she loves to teach. Haddad says she does not ever intend to retire. (Courtesy Charley Haddad.)

Maria Lupe Macias

Maria Lupe Macias enjoys cooking. Perhaps that explains her popularity as a cook at Whataburger in Lake Worth, Texas. She used to make pancakes with ears that delighted those struggling with health issues. Ben Mauldin would perk up when he saw them, and in spite of poor health, ate every bite of her funny pancakes.

Macias lives in nearby Sansom Park and has two children, Amelia and Brenda. (Courtesy Maria Macias.)

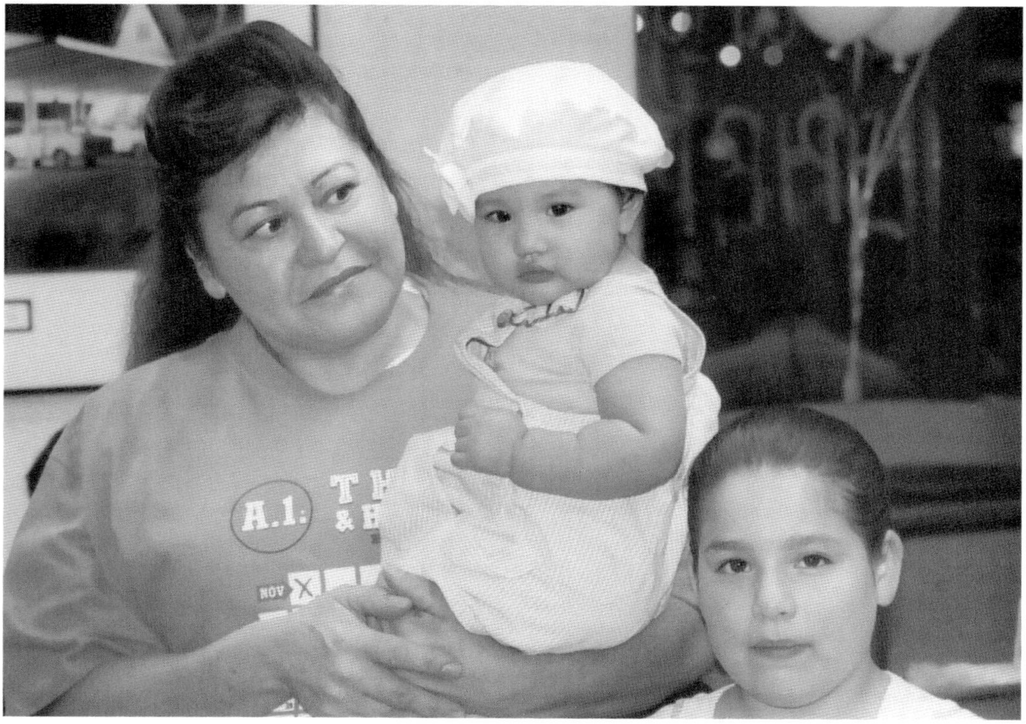

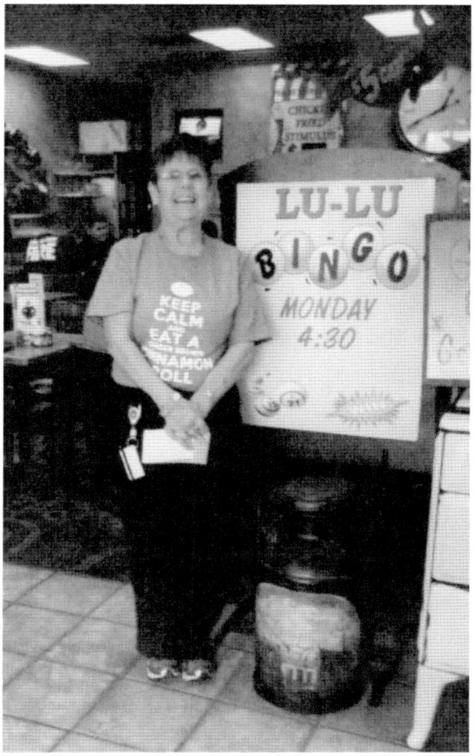

Linda Pruitt Ferris "Lulu"
Linda Pruitt Ferris, known as "Lulu," celebrated her 25th anniversary as head waitress and manager of Ginger Brown's Old Tyme Restaurant and Bakery in Lake Worth, Texas, on October 28, 2012. She once won recognition as employee of the month. She received a seven-day cruise on her 20th anniversary by the owner, Ginger Brown, who initiated "Lulu Bingo," one of Ferris's best-loved hobbies. (Courtesy Lawana Mauldin.)

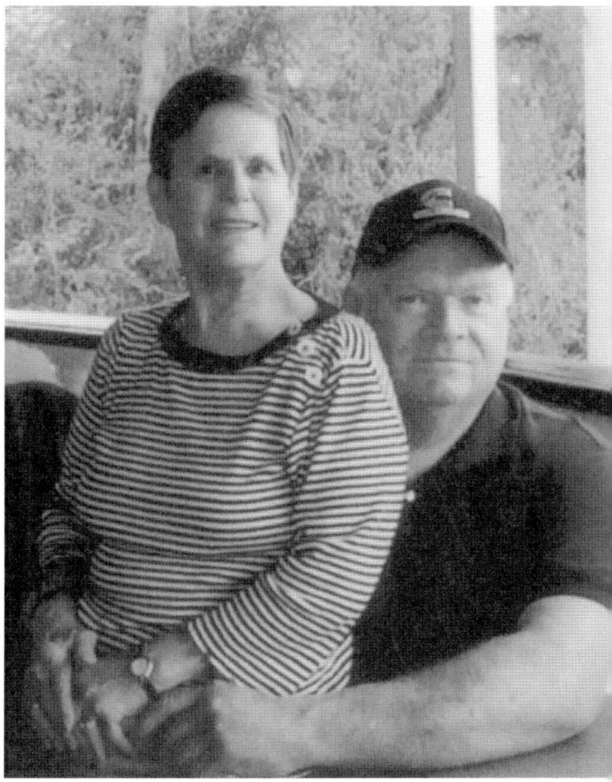

Linda (Pruitt) Ferris and Husband
Linda Pruitt worked diligently as a child, sometimes ironing clothes for others. She continued this work ethic at various jobs including private home employment.

She worked as the youngest employee at a local restaurant at age 15, and she met Lee Wayne Ferris there. Five years after their marriage in 1970, she had Russell, her son. Ferris presently works for Ginger Brown's Old Tyme Restaurant and Bakery, where her acute awareness of her customers brings joy to many. (Courtesy Linda Ferris.)

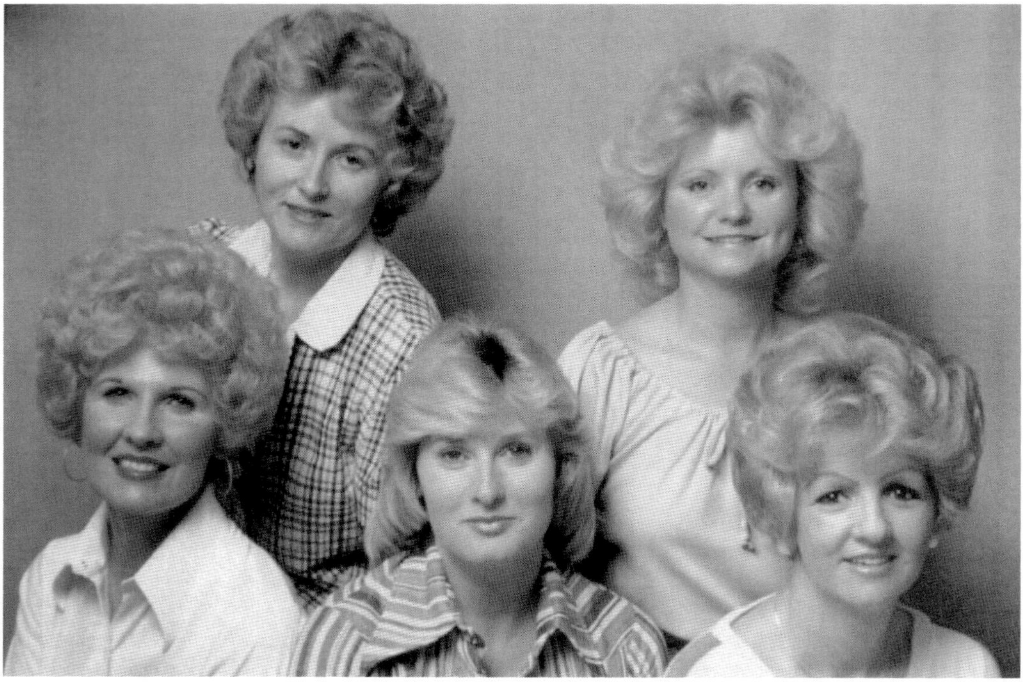

Beautician's World
This group of ladies worked together in the legendary beauty business when terms such as *beauty school* predated terms such as *beauty college*. Cost of acquiring a beautician's license averaged in the range of $1,000, as opposed to current cost of approximately $10,000. Also, customers later became known as clients. Two of those in this photograph, Reba Thurman (lower left) and Opal Beauchamp (behind Reba), eventually opened their own salon. The first names of the other beauticians pictured are Sandy (middle of first row), Linda (next to her), and Marsha (standing behind Linda). (Courtesy Opal Beauchamp.)

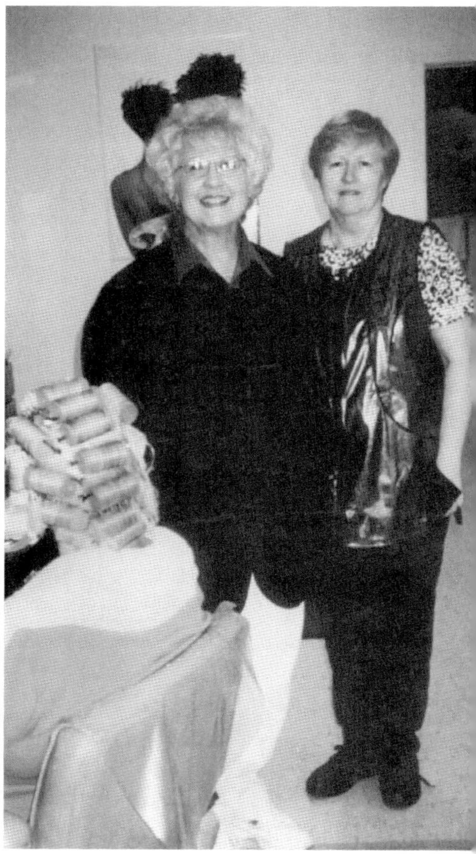

The Beauty Salon
Reba Thurman, on the left, dressed hair for 30 years, mostly in Lake Worth. She married Duane Thurman and held a number of offices in the Lake Worth Parent Teacher Association including that of secretary and served as a Girl Scouts Leader.

Opal Beauchamp, on the right, a hairdresser for 50 years, worked mostly in the Lake Worth area. She eventually wound up as co-owner with Reba Thurman of The Beauty Salon. Beauchamp graduated high school as salutatorian in Perrin, Texas, and then went to beauty school and took her first job at 17. She married Jerry Beauchamp in 1973. These talented women recently sold their shop and now enjoy their retirements. (Courtesy Opal Beauchamp.)

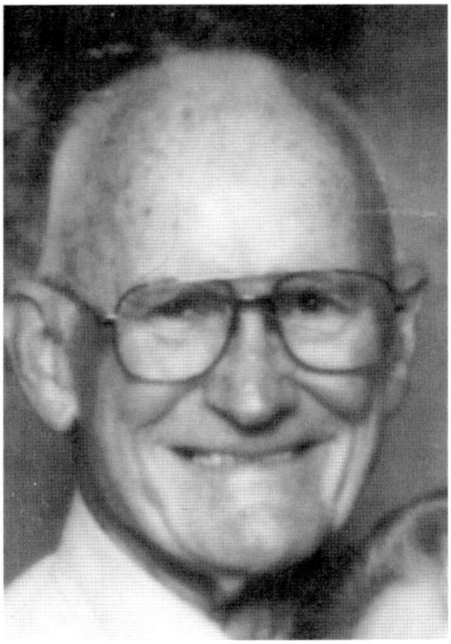

David Ford

David Ford combined a quick wit with a hearty laugh to entertain his customers. He owned and operated Ford's Barber Shop for more than 30 years. He served in the Army in World War II. He and his former wife, Mary Sanders, moved to Lake Worth in the 1950s.

Ford opened his first barbershop two miles northwest of Lake Worth. In the late 1970s, he moved his shop to Lake Worth. As an avid supporter of school and community affairs, he served on the Lake Worth School Board in the 1960s and 1970s. Mary Ford died in 1998. He then married Marlene Nabors. He supported HIV and antiprostitution missionary work in Argentina. Ford died in 2012. (Courtesy Carlus Nabors.)

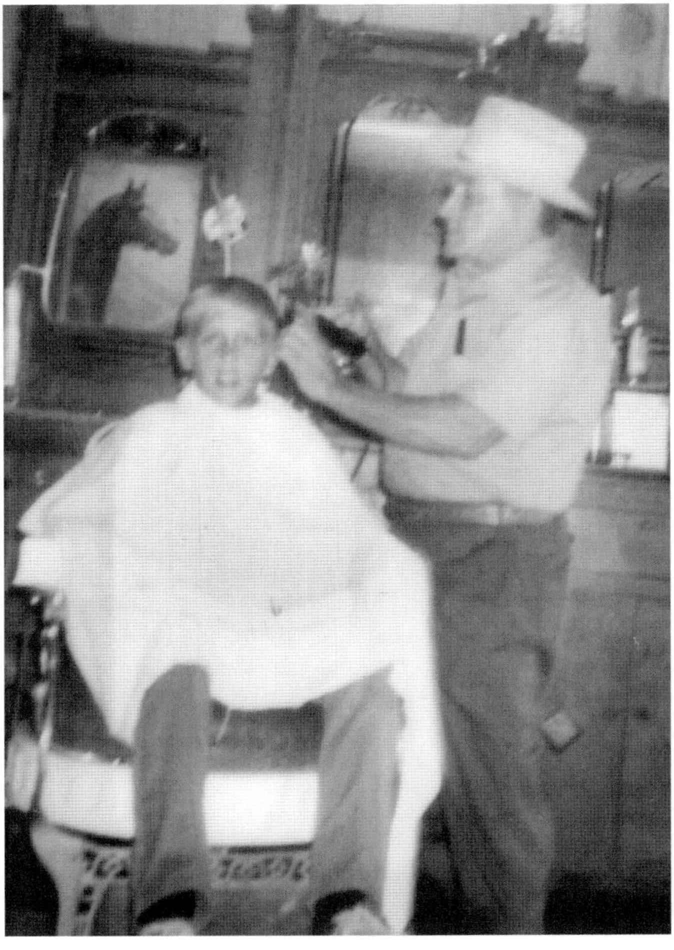

Bill Mowell

Bill Mowell moved to Lake Worth in 1954 and opened his business, Wild Bill's Barber Shop. He operated it for more than 30 years. He never cut anyone's hair without treating the customer to his singing, guitar strumming, or French harp playing. He also owned a horse, donkey, and buggy and gave many schoolchildren rides in the buggy, teaching some how to ride his horse, Pancho.

Additionally, he wrote songs such as "On Mother's Day" and "Old Shank," both hits with Lake Worth High School students. He also wrote songs he sent to several presidents and received their thank-you notes in return. This photograph shows Mowell giving his grandson, Billy Heiser, a haircut. (Courtesy Nancy Mowell Heiser.)

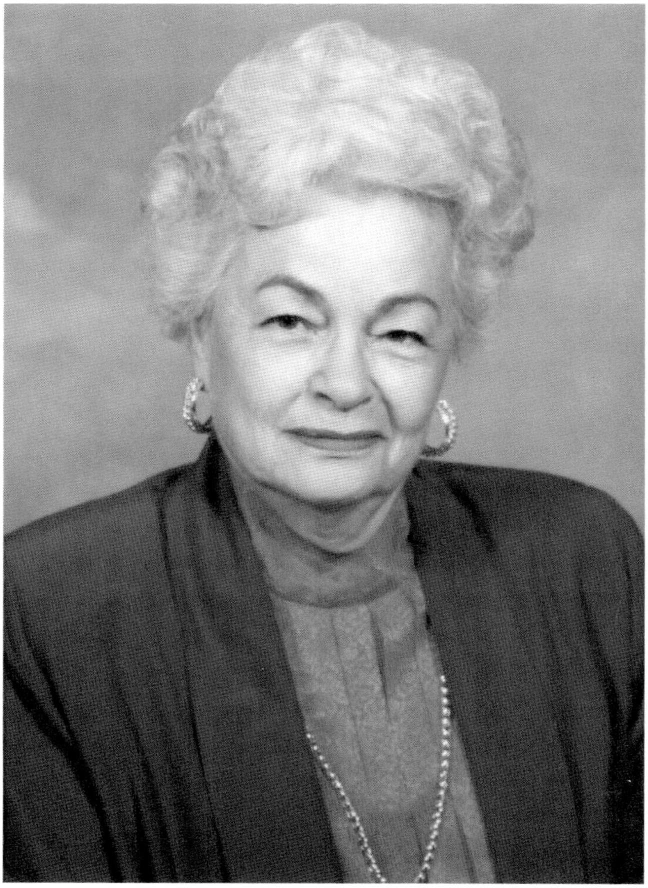

Eddie McKay

Eddie McKay, longtime resident of Lake Worth, met her future husband after starting to work at Southwestern Bell Telephone Company in 1952. She worked until the birth of her child Sonja. When she grew older, McKay started working in the insurance business. In 1982, she became president of the National Association of Insurance Women. This organization adopted a family at Christmas and provided for their needs. They also held fundraisers selling pecans.

Additionally, they made and sold cookbooks to raise money to fund the cost of helping others. In that same year, McKay received the distinction of being named Insurance Woman of the Year.

Women belonging to the NAIW from all over the nation met every year for a conference in different states. McKay recalls how informative and enjoyable she found the conferences to be, partially because the women dressed "to the hilt." In 1982, McKay spoke to the Lake Worth City Council concerning the changes in the insurance business, particularly about the use of computers. McKay indicated that the company she worked for became one of the first to install computers.

Another of McKay's community volunteer services included co-leading a Girl Scout group in Lake Worth with Doris Thomas. One of the girls belonging to that group, Lisa Whelchel, became a well-known star from television's *Facts of Life* series, a writer, and a speaker. She also starred as a contestant in the television show *Survivor.*

McKay's attention to detail and reliability coupled with her faith in God landed her two terms on The Session at John Knox Presbyterian Church. This group ensures that the original bylaws of the church stay intact. Eddie McKay loves her home in Lake Worth where she has lived for 53 years. She continues to do various things for her church and community. (Courtesy Eddie McKay.)

CHAPTER EIGHT

Volunteers and Others

Communities need volunteers to advance various endeavors that affect the lives of their citizens. They also need qualified builders to provide durable homes. This chapter highlights residents who propel a number of ideas and things that impacted the community of Lake Worth.

Earl Fowlkes served his country well in the Navy Air Corps during World War II. His service in other areas in Lake Worth deserves acknowledgement as well, including special assignments and membership in the Lions Club and Kiwanis Club.

Another caring individual, Carla Bezner, helps keep her community safe by serving on the Neighborhood Watch Association. She also has done extensive volunteer work at the L.O. "Bud" Irby Senior Citizens Center and various other places. Emma Pritchard has volunteered there for a long while in several capacities. Additionally, she belonged to the Allied Youth Association in high school.

Jerry Pritchard, like his wife, Emma, participated in a number of events in high school and belonged to the Boy Scouts of America. He enjoys studying the Bible with others.

Many times, a person's creativity produces amazing encouragement that enhances the lives of people. Terry Purdom, a cancer survivor, did just that as he traveled the United States on his motorcycle distributing a unique coin and giving hope to those he encountered.

Ben Mauldin, now deceased, enjoyed civic involvement in Lake Worth. He belonged to a number of service organizations. After his death, his wife, Lawana, donated a number of items to the Lake Worth Museum.

David Woodall has a family history involving one of the founding fathers of Lake Worth, which he shared with the community. He gave a number of donations to the museum, including a beautiful cement bench belonging to his grandparents.

John DeGroat and his wife, Dottie, also donated items to the museum. He amassed a large collection of photographs, which he generously shared with several authors to write about Lake Worth.

James Coley, an interesting person, built a charming home on the shores of Lake Worth that still stands and belongs to his step-granddaughter Cindy Bozart. She and her husband allow for baptisms in the lake behind their home.

One talented woman, artist June Kittrell, has an interesting background. She sometimes donates her paintings and makes items for cancer patients.

Sara Riley has the heart of a teacher in that she tutored elementary students twice a week for a number of years in Lake Worth. She and her husband, Don, also served in the Lake Worth Youth Association and Lake Worth Athletic Association.

Ann Hooper, who lives just outside Lake Worth, often participates in activities there. She has served over 11,000 hours as a hospice volunteer. Her husband, Johnnie, now deceased, had a fine reputation for his honesty and dedication when building homes or other structures.

All of the above served generously in one way or another to this community.

Earl Sanford Fowlkes

Earl Fowlkes served in the Navy Air Corps during World War II. After just three weeks of boot camp and high scores on his aptitude tests, he attended the Air Technical Training Center in Norman, Oklahoma, for Aviation Ordnance School to learn about bombs, rifles, pistols, machine guns, rockets, the associated equipment and electronics. With more transfers and more training, he serviced American aircraft, plus Canadian aircraft that ran submarine patrol and participated in shooting down Japanese balloons.

After his honorable discharge, he had various jobs such as running steam generators for the Texas Power Plant on North Main Street in Fort Worth, Texas, and industries including the lumberjacking business in another state. After breaking his ribs in a fall and nearly cutting off his big toe with an axe accident, he decided to find a different line of work.

Later, he received more training in electronics and worked in various positions for General Dynamics for 14 years in Fort Worth, Texas, and 18 years in the Pomona California Missile Division.

Other employment led him to live in Mesa, Arizona. While there, he became head usher at the New Life Assembly of God Church and later held the same position at the Red Mountain Christian Center.

Raised in Lake Worth, Texas, as a teenager, Fowlkes played on the first football and basketball teams in school. After graduation and serving in the Navy and working in several other states, he returned to Lake Worth where he served as president of the Lions Club in 2003–2004.

He also became a member of Texas Lions Club Children's Camp and the Kiwanis Club, where he has worked with the Christmas Express program. In addition, he served on the Steering Committee to establish the Lake Worth Area Historical Society of which he became a member. In addition, he served as program chairman for the society.

With much enthusiasm, Fowlkes, along with his wife, Myrtle Belle, and others, helped establish the museum in Lake Worth in 2003. Fowlkes, appointed to the Planning and Zoning Commission in 2012, served as president. He also served on the Historical Preservation Commission and the Police Training Advisory Committee. Earl Fowlkes's interesting life has made a positive difference in Lake Worth, Texas. (Photograph by Lawana Mauldin.)

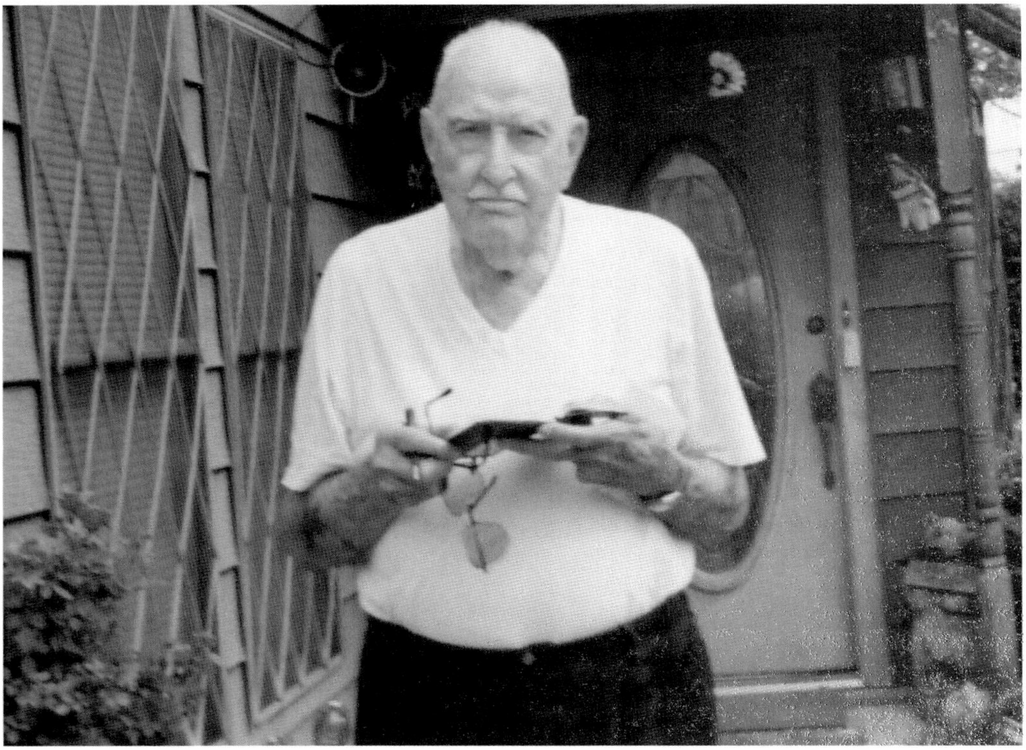

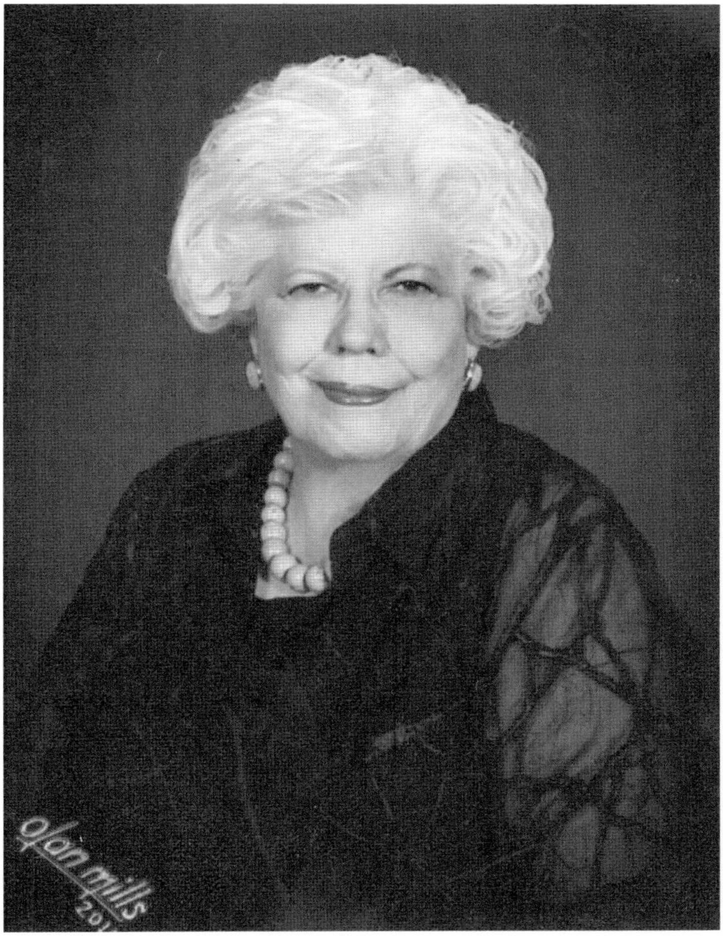

Carla Bezner

Carla Bezner, a Eucharistic minister, belongs to the Women's Organization at St. Thomas the Apostle Catholic Church. She has been a member for 56 years.

Born January 16, 1938, in Mesquite, Texas, her family moved to Lake Worth in 1948. After high school, Bezner went to work for an important aircraft plant, built on the nearby shores of Lake Worth. The plant underwent many name changes over the 37.5 years she worked there. Commonly known as the Bomber Plant, the correct names over the years include Consolidated Vultee Aircraft Corporation, Convair, General Dynamics, and Lockheed Martin. Bezner retired from this famous aircraft institution as a senior financial analyst.

Now retired, she spends much of her time as a volunteer in areas such as the Neighborhood Watch Association. Bezner spent many happy hours with the volunteer Lake Worth Youth Association with her husband before his death on March 20, 2006.

In addition, this busy woman has served as president of the Lake Worth Senior Association and as secretary-treasurer of the Lake Worth Alumni Association. She also served on the Oil and Gas Lease Committee for her neighborhood. Quick to inform the neighborhood of any needs for prayer for others, or to keep them abreast of anything affecting the area, she sends out details via e-mails.

One of her favorite hobbies, quilt making, keeps her busy also. She belongs to a quilting group at the senior citizens complex. She has been involved in groups making donations to James L. West, a hospice institution, the Tadpole Learning Center, the Union Gospel Mission of Fort Worth, and other organizations needing warm bedding. Lake Worth citizens appreciate Carla Bezner. (Courtesy Carla Bezner.)

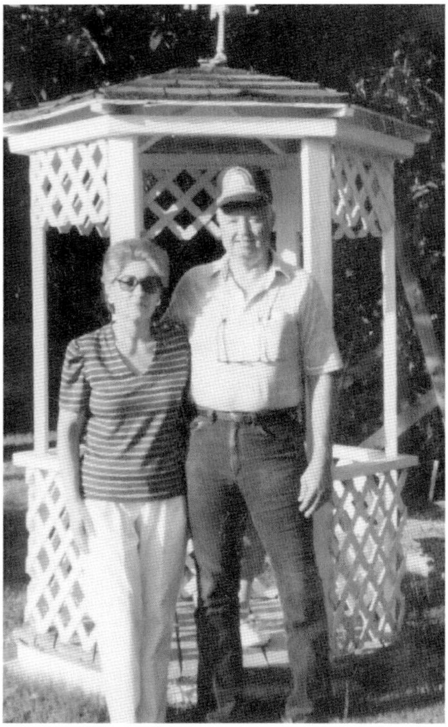

Emma and Jerry Pritchard

Emma Pritchard, a volunteer, moved to Lake Worth in 1951. She attended five years of school, becoming active in band, the school newspaper, and the Allied Youth Association. She graduated in 1955. She served as secretary to the Lake Worth Senior Association at the L.O. "Bud" Irby Senior Center. She also helps with Friday potluck lunches.

Jerry Pritchard moved to Lake Worth in 1942 and graduated high school in 1956. Involved in school sports, band, and the school's annual staff, Pritchard also belonged to the Boy Scouts. He enjoys studying the Bible and encouraging others. Both he and his wife, Emma, remain active members of Bethesda Community Church in Haltom City. His sense of humor stands out in the picture below as he pretends to be a dentist using a headlight received in a gift exchange. (Courtesy Jerry Pritchard and Lawana Mauldin.)

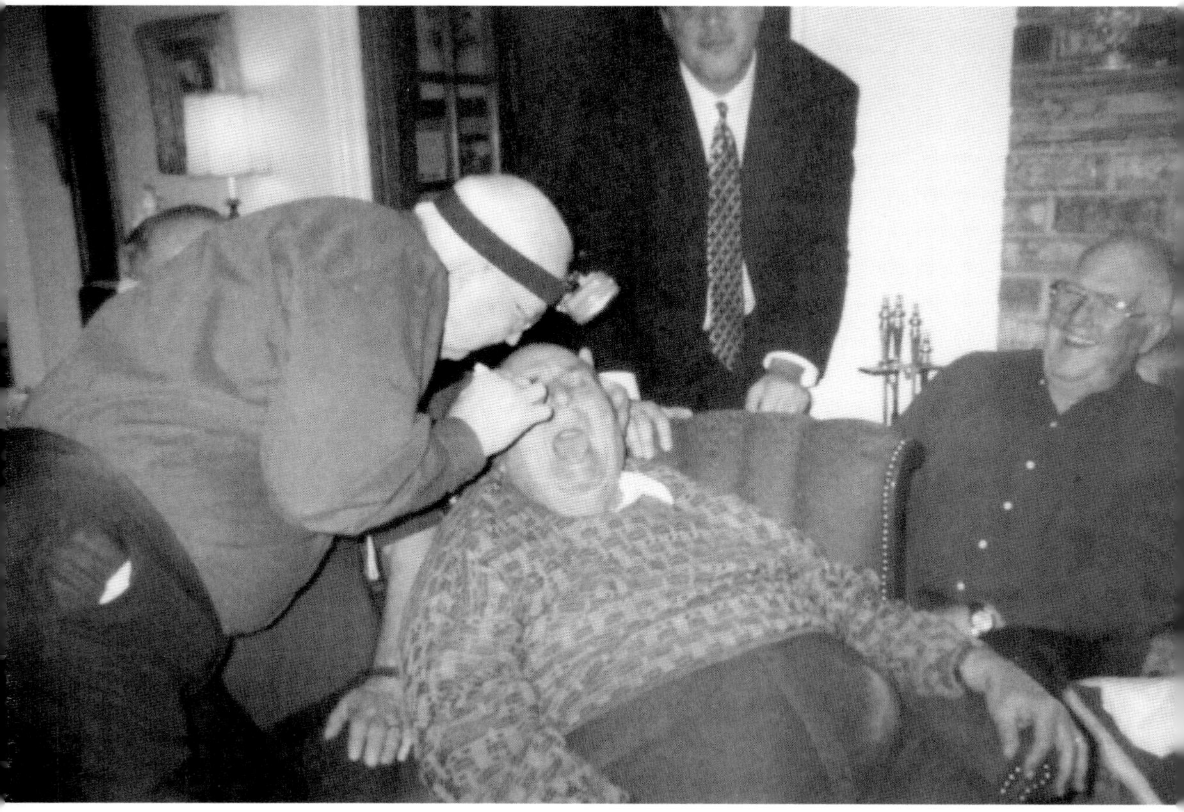

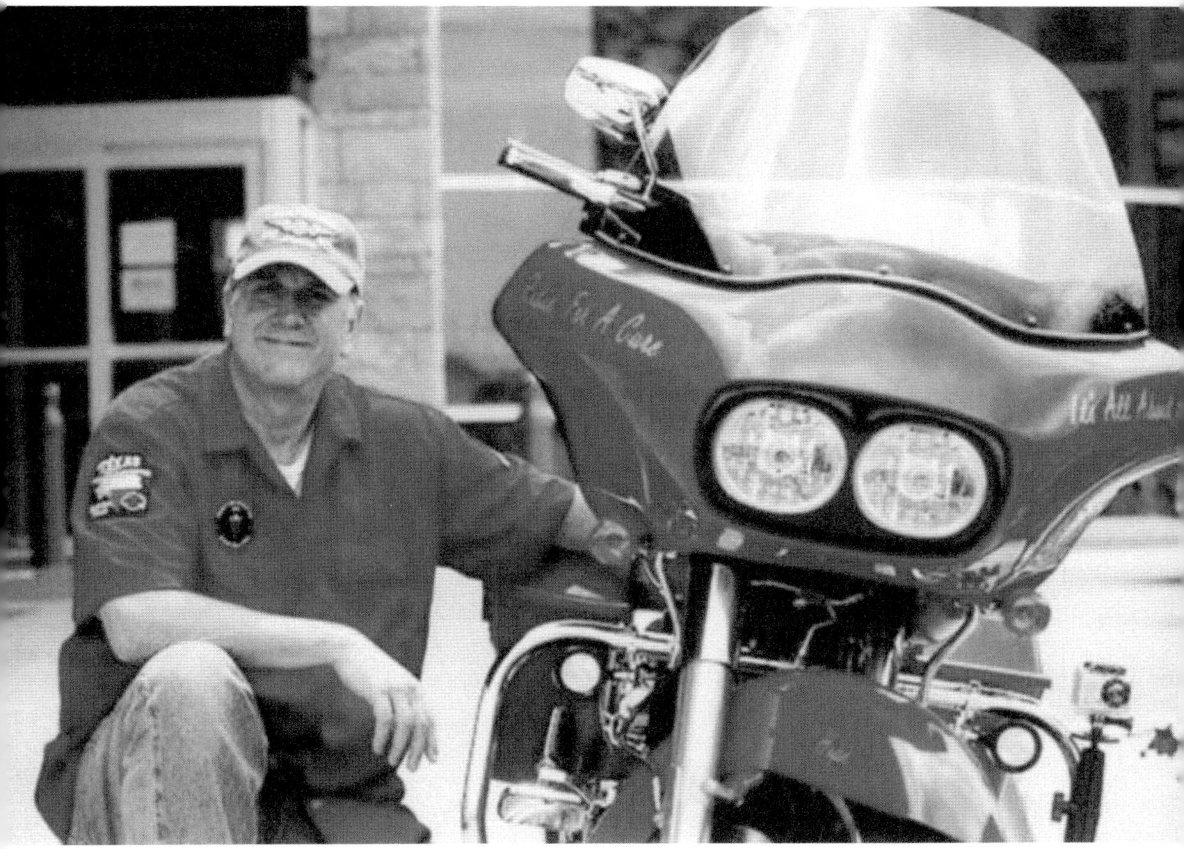

Terry Purdom

Terry Purdom's home has always been in Lake Worth, Texas. His cousin Rue Dean Purdom loved and raised him beginning when he was three days old. He called her "mother," just as her two older biological sons did. All three of the boys considered themselves brothers.

His six-foot-six-inch height helped him in playing high school basketball. Sometimes, the team went out of town for the games. On these occasions, June Kittrell, wife of Coach Kittrell, drove the bus. When they returned to Lake Worth, Purdom rode with her to park the bus. With his home across the street, this arrangement worked well for both.

He fondly remembers his teachers and the times that coaches Kit Kittrell, David Choate, and N.A. Howry "busted his butt." He believes each one helped make him become the Terry Purdom of today. Well liked in school and elected senior class president, Purdom also became a member of The Lake Worth Volunteer Fire Department while still in high school. He remembers his excitement to get out of a few classes to do this important job when an intercom message from the office called, "All junior volunteer firefighters report to the fire station." He also got paid $2 for every trip.

Diagnosed with cancer in 2004, Purdom did not know how long he might live. One medicine had complications, but in 2008, a new medicine made him feel better. One of the things on his bucket list included a trip across America to give hope to others who had cancer. Already with many Facebook friends, he gained hundreds more as he chronicled his "Summer of Hope" travels of 12,000 miles across America on his red Harley Davidson motorcycle. He created a simple coin, called the Hope Coin, that he sold, which helped him finance his trip, although most of the cost he paid himself. He met thousands of people, many with cancer, whom he encouraged never to give up hope. His own hope, faith in God, the new medicine, and the encouragement of many friends brought him safely home with his cancer in remission. (Courtesy Terry Purdom.)

Ben and Lawana Mauldin

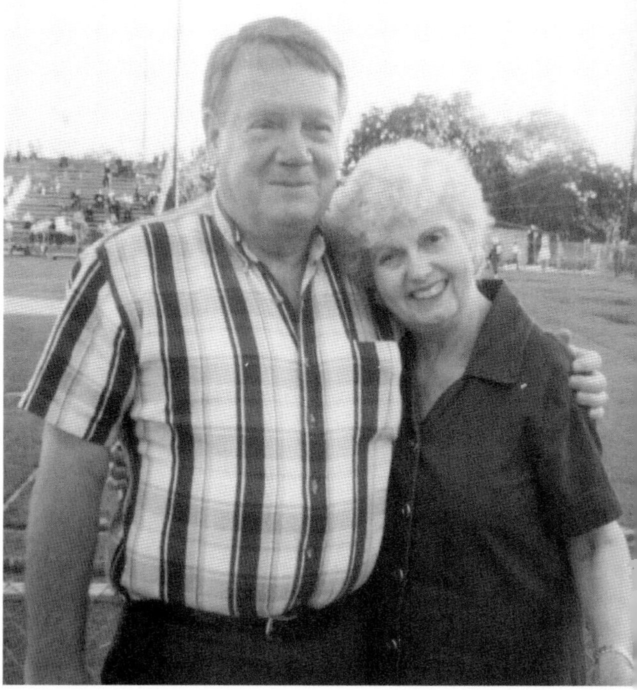

Ben Mauldin married Delores Lawana Allred in 1950. A former banker, Mauldin served on the Economic Development Committee for the City of Lake Worth. He became the first president of the Lake Worth Area Historical Society and collaborated with the high school allowing students to work in his printing business.

He belonged to the Kiwanis Club, Northwest Chamber of Commerce and participated in Meals on Wheels. In the photograph below, he holds a treasured gift. Sadly, Mauldin passed away in 2010.

Lawana Mauldin, a published author, taught elementary school for 20 years and holds membership in the Lake Worth Area Historical Society. As a former member of the Lake Worth Garden Club, she helped with the Kids and Trees Program. She also donated many items to the Lake Worth Museum. (Both photographs courtesy Lawana Mauldin.)

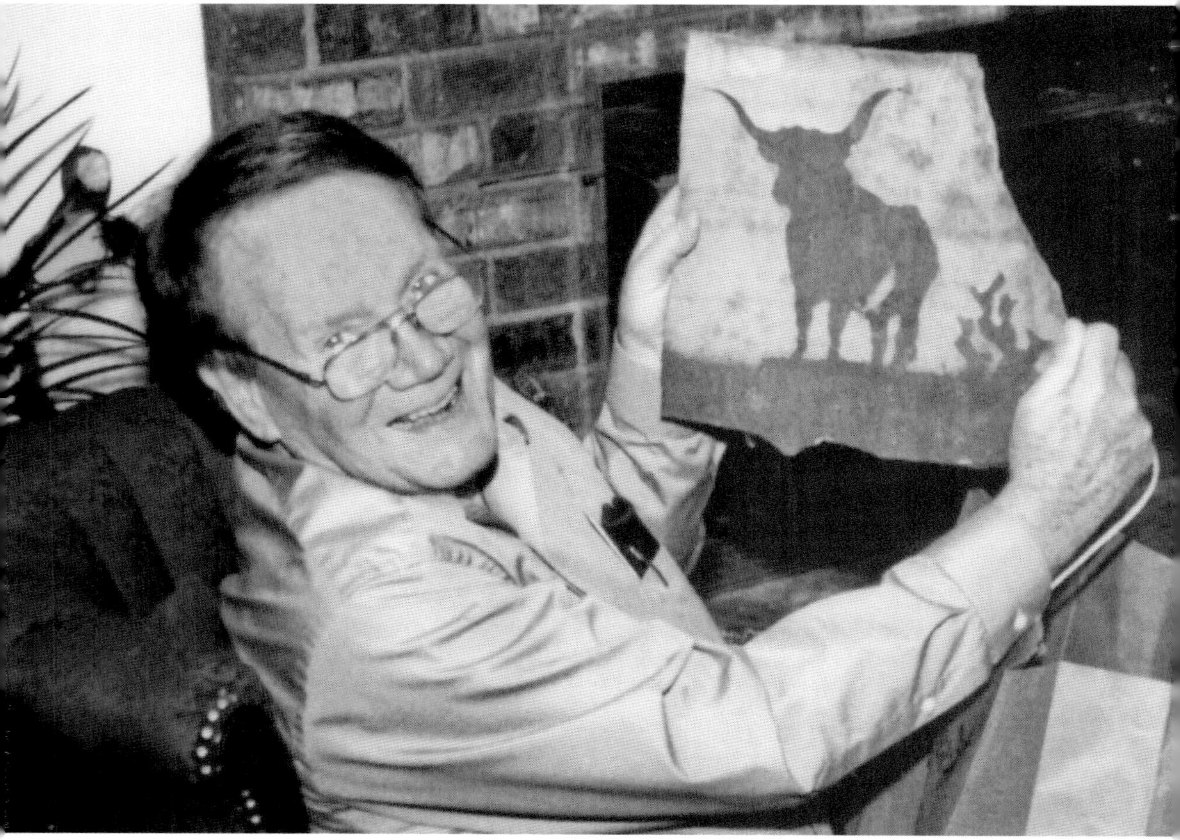

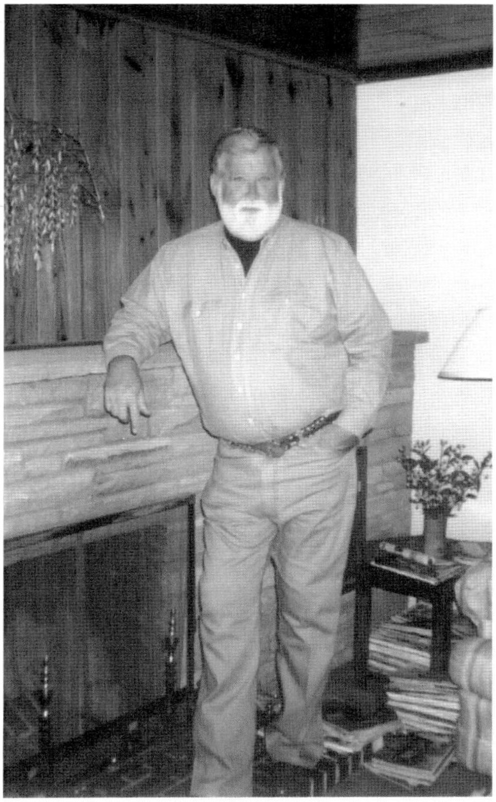

David Woodall

Born in 1934, David Woodall's grandfather J.R. Foster became his father figure. Foster died in 1946, the year Woodall became a Boy Scout. After college, Woodall joined the US Marine Corps. While attached to the Navy, he toured several foreign countries.

He married Carolyn Collins in 1959. They have two daughters and three grandchildren. Woodall spent 40 years in insurance. He helped organize the Lake Worth Jaycees, eventually becoming president and the Mid-Cities Toastmasters Club, holding many positions. Woodall served as charter vice president of the Lake Worth Area Historical Society. He donated a treasured bench to the society. A member of the Azle Christian Church, he has served on the church board. (Courtesy of David Woodall.)

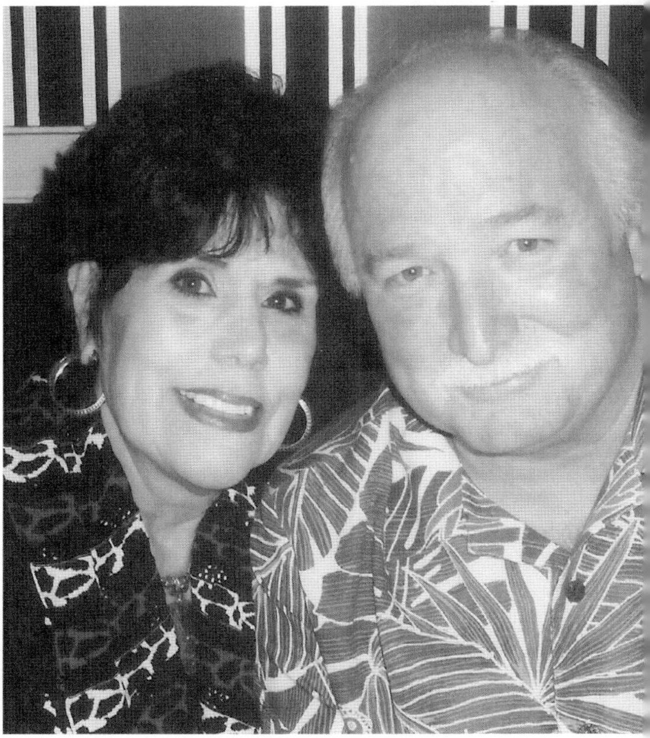

John and Dottie DeGroat

John and Dottie DeGroat contributed generously to the preservation of Lake Worth history. In 2005, he amassed a vast collection of high-resolution pictures of the lake, which he has generously shared. He and his wife also donated articles to the Lake Worth Museum.

DeGroat and his family moved to Fort Worth in 1953 where his father took a job at Convair. He attended Castleberry schools from first through eighth grade. He attended Azle High School, and then paid tuition to transfer to Lake Worth High School for the school's Distributive Education class. DeGroat also served as class president and later graduated from the Academy of Computer Technology.

In 1979, he married Dottie Allbritton. After working at several jobs, DeGroat retired in 2009 and enjoys his retirement residing in their home by the lake. (Courtesy John Degroat.)

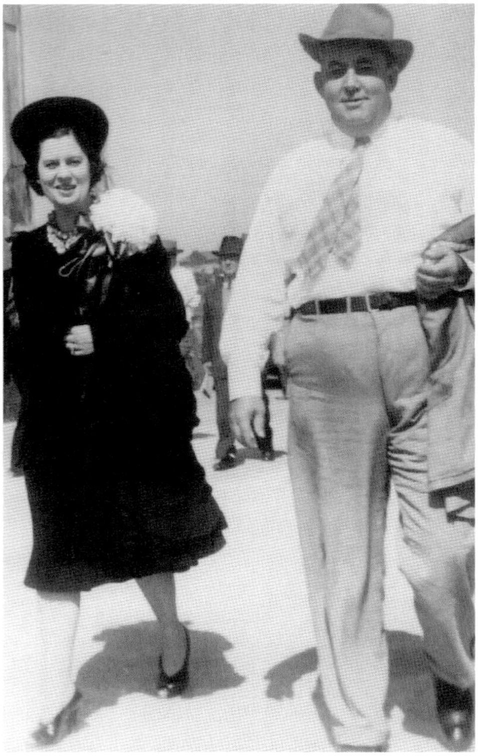

James E. Parker and wife, Laura Belle (Colbert) Parker

James E. Parker, a successful wildcatter dug only one dry hole out of sixty to seventy good ones. He decided where to drill by using a divining rod (forked tree branch). When it moved, he bent over and smelled the dirt and sometimes tasted it. Most people called this hocus-pocus, but he had faith in it.

In 1938, he bought his house on Cahoba Drive once known as Meandering Road. In the 1950s, Parker married Laura Belle Colbert, Cindy Bozart's grandmother. Bozart appreciates the history connected to the home, now hers, where sometimes she holds church-related events. (Courtesy Cindy Bozart.)

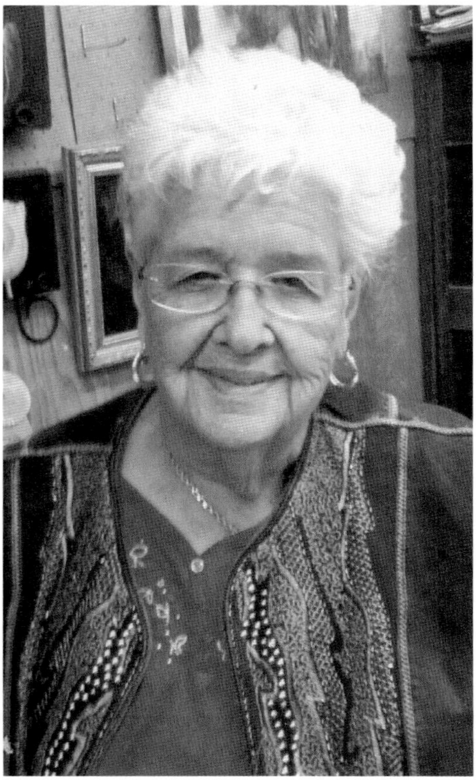

June Kittrell

June Kittrell drove a Lake Worth school bus for 22 years while her husband, Kit Kittrell, served as teacher, coach, and principal in the schools. She also served as director of transportation for the school district for 10 years.

After raising three children, in retirement, Kittrell knits crocheted caps for premature babies and cancer patients. In addition, she sometimes donates oil paintings she painted and does bookkeeping once a week for a Lake Worth restaurant. (Courtesy June Kittrell.)

Sara and Don Riley

Sara Riley has served Lake Worth and Tarrant County in various ways. She tutored children in elementary school in the Lake Worth School District twice a week for several years as well as volunteering playground duty to relieve teachers. In addition, she served as room mother and belonged to the Parent-Teacher Organization (PTO) for 14 years. She also maintained membership for many years in both the Lake Worth Youth Association and the Lake Worth Athletic Association. Riley coached girls' softball for one year and participated in Special Olympics.

Further service includes Riley's work for four years in the Tarrant County District Clerk's Office. She served 20 years as court coordinator for the 297th District Court. As a member of Texas and Tarrant County Coordinators' Association, she held offices as president, vice president, and secretary for a local association for a number of years. She served on the Tarrant County Grand Jury, volunteered at the Tarrant County Food Bank, and currently serves on the Lake Worth Economic Development Board.

Don Riley also served with his wife, Sara, as a member of both the Lake Worth Youth Association and Lake Worth Athletic Association. During the time their children attended Lake Worth schools, he served as vice president and later as president of the school board. In the late 1960s, Riley served as a reserve police officer in Fort Worth as well as working at General Dynamics. He attended court-reporting college in the 1970s and worked as a freelance reporter full-time. Riley worked as a freelance and official court reporter for almost 40 years, including 26 years serving in County Courts No. 1 and No. 2.

Since his retirement in 2009, Riley joined the Texas Court Reporters Certification Board where he holds the position of freelance member and chairman of the Review Panel Committee. He also serves on the Uniform Format Committee and the Continuing Education Committee.

Don and Sara Riley, members of the Hills Church of Christ since 1982, became involved in ministry, making trips to Russia. She went three times, and he went once. Sharing the story of this unselfish couple's years of service to others fits well in this chapter. (Courtesy Sara Riley.)

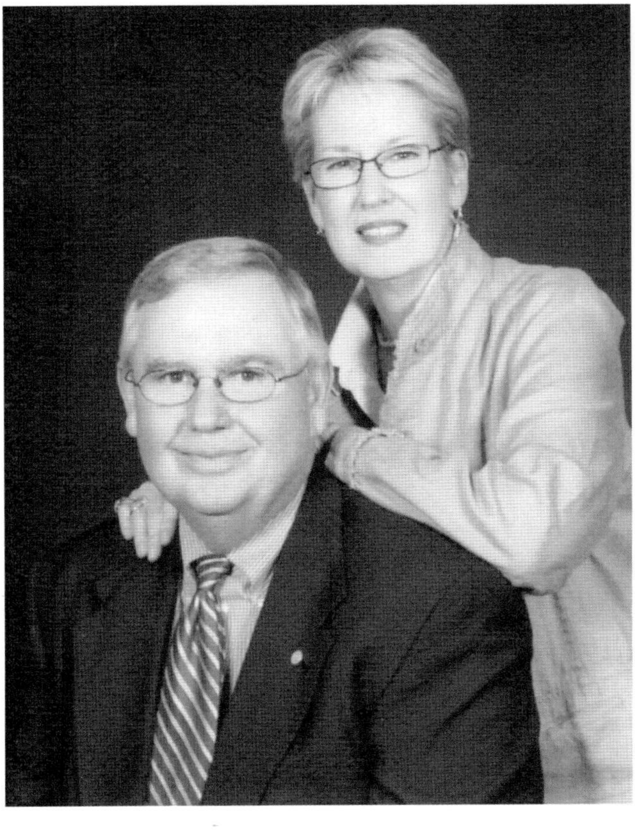

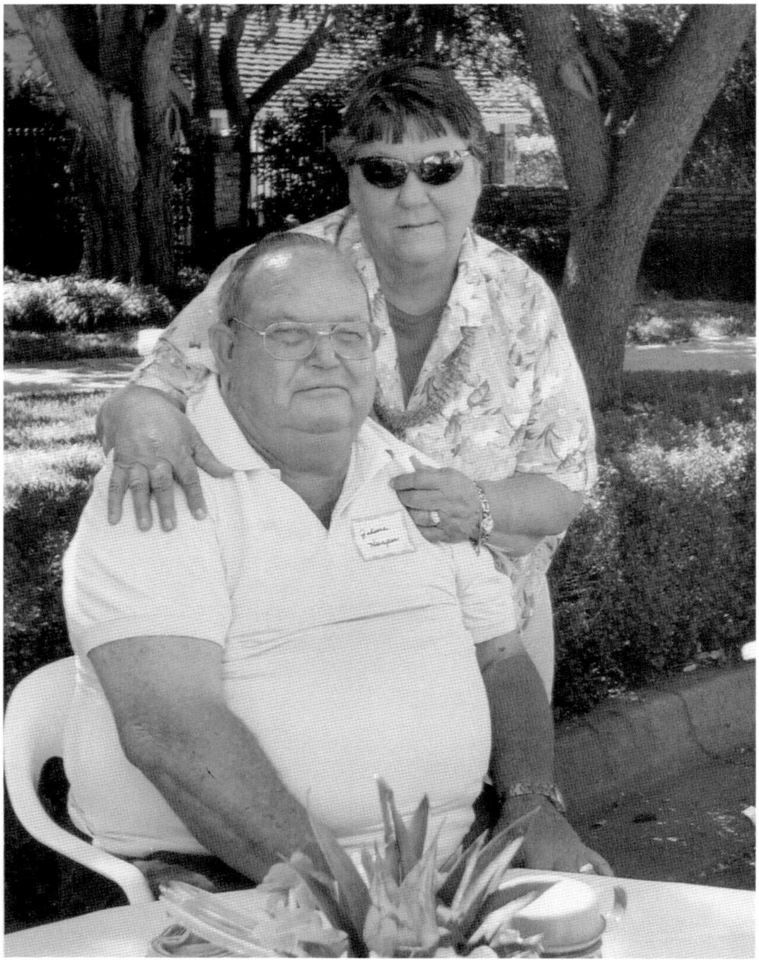

Ann and John Hooper

Ann Hooper has served a total of 31 years and over 11,000 hours as a hospice volunteer. She assists home patients and their families with transportation, outings, sitter services, and supports the inpatient staff at Hospice House doing volunteer work with St. Joseph Hospice and Community Hospice of Fort Worth.

In addition, Hooper assists in the bereavement services for the families of deceased patients, attending weekly and monthly meetings. Her supervisor has said her unconditional acceptance of all patients and "can-do" attitude makes her invaluable to the hospice team and those patients she serves. She also has a delightful sense of humor that sometimes catches her friends off guard, but makes them cherish her even more.

Hooper and her husband, John, moved in 1958 to Greenfield Acres, a nearby area of Lake Worth. They developed many friendships in Lake Worth and other areas.

John Hooper, who built homes and other structures all over Tarrant County, had tireless energy. His customers knew he would be right on the job supervising every nail hammered and hole dug. This dedication profited him a good reputation as a highly responsible builder. Many loved and respected him and mourned his death in 2007.

Both of these fine people enjoyed going to breakfast for a number of years in Lake Worth with friends five or six days a week. Ann Hooper continues this tradition with others who also find Whataburger breakfast meals delicious. (Courtesy Carla Bezner.)

CHAPTER NINE

Athletes

Countless Lake Worth citizens have competed in and excelled in various sports over the years. Some have done well enough to win numerous awards and gain national fame. A few have succeeded in the major sports of football, basketball, and baseball, while others have gained acclaim in minor sports such as rodeo and water sports.

The Sperry family has earned honors in water skiing competition. The family of six has shared a love of water skiing that fueled their competitive desires. That desire translated into national honors for some. When Richard and Lucille Sperry married, they perpetuated their love of water skiing. Richard Sperry Sr. taught his four children how to ski. He enhanced his skills by joining a prominent ski club and school located near the family home on Lake Worth. He and his son Richard Sperry II earned honors with regional championships in 1952. However, another son—Glenn—excelled even further. He won regional championships in 1956, 1957, and 1958, and won a national championship in 1957. At age 16, he earned a record high score that still stands. Fifty years later, he won another national title. The skis he used then now may be found in the Water Ski Hall of Fame in Florida. He had such talent that he later skied nationwide with a traveling show. He also ran his own traveling show eventually and performed exhibition skiing on Lake Worth. His mother, Lucille Sperry, did not allow age to put limits on her talent for water skiing. She skied most of her life and for the last time at age 100, only two years before her death.

The Purdom family honed their skills in riding bucking horses and in trick roping. As a youth, E.C. Purdom developed into a talented horseman, trick roper, and worked in Hollywood for a while. He shared his knowledge of horses with his wife, Rue Dean. His sons Donnie and Ronnie Purdom learned trick roping from him. Donnie went on to be a competitive "bronc rider" and sponsored the Lake Worth High School Rodeo Club for a time. Rue Dean became a natural with horses as well. She proved her athletic ability in helping her husband handle horses and riding in several local parades.

As a fierce competitor, Zachary Lopez excelled in sports at Lake Worth High School. He received several offers from colleges to play football and basketball. He went on to play college football for a few years before devoting his life to the Christian Ministry.

Each of these entries earned a place in this chapter. Their abilities may inspire others to follow through on their own efforts to master a rewarding challenge.

E.C. Purdom

E.C. Purdom, known as Duke in his earlier years, later changed the spelling to Dook. Born in Fairy, a Chalk Mountain area of Central Texas, he graduated as valedictorian in Hico, Texas.

A rodeo cowboy, Purdom rounded up wild horses in New Mexico, and in the early 1930s became a world-class bull rider. In addition, he performed trick roping for the circus and became a stunt man in Hollywood as well as being in westerns as an extra. He auditioned for the part of Geronimo but wound up selling ice cream from a cart on the University of Southern California campus. As time passed, he practiced trick roping with Will Rogers on the weekends. His love of horses led Purdom to become a founding member of the Texas Cutting Horse Association.

This horse lover obviously had an upbeat personality, which served him well after an accident occurred. Purdom fell when the cinch on his saddle broke as he sat astride in demonstration for an observing prospective buyer. He broke his neck and was paralyzed. After three months in the hospital, he miraculously recovered.

Purdom owned ranches in different places, but after several years, he sold them and focused his attention in cars. This interest eventually led him to own several car lots. At one of his car lots, he met his future wife, 18-year-old Rue Dean Jackson who had accompanied her father to purchase a car. They married a year later in 1939. They had two sons, Ronnie in 1940 and Donnie in 1943.

In 1949, the Purdoms moved to Fort Worth, Texas, and started The Cowtown Auto Auction on Jacksboro Highway. They also bought their home in Lake Worth on Charbonneau Road, where they raised their family. Many consider them both as legendary locals. (Courtesy Donnie Purdom.)

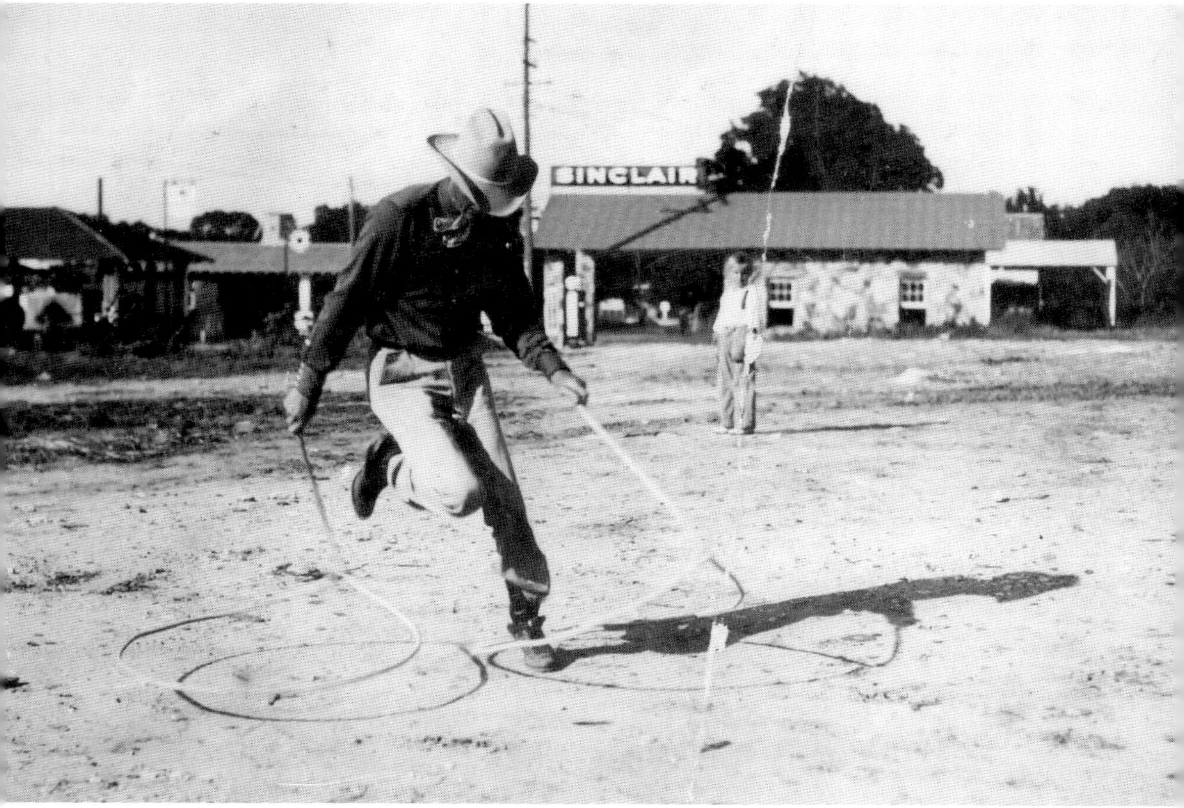

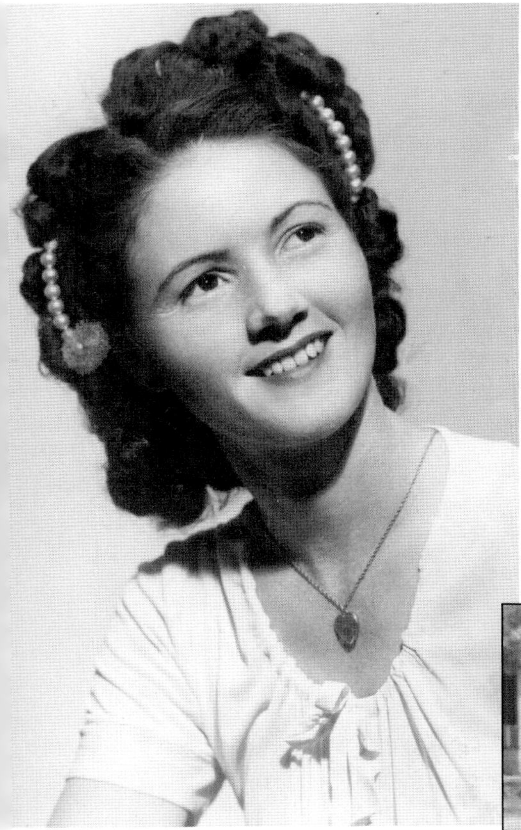

Young Rue Dean Purdom
Attractive 18-year-old Rue Dean Jackson caught the eye of her future husband, E.C. "Dook" Purdom, in 1938. They married in 1939 and later had two sons, Donnie and Ronnie. Early on, Purdom helped her husband run his ranches. They later moved to Fort Worth where they began various business ventures. (Courtesy Donnie Purdom.)

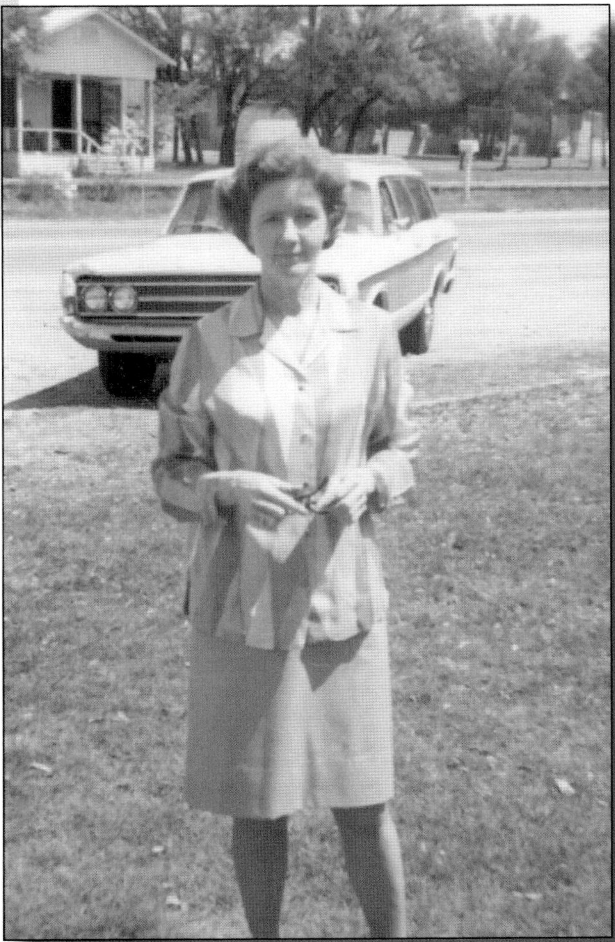

Rue Dean Purdom
Rue Dean Purdom moved to Lake Worth in 1950 and started the School Bell Cafe across the street from the school. She later turned the cafe building into the family home where she opened a day care, "The Wigwam Nursery." After having the home's front porch removed, she had a 15-foot teepee built as an entrance.

Other business endeavors included raising chinchillas, providing notary service, and auto license sales out of her home. This information provides an insight of this talented woman who appears in this chapter because of her athletic abilities with horses. (Courtesy Donnie Purdom.)

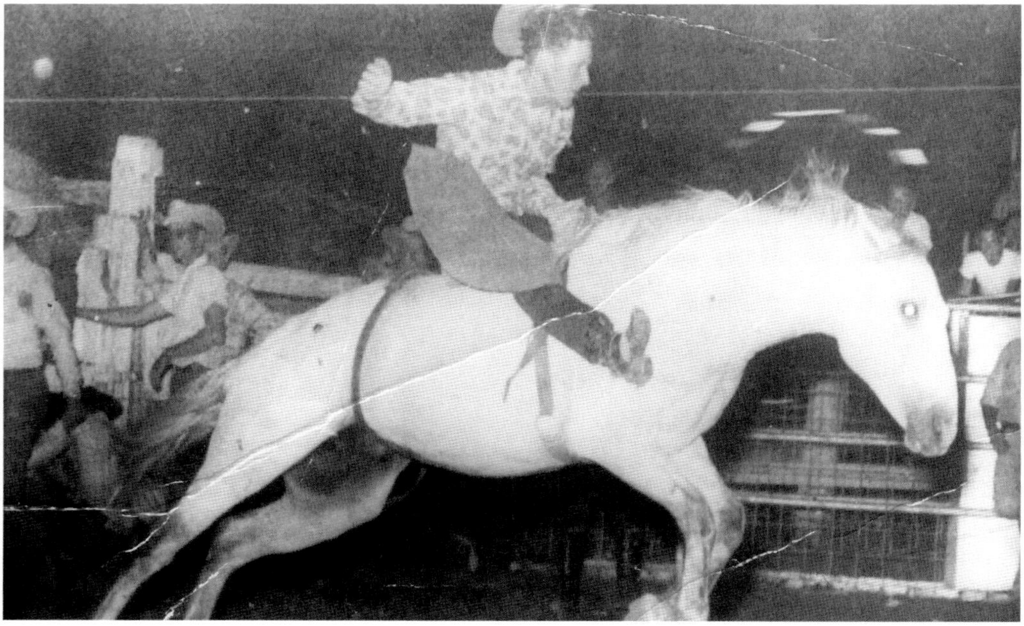

Donnie Purdom

Donnie Purdom attended Lake Worth Schools until he married a lovely girl named Glenda Godbey. In the late 1950s, he served briefly in the US Navy, receiving an honorable discharge.

Purdom's various interests included riding bucking horses and doing trick roping. He learned about both from his father, E.C. Purdom. It appears he learned well, as demonstrated in the photographs. Donnie Purdom is pictured above. In the photograph below, Donnie, the tallest child, stands with his younger brother Ronnie.

Although Purdom ceased riding broncos after having suffered many broken bones over the years, he did sponsor the rodeo club at Lake Worth High School. (Courtesy Donnie Purdom.)

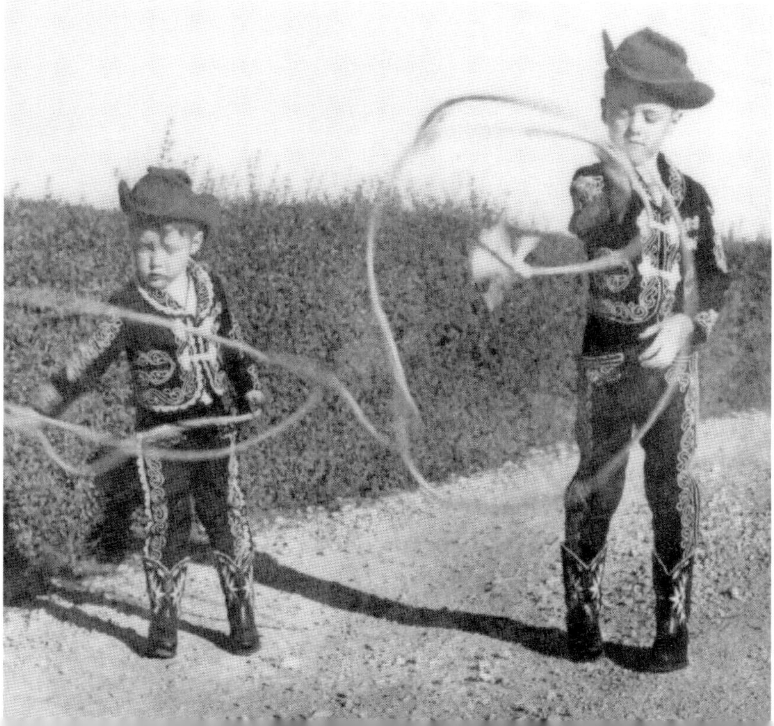

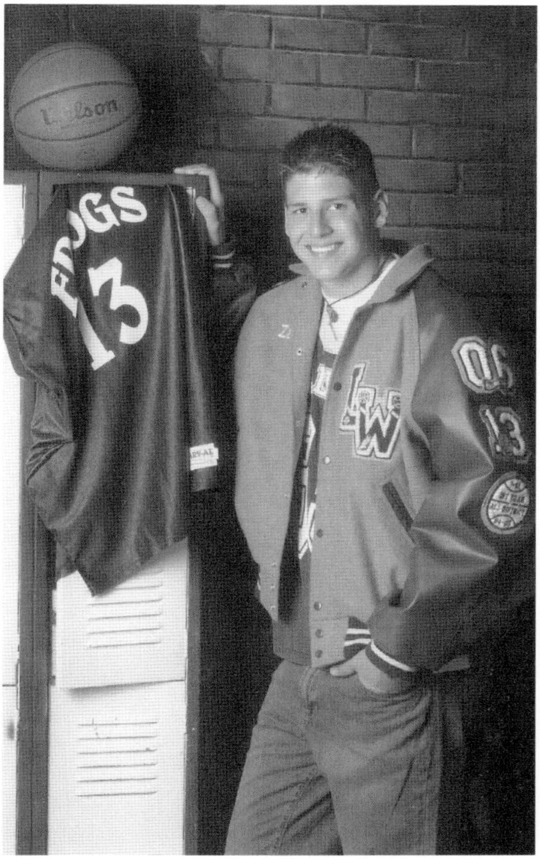

Zachary Lopez
Zachary Lopez excelled in sports at Lake Worth High School. As a senior, he received offers from several colleges to play football and offers to play basketball from two other colleges. After graduating high school, he played football at West Texas Agricultural and Mechanical University, and then Trinity Valley Community College. Lopez returned later to West Texas, where he felt comfortable sharing his faith in Jesus. He played football until March of 2010. (Courtesy Carla Bezner.)

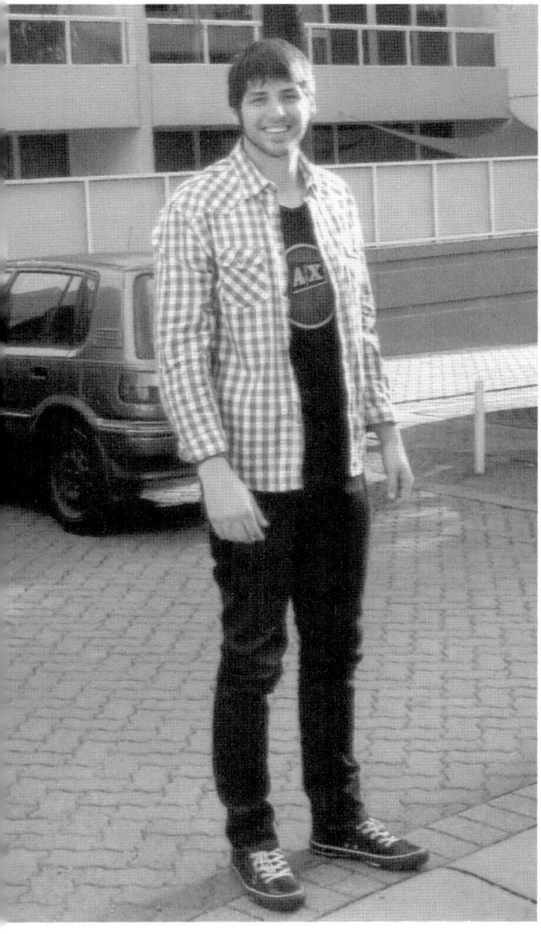

Zachary Lopez, Today
At age 14, Zachary Lopez felt called to the ministry, but at age 16, sports became the center of his life. He later reconnected with God, and his faith led him to Sydney, Australia, studying at Hillsong International Leadership College. He says he has discovered purpose that God gave him through Jesus. He has graduated and returned to the United States. (Courtesy Kim Lopez and Carla Bezner.)

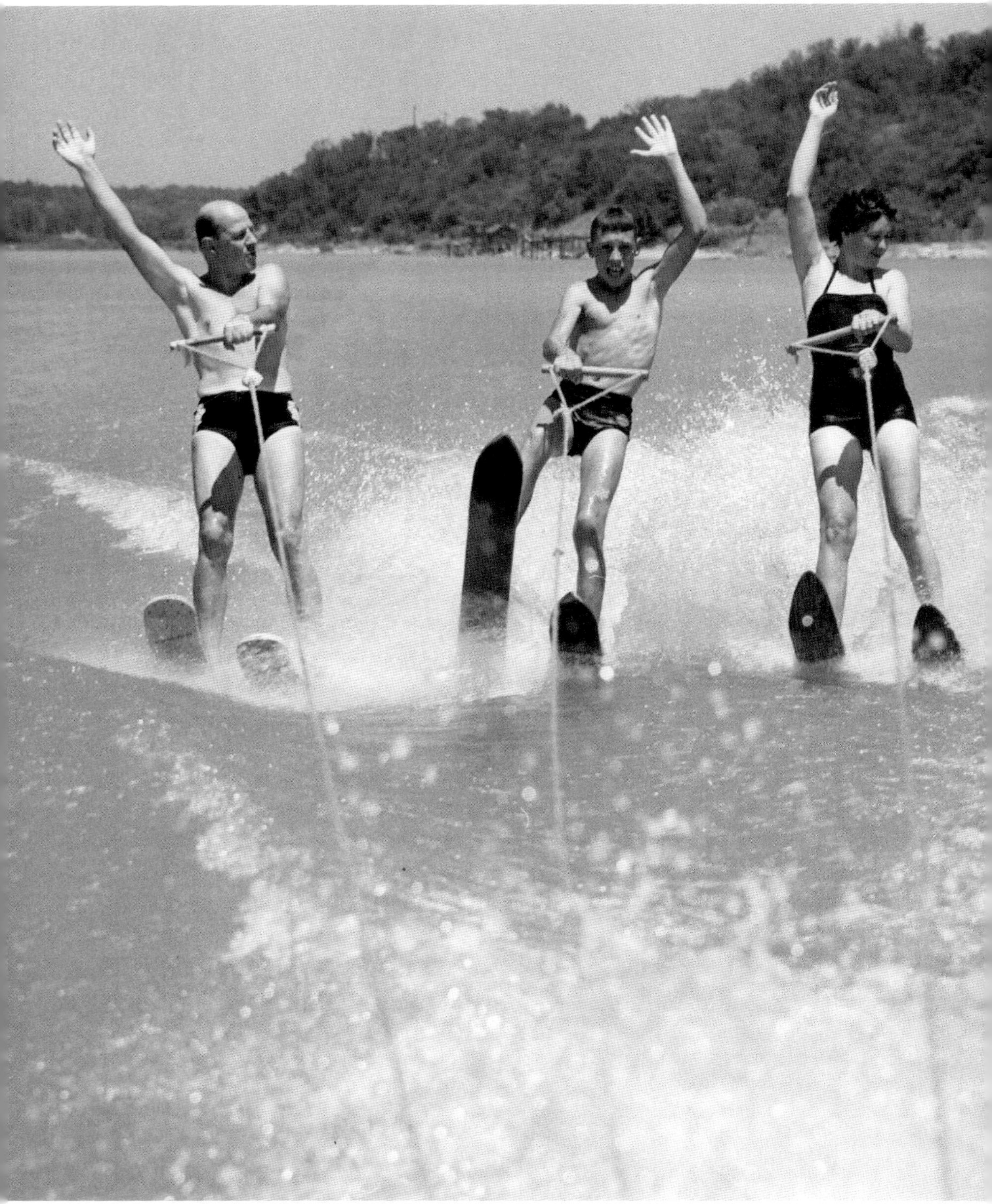

Richard Sperry Senior and Family

Richard Sperry Sr. and his wife, Lucille, shared the love of water skiing. Sperry taught all four of their children to ski. In 1952, he and his son Richard II won regional championships respectively. His son Glenn

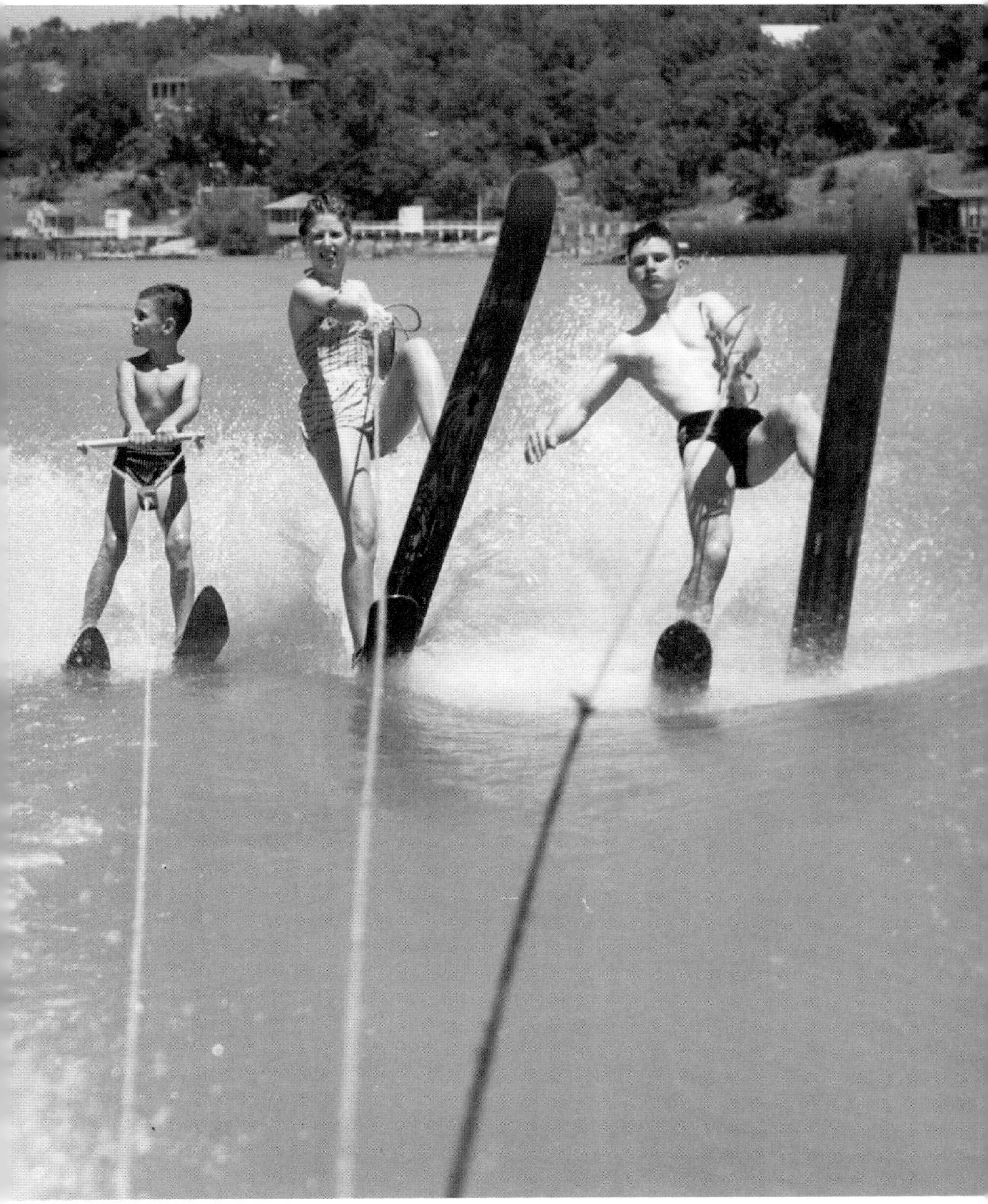

also won many awards. The entire family was photographed skiing and identified from left to right as father, Richard "Dick" Sperry; son, Glenn; mother, Lucille; youngest son, Philip; daughter, Thelma; and Richard II, their eldest son. (Courtesy Glenn Sperry.)

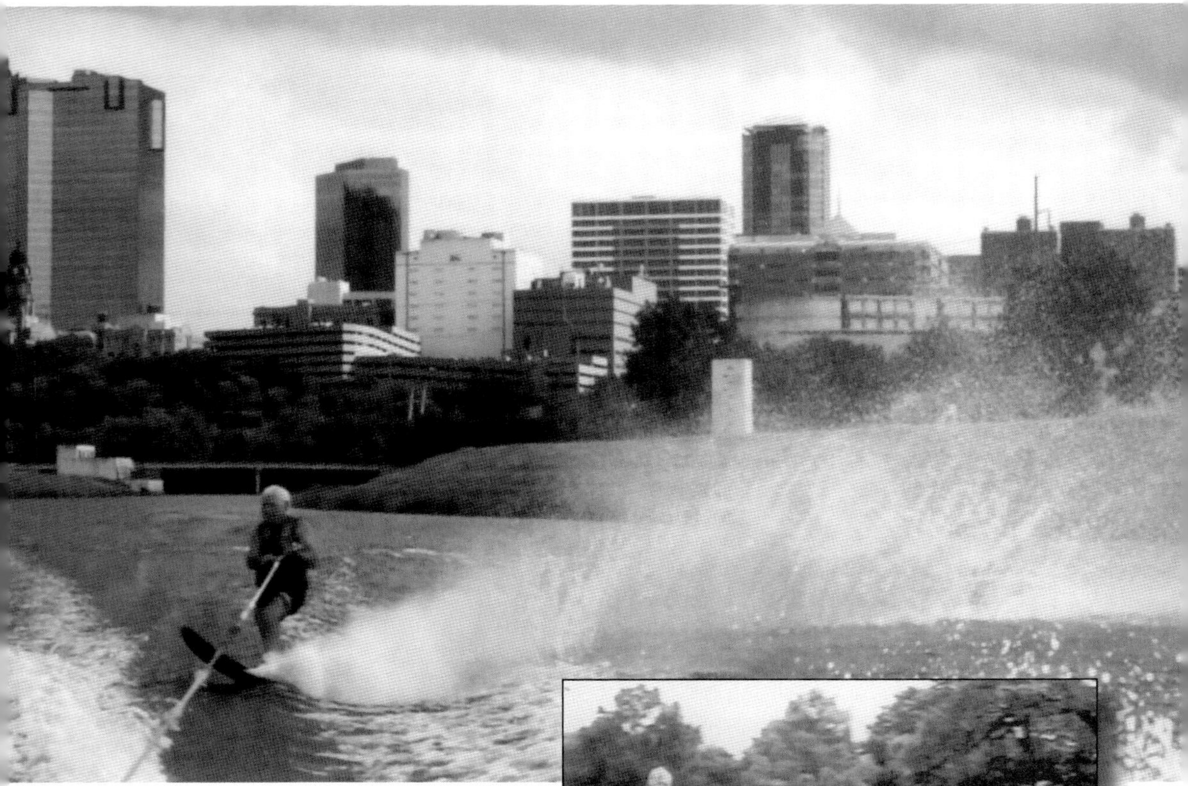

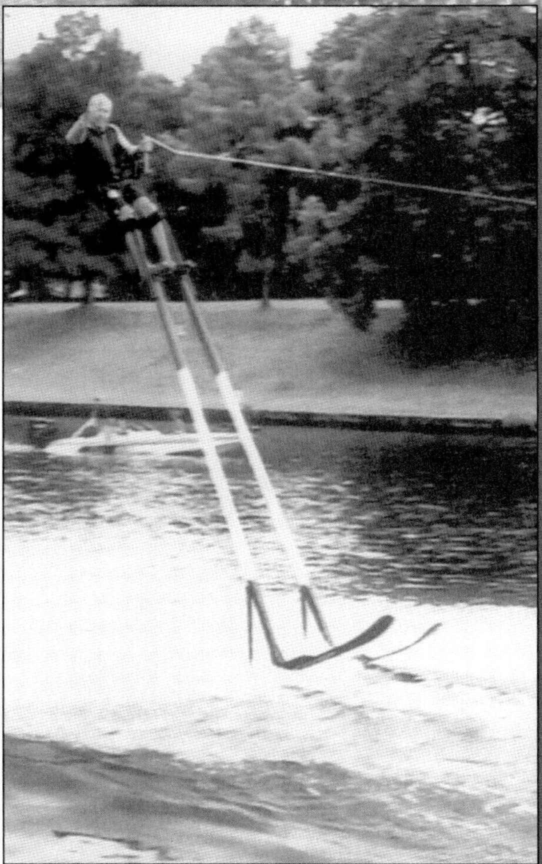

Glenn Sperry
Glenn Sperry, 72 as of this writing, has honed his water skiing skills on Lake Worth near his waterfront home for many years. He also skies other area lakes and rivers. Incredibly, Sperry has earned the title of National Water Skiing Champion twice, 50 years apart, in 1957 and in 2007.

Photographed here, Sperry skis on the Trinity River in 2010 with Fort Worth's beautiful skyline in the background. (Courtesy Glenn Sperry.)

Glenn Sperry on Stilts
Glenn Sperry, national champion skier, appears in this photograph skiing on 10-foot-high stilts connected to his skis. He has practiced extensively on four ski jumps and six slalom courses located around Lake Worth. His 7.5-foot-tall skis, which he used to win a national record, may now be found in the Water Ski Hall of Fame in Polk City, Florida. (Courtesy Glenn Sperry.)

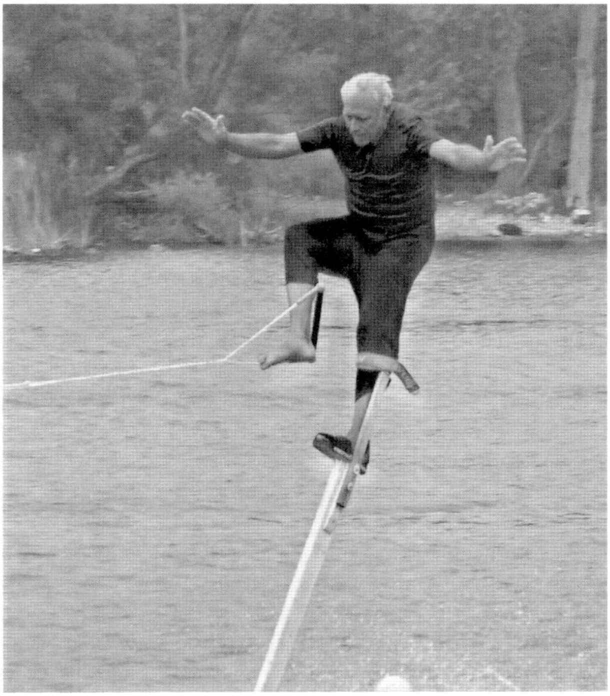

Glenn Sperry Water Adventures
Skiing for Glenn Sperry and his family became a tradition, impacting the history of water events in Lake Worth as well as other areas across the country. A longtime resident of Lake Worth, Sperry recalls such occasions that involved himself and his family.

After moving to Texas in 1952, the Sperry family discovered the Herman and Midge Aston Ski School operating off Casino Beach at the Lake Worth reservoir. The next year, the Astons opened the Aston Ski Club, which they could access just out their back door, as their home sat on the shores of Lake Worth.

For excellence in instruction and its ability to produce winners, the Aston Ski Club was voted fourth in America by students in 1956. Sperry and his father, Richard Sr., spent the summers skiing with that club. With four ski jumps and six slalom courses located around the lake during the 1950s and 1960s, a challenging environment awaited the skiers.

Another important event was The Lone Star Championship Tournament held for several years in the mid-1950s on Lake Worth. These courses provided skilled athletes an opportunity to showcase their talents.

One particular practice became an embarrassing event Sperry recalls in the 1950s as he practiced the slalom run. He took a fall and lost his bathing suit. He refused to get back into the boat, so he swam back to the Aston's boat dock and got a towel before coming out of the water.

In 1956, 1957, and 1958, Glenn Sperry won regional champion. In 1957, he also won nationals, and became the last person to ski the slalom course on two skis. He had the highest score at the age of 16, a record that still stands. Amazingly, he went back 50 years later and won the nationals again.

Tommy Bartlett, who owned the Tommy Bartlett Water show in 1958, included Sperry in his traveling show, but they did not perform on Lake Worth; however, Sperry did perform later on in exhibition skiing with the Lake Worth Boat and Ski Club in the early 1960s. Sperry ran his own traveling ski shows in the 1970s and 1980s. They performed on Lake Worth and in various other states. He also sponsored the first high school ski club at Castleberry High School, where at one time he taught woodworking.

He still teaches skiing at his present home on Lake Worth and credits God for his skiing and teaching ability. (Courtesy Glenn Sperry.)

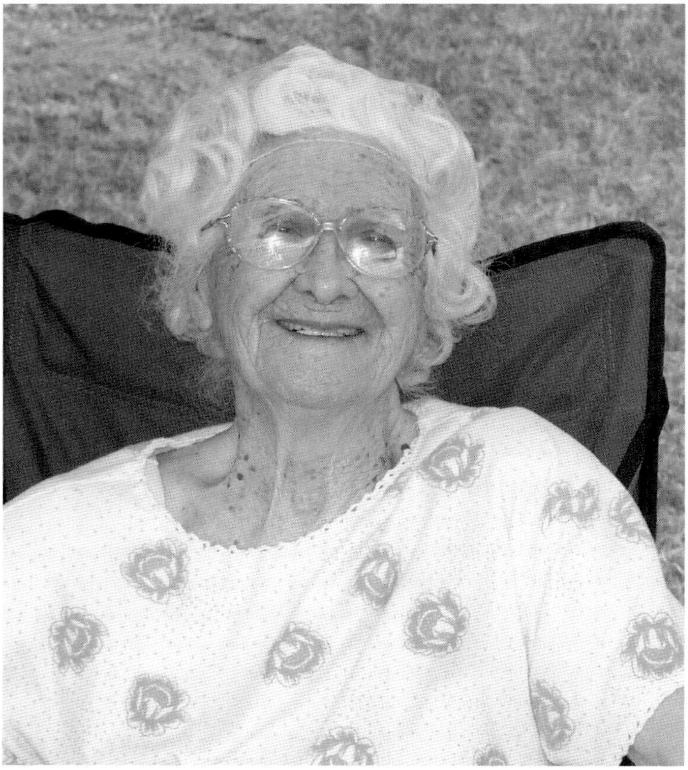

Lucille Thelma Sperry
Lucille Thelma (Hughey) Sperry, the mother of four children, spent much of her life on skis, sometimes with family members. This courageous and talented woman skied her last time at the age of 100. Shown here smiling in the photograph, she lived to the age of 102. (Courtesy of Glenn Sperry.)

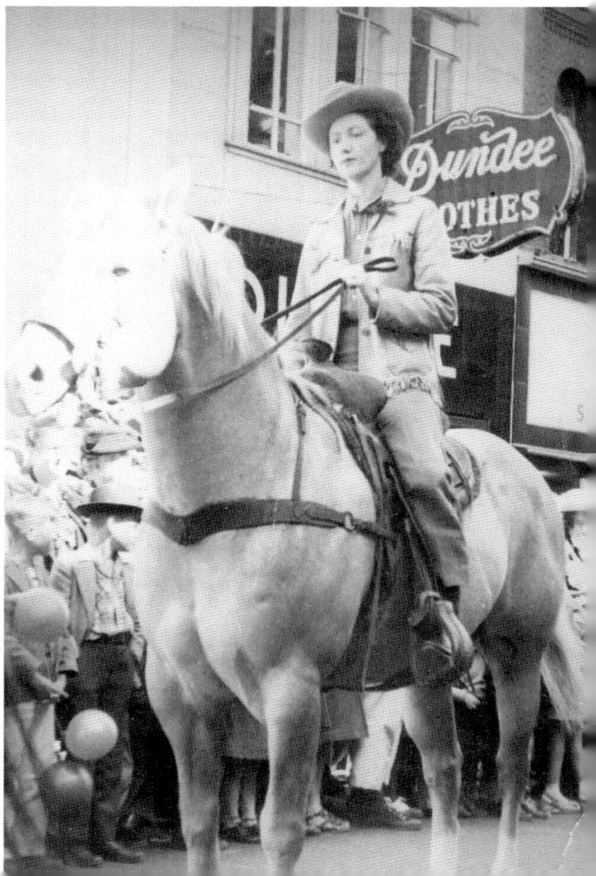

Rue Dean Purdom in Parade
Rue Dean Purdom rode proudly on her horse in the Fort Worth Stock Show Parade. She rode in this annual parade at least a dozen times. Her husband, E.C. Purdom, had many horses entered in Stock Show Rodeo events.

Purdom came to love horses as she helped him tend to approximately 50 horses on their Stephenville ranch in the 1940s. (Courtesy Donnie Purdom.)

CHAPTER TEN

Destructive Past, Recovery, and the Future

In the 1920s, Lake Worth shores soon had mom-and-pop shops all over the beach. A pleasant park for many, it soon became home to a famous amusement park and to government-related projects. Ohio-based A.J. Miller and Company built the park, the largest in the southwestern United States at that time. The park featured a mile-long roller coaster, bumper cars, a merry-go-round, and other rides.

In 1928, tragedy struck when a fire consumed many of the park's wooden buildings. The park recovered and flourished for a while, but times worsened nationwide, prompting the government to initiate a program called Civilian Conservation Corps to provide jobs for hundreds.

Tara School provided an education for the workers. Additionally, the Federal Transient Camp provided living quarters. Gangsters created havoc near the area in the 1930s and 1940s. Fires and financial difficulties added to the turmoil of the amusement park. It thrived for a while through the economic depression but later suffered other tragic times, eventually causing its demise.

"Bud" Irby became a true legendary local, who had much involvement with the old Casino Beach Amusement Park and Ballroom. He also served the city of Lake Worth. During much of the up-and-down days of the park, gangsters like Tincy Eaggelson, Frank Cates, Gene Paul Norris, and George Keen caused their own disruptions by gambling and killing each other. They often used Jacksboro Highway, which runs through the city of Lake Worth, as their road of travel.

With that era far into the past, during the early years of the 21st century, citizens in Lake Worth currently enjoy a beautiful multipurpose complex headed up by Cheryl Vess. Mary Ann Kozel, Betty Cross, Anne Floyd, and Barbara Howard come there to make quilts.

The nearby new library offers residents reading materials and more. Lara Struthers, the director of the library, initiates a variety of programs. A few yards west, a memorial park honors military personnel who served our country in uniform.

Other parks and plaques honor various people, places, or things. The Lake Worth Garden Club has participated in some of the events to enhance Lake Worth. Members Thelma Smith, Barbara Bateman, Nancy Keylon, Georgeanna Metts, JoAnn Zwald, Lois Sumerlin, and others provided a butterfly garden and more.

New life for the beaches of Lake Worth looms ahead as the Casino Beach Partners, LLC, plan a development to possibly include a boardwalk, riverboat, restaurants, marina, and Casino Beach Hall. The centennial year of the lake, 2014, brings opportunities for events honoring its development.

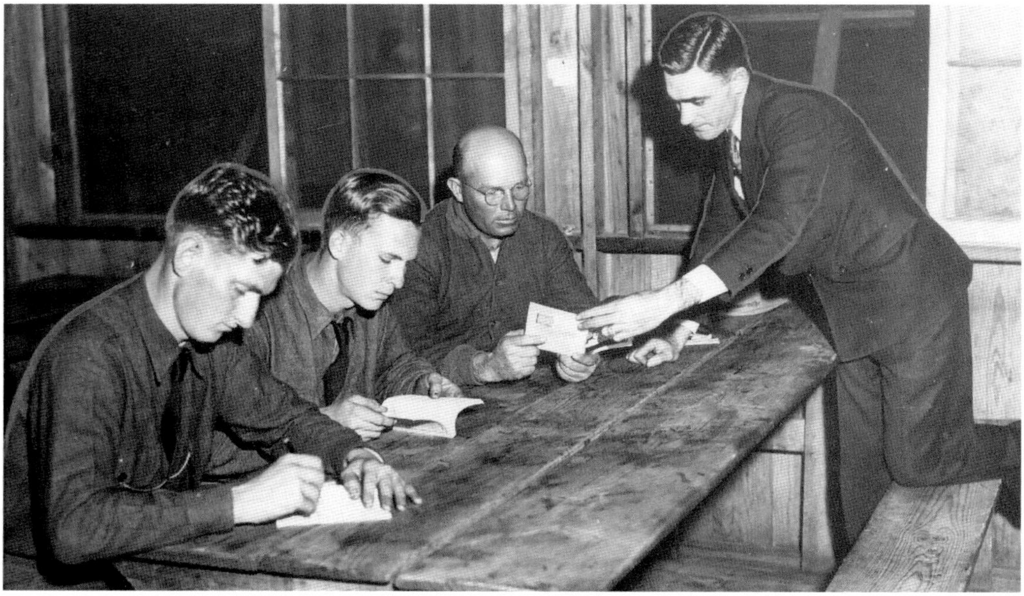

Tara School for Civilian Conservation Corps

During the years of 1933 to 1942, Pres. Franklin D. Roosevelt created an emergency plan, the Civilian Conservation Corps, to bring relief to families. With 3,000 camps, each had 200 men, some assigned to projects in their own state or assigned elsewhere in the United States. Those assigned had to be at least 17 years of age. Some workers had not completed elementary school or high school. Many took advantage of courses offered within their camp.

The photograph has unidentified males attending classes in a camp named Tara, possibly located near Lake Worth. (Courtesy John DeGroat.)

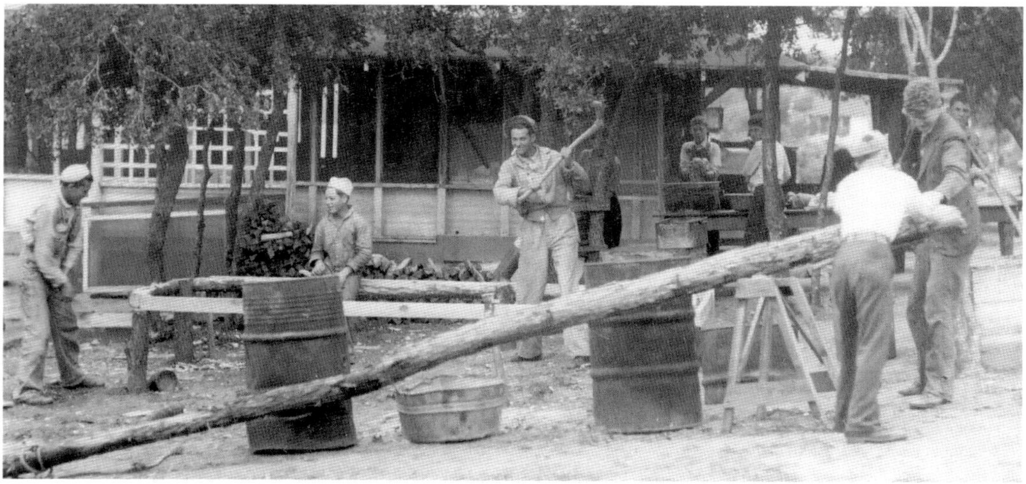

Civilian Conservation Camp

Sleeping quarters and meals provided for workers made their jobs a little more convenient, especially at times when they worked near their camp. Although much of their monthly $30 paychecks had to be sent home to their families, they kept $5.

In the photograph unidentified men work outside. A few structures built by men in the Civilian Conservation Corps still remain in Lake Worth, some with a lake view. (Courtesy John DeGroat.)

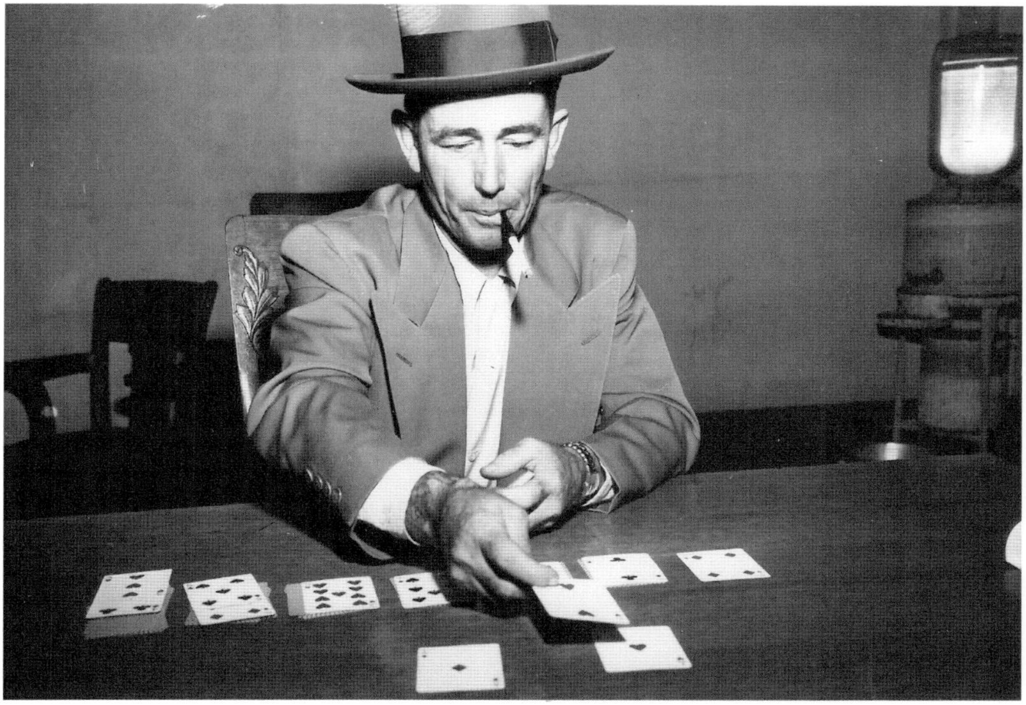

Tincy Eggleston

Tincy Eggleston, above, became a suspect many times in the courtroom as the initiator of illegal gambling incidents and murders. A quarrel between Eggleston and Edell Evans ended in Evans putting a hit on Eggleston. Being confronted by the hit man, Eggleston offered the hit man more money to go and kill Evans. A newspaper story related that Eggleston and crime partner Cecil Green lured Evans to a place near Lake Worth and knocked him unconscious. When Eggleston and Cecil Green tried to bury him, Evans awoke from his unconscious state and rose up enough to bite Eggleston on the ankle. Police later found Evans in a shallow grave near Lake Worth with two bullet holes in his head. Eggleston gained further notoriety when he was found at the bottom of a well, according to reports. (Courtesy Fort Worth Police Historical Association, Dale Lee Hinz, trustee.)

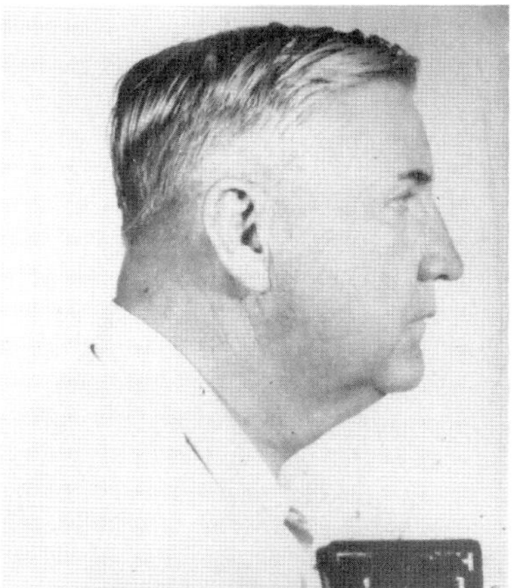

Frank Cates—1956
bombed. then shot

Frank Cates

Frank Cates made his money as a gambling hall owner and by transporting illegal liquor for gangsters. In 1956, he rented a home on Roberts Cut-Off Road that he turned into a small casino and angered many residents. He survived severe injuries from an explosion; apparently the explosives were under his house. The explosion severely injured Cates. A few months later, he did not survive a trip to deliver liquor to a Wichita Falls warehouse. Someone found his body riddled with bullets next to his car. Bandages still covered his body from injuries sustained in the house explosion. (Courtesy Fort Worth Police Historical Association, Dale Lee Hinz, trustee.)

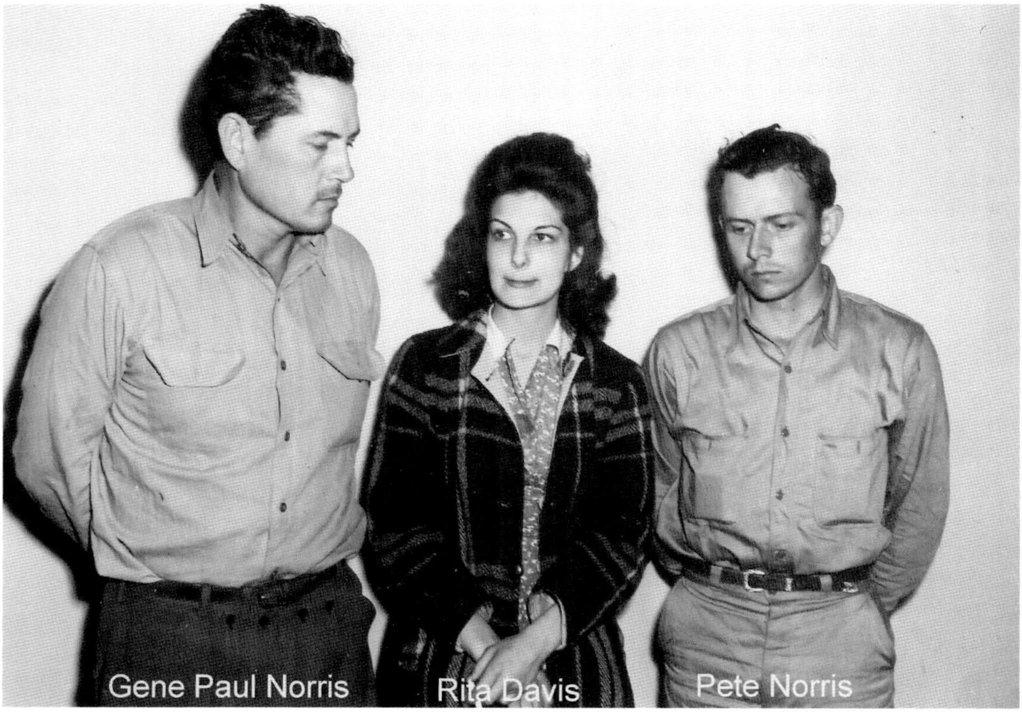

Gene Paul Norris

Notorious gangster Gene Paul Norris planned to rob a bank at Carswell Air Base. He plotted to kidnap the cashier at her Lake Worth home and steal her car, which had a base-entry sticker.

The Federal Bureau of Investigation received a tip about the planned heist. The FBI investigators, the Fort Worth police chief, the Tarrant County sheriff, and a Texas Ranger prevented the incident by securing the cashier and setting a trap to capture Norris.

Police officers noticed their car passing through Lake Worth, and a chase followed. Norris and his bodyguard William Humphrey never robbed again for the officers gunned them down on the spot just a few miles down the road near Springtown. (Courtesy Fort Worth Police Historical Association, Dale Lee Hinz, trustee.)

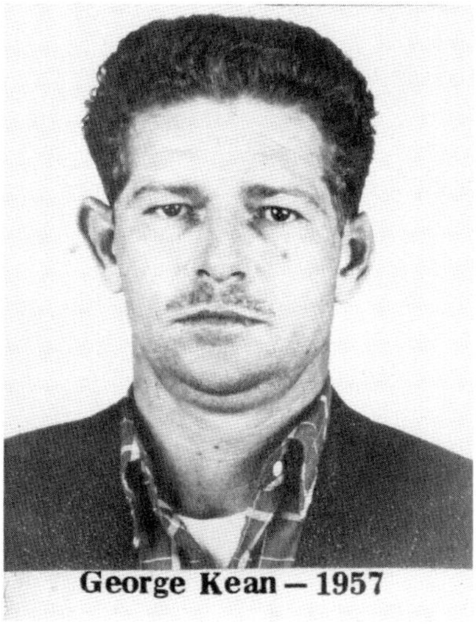

George Keen

George Keen wanted to take advantage of being one of the last gangsters alive in the area. Keen, according to police information, planned to take over the gangs of slain gang leaders and be a kingpin in the Dallas-Fort Worth area.

He made progress until someone tried to kill him in November 1957. Lawmen found a bomb in his car, and Keen apparently went into hiding. He ended up in Michigan, but encountered dissension within his own gang. A newspaper report revealed that one of his gang members there shot him at close range after an argument. The report stated that the men fought over "who was the toughest." Police officers found Keen's body in a shallow grave. He lived to age 32. (Courtesy Fort Worth Police Historical Association, Dale Lee Hinz, trustee.)

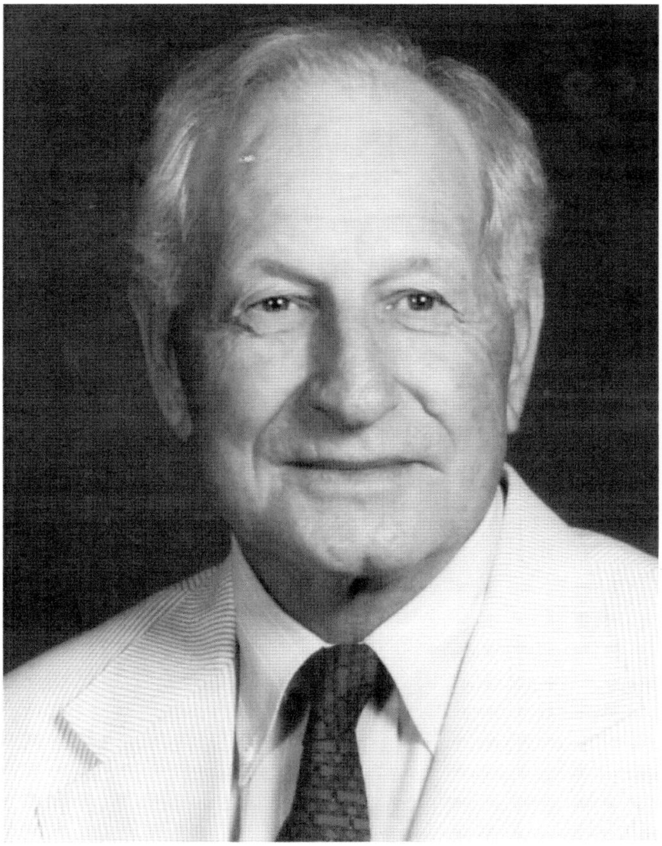

L.O. "Bud" Irby

L.O. "Bud" Irby, a native Texan, moved to Lake Worth in 1927. At the age of nine, he did odd jobs at the Lake Worth Casino, a well-known entertainment mecca located on the banks of the reservoir. In lean times, a local newspaper reported Irby said he often raced to beat another employee to go underneath the ballroom to look for coins dropped by the dancers through a few cracks in the floor. He later became assistant manager and then manager of this grand ballroom. He booked famous acts such as Harry James' band. James, once an unknown trumpet player, had to move to the back because of his loud playing. He later led his own band to fame. When playing the Casino Ballroom, Irby sometimes slipped James a cold beer, which the musician said he really appreciated.

Irby also booked Tommy Dorsey and several lesser-known stars at the time such as Frank Sinatra and Cab Calloway. Irby's employment there spanned 37 years, but he never had Glenn Miller's band because the musician, while in the military, died in a plane crash over England.

When World War II broke out, Irby served as an infantryman and became involved in the invasion of Normandy. In 1960, as the chief of Veterans of Foreign Wars, the VFW News tagged him as "the most engaging and pleasing host ever." His wife, Bernice, also joined in the planning of various events with the VFW. Later, Irby became manager of The Guys and Dolls Ballroom. In 1968, the City of Lake Worth asked this busy man to become the city manager on a temporary basis. Irby stayed 16 years. Later at age 66, he decided to leave his temporary work. He told a reporter, "I've enjoyed the work, but I'm at an age where I feel I'm losing some pizzazz, so to speak."

Later, when the city purchased 40 acres of land from the federal government and dubbed it the Carswell Annex, Irby expressed his approval. The land eventually served as a Lake Worth city park. Irby passed away in June 1996. His genuine love of Lake Worth left a legacy for all to treasure. His daughters were kind enough to supply the photograph. (Courtesy Patti Williams and Carolyn Irby.)

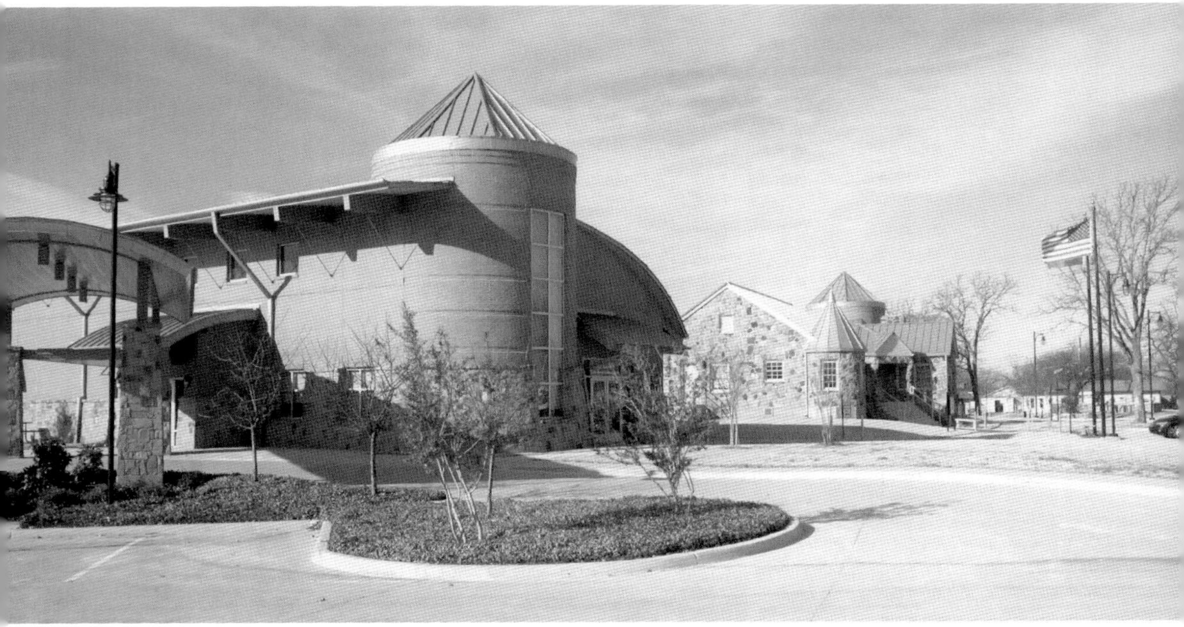

The L.O. "Bud" Irby Senior Center and Lake Worth Museum

The center was named after Bud Irby in 1985 because Irby's outstanding service to Lake Worth has become legendary. The original center, located elsewhere in Lake Worth, provided many activities for seniors to enjoy. The new center, an important part of a recently developed multipurpose complex in Lake Worth, continues various activities for a combined period of 37 years.

Located next to the senior center, the Lake Worth Museum, former home of J.R. Foster (early resident of Lake Worth), contains many interesting antiques and memorabilia. The city relocated the house to its present site in 2009. (Both photographs courtesy Ken Brower.)

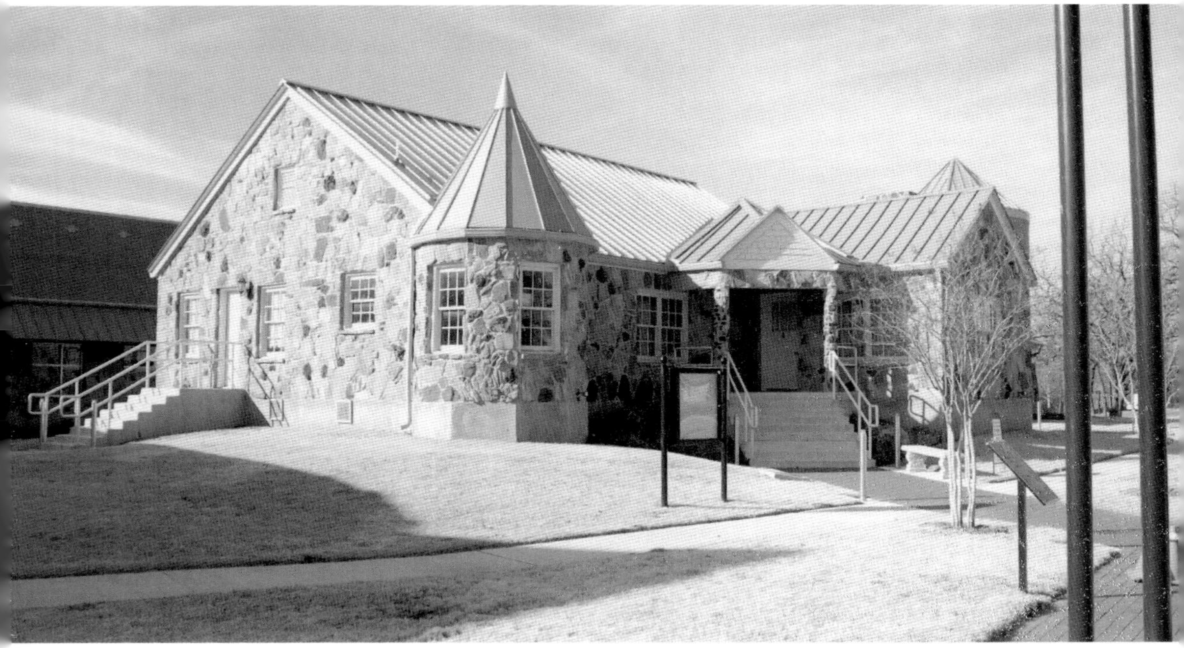

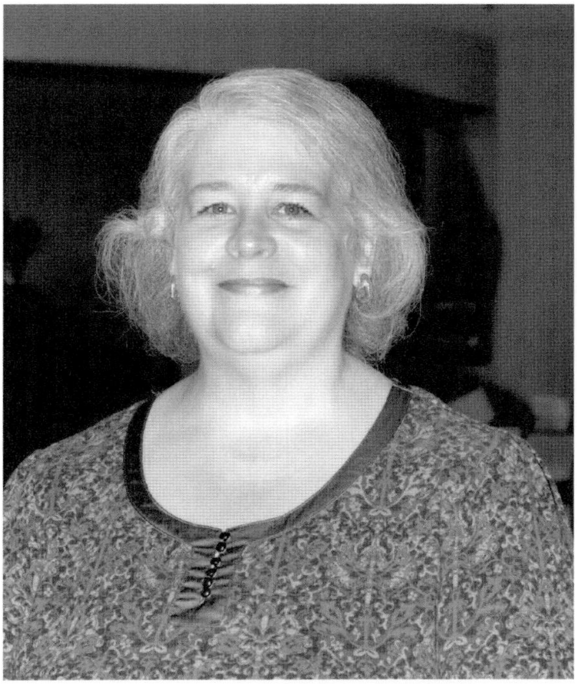

Cheryl Vess

As coordinator of the L.O. "Bud" Irby Senior Center since 2005, Cheryl Vess has promoted many new classes and activities. She has worked with city departments to coordinate several Lake Worth events, which include the annual winter Christmas Tree Lighting and the spring Easter Egg Hunt. In addition, she added an annual craft fair held during December that raises money to sponsor programs for the seniors. Vess and others make the center a special place. (Photograph by Ken Brower.)

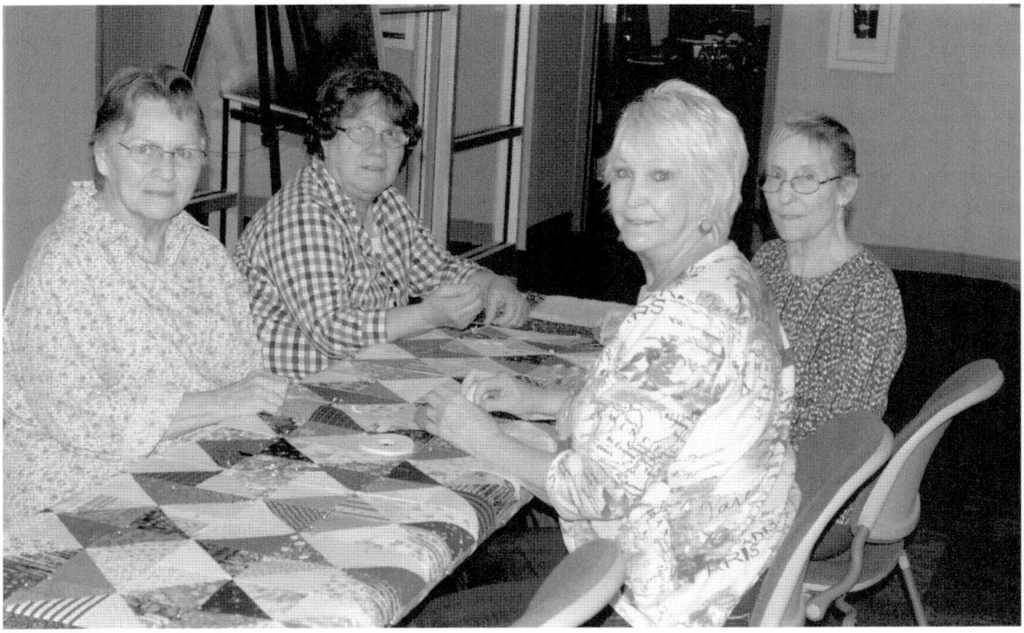

Quilting Ladies

For many years now, women from various areas come to L.O. "Bud" Irby Senior Center to make quilts. Each quilt is worked on by several people helping the owner.

On an individual basis, some quilts donated to community service organizations, such as Teenagers at Risk for Suicide, may provide means for organizations to raise money. Shown on the left in the first chair, Mary Ann Kozel sits next to Betty Cross. On the right, Ann Floyd sits in the first chair with Barbara Howard next to her. (Photograph by Ken Brower.)

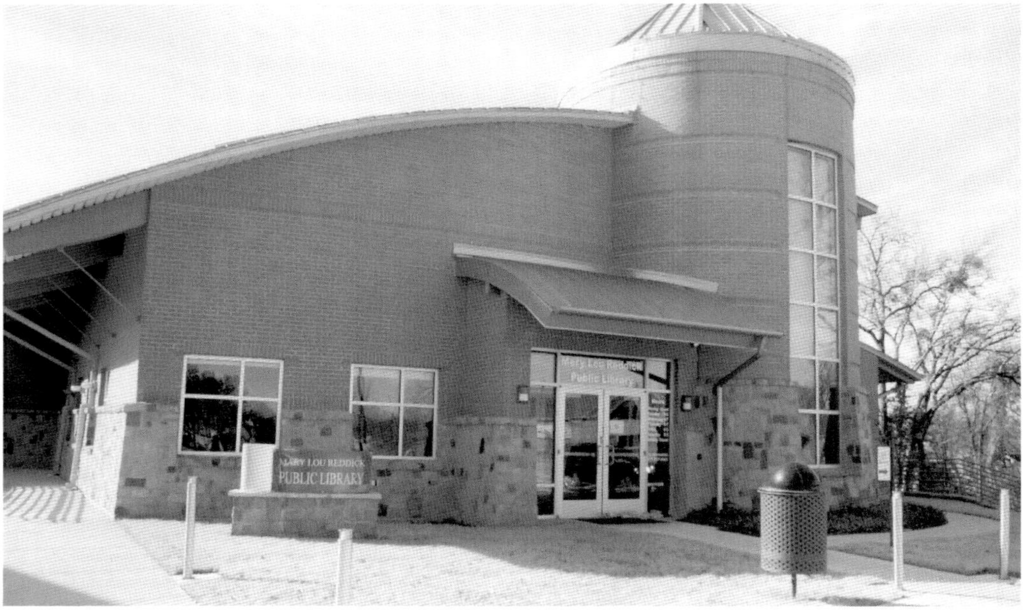

Mary Lou Reddick Public Library
The Mary Lou Reddick Public Library's architectural dome resembles the one on the nearby historical museum. The library offers a wide variety of reading material and other amenities set in a beautiful and comfortable arrangement. There may be found research materials, videos, and often groups of children who gather for book reviews. (Photograph by Ken Brower.)

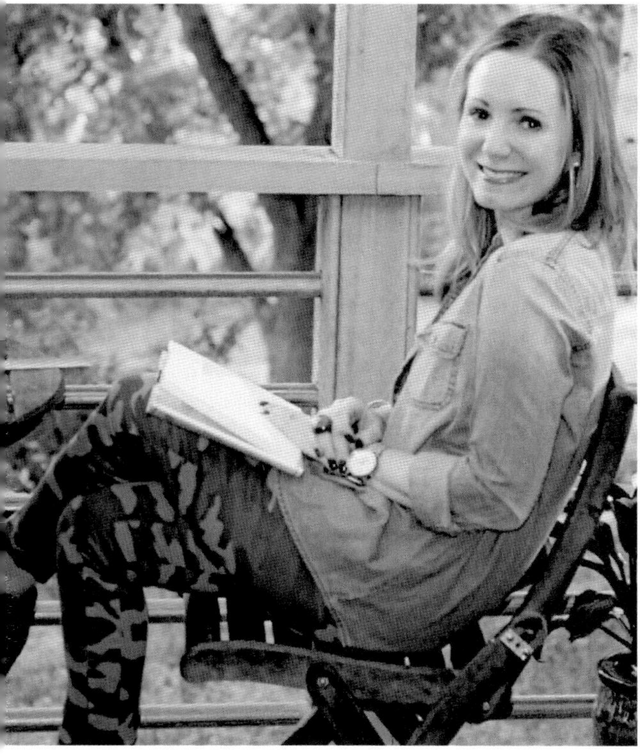

Lara Strother
Strother, born in Fort Worth, has been library director for Lake Worth's Mary Lou Reddick Public Library since 1998. She earned her undergraduate degree from Texas Wesleyan University, and her master's degree is from Texas Woman's University. She belongs to the Texas Library Association and the American Library Association.

Strother enjoys assisting the community with their learning endeavors. With a knack for planning programs, her skills initiate a variety of interesting events at the library including book reviews and children's programs. She also volunteers for Meals on Wheels for Tarrant County and runs a weekly delivery route in the Lake Worth area, although she lives in Arlington with her husband and poodle.

A few of the things Strother enjoys include reading, exploring the world, riding her bike, and practicing yoga. (Courtesy Lara Strother.)

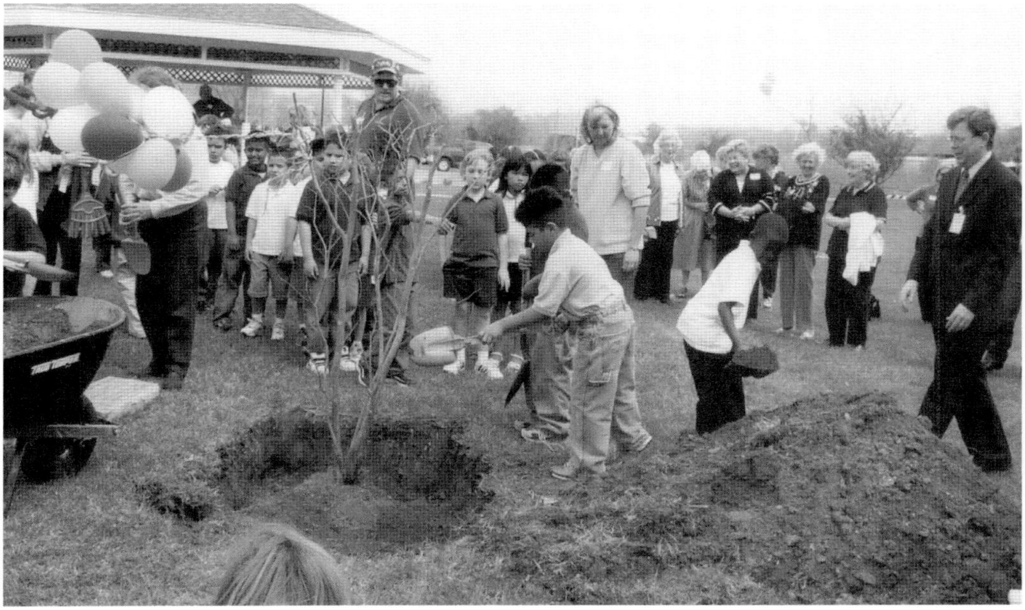

Lake Worth Garden Club Projects

On March 7, 2003, the Lake Worth Garden Club celebrated Arbor Day in a park named Effie Morris Park, along with elementary students who went to Effie Morris Elementary, located across the street.

Also invited to participate, a few city dignitaries and educators attended. In this photograph, a child digs a hole where a special tree, believed to be a Bur Oak, found its resting place. (Courtesy Lake Worth Garden Club.)

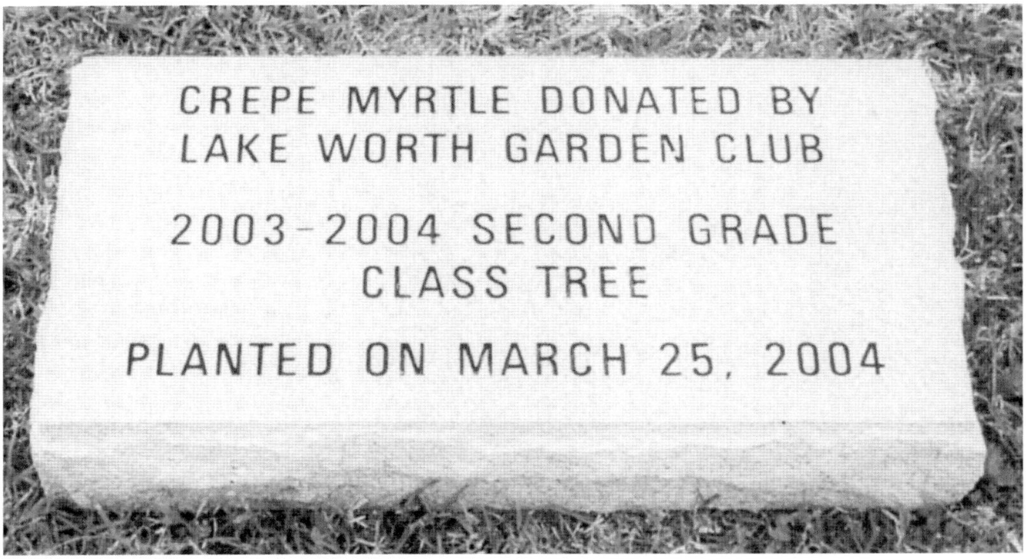

Another Lake Worth Garden Club Involvement

In 2004, a Crepe Myrtle tree donated by Lake Worth Garden Club members made another nice addition to Effie Morris Park. The honors appear on the image of the plaque. Over the years, many of the trees planted have reached a nice height and look beautiful. Those who helped made this a successful endeavor must feel a sense of pride. (Courtesy Lake Worth Garden Club.)

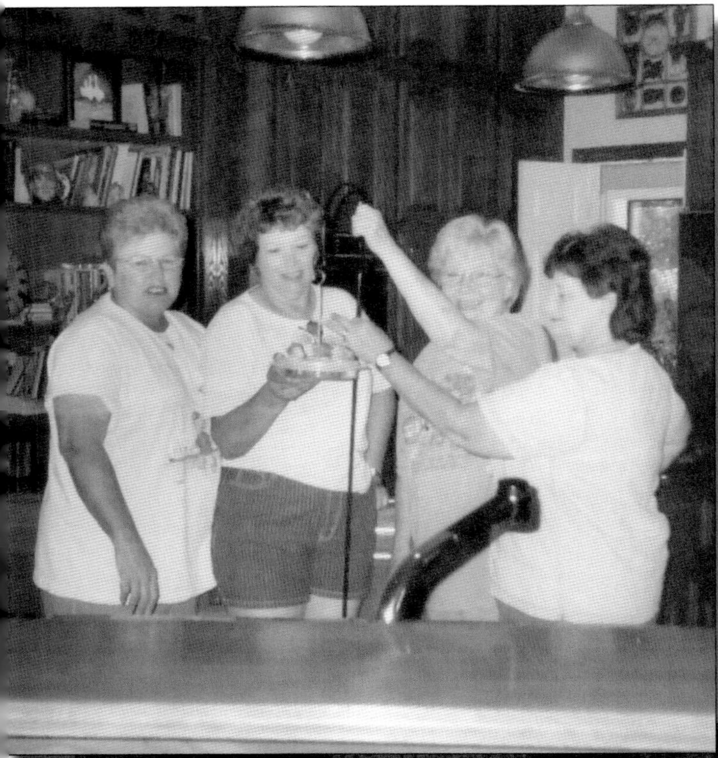

Thelma Smith Butterfly Garden
Thelma Smith has opened her home to members of the Lake Worth Garden Club for many years. Her kitchen often has been the setting for meetings where speakers have given interesting programs including what plants attract butterflies. Pictured from left to right are Nancy Keylon, Barbara Bateman, Thelma Smith, and Georgeanna Metts. (Courtesy Lawana Mauldin.)

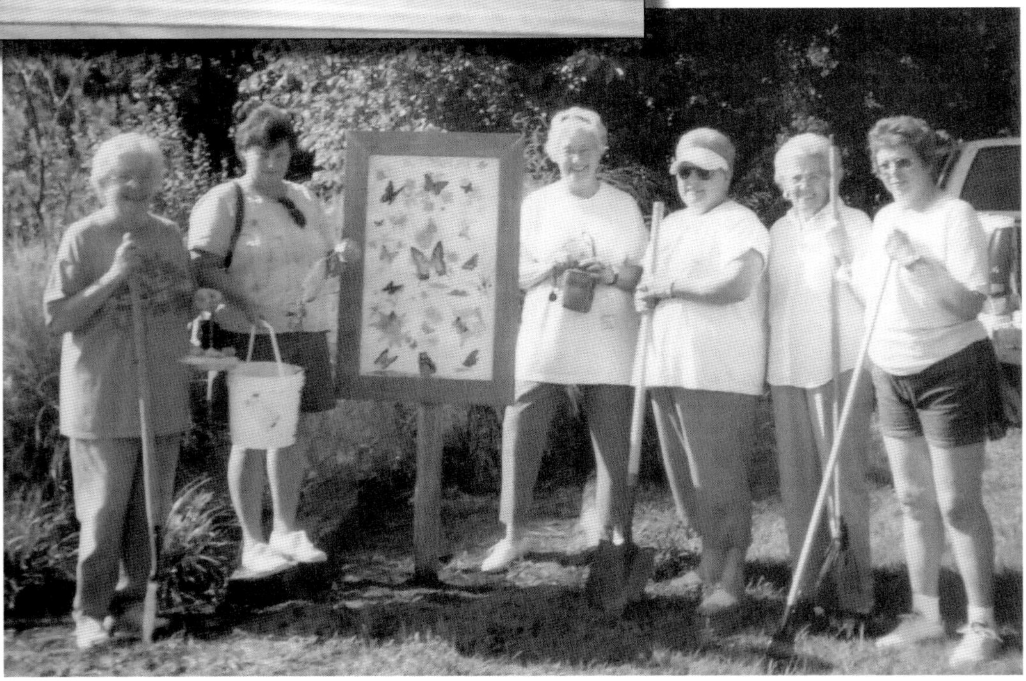

Garden Club Butterfly Activity
This garden club plants a variety of species that specifically attract butterflies. The images on the poster shown in the photograph help to identify the butterflies. Garden club members participating in the activity photographed include, from left to right: Thelma Smith, Georgeanna Metts, Joann Zwald, Nancy Keylon, Lois Sumerlin, and Barbara Bateman. (Courtesy Lawana Mauldin.)

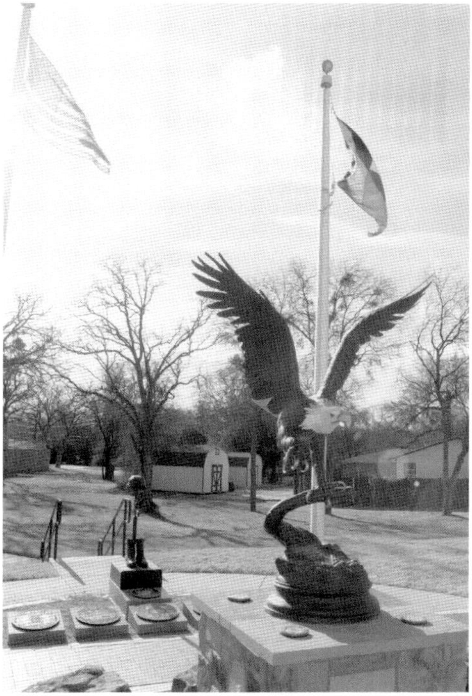

The Memorial Park

The new Veterans Memorial Park brings honor to many. Within the memorial setting, a large bronze eagle represents the American symbol. In addition, the fallen soldier's rifle, helmet, and boots, also in bronze, symbolize and honor those lost in battle.

The American and Texan flags wave gently over the park. Around the west side, a half-moon-shaped wall with granite podiums has names inscribed of some of the major military conflicts veterans have served. (Both photographs by Ken Brower.)

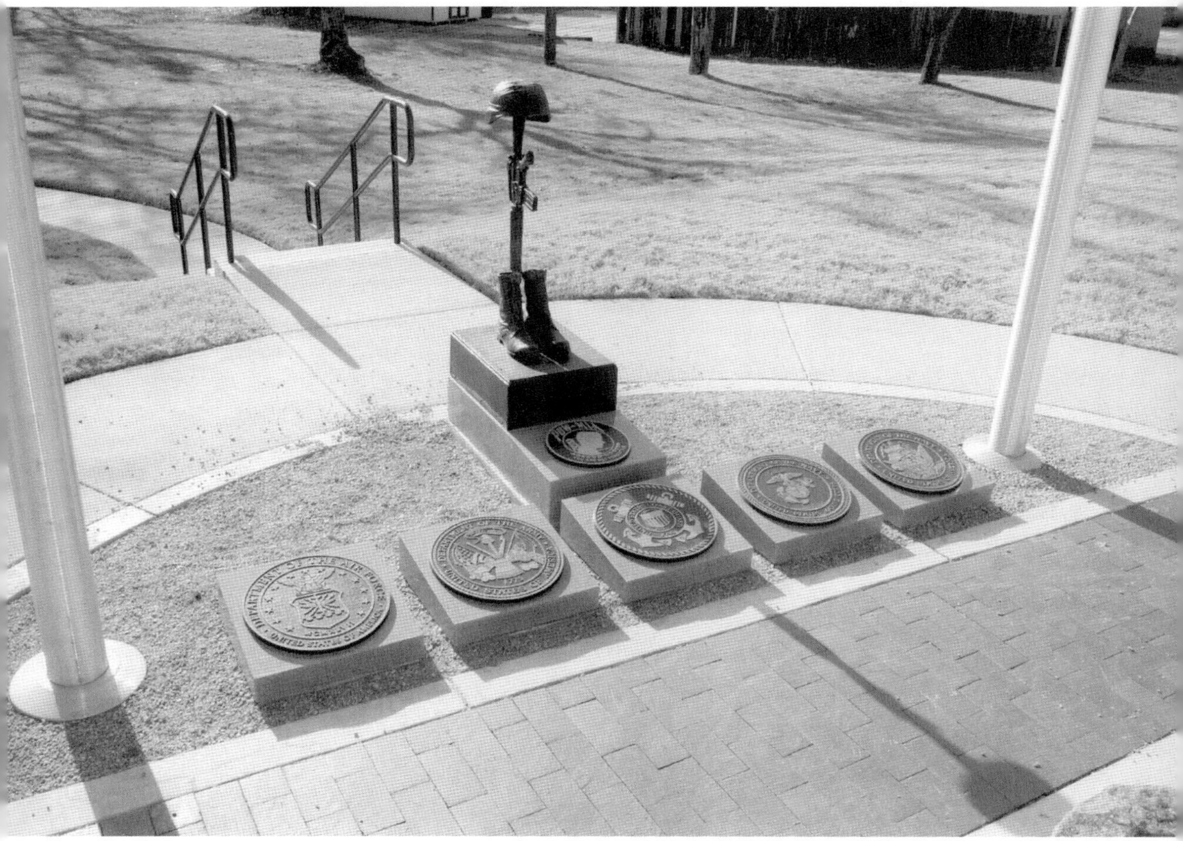

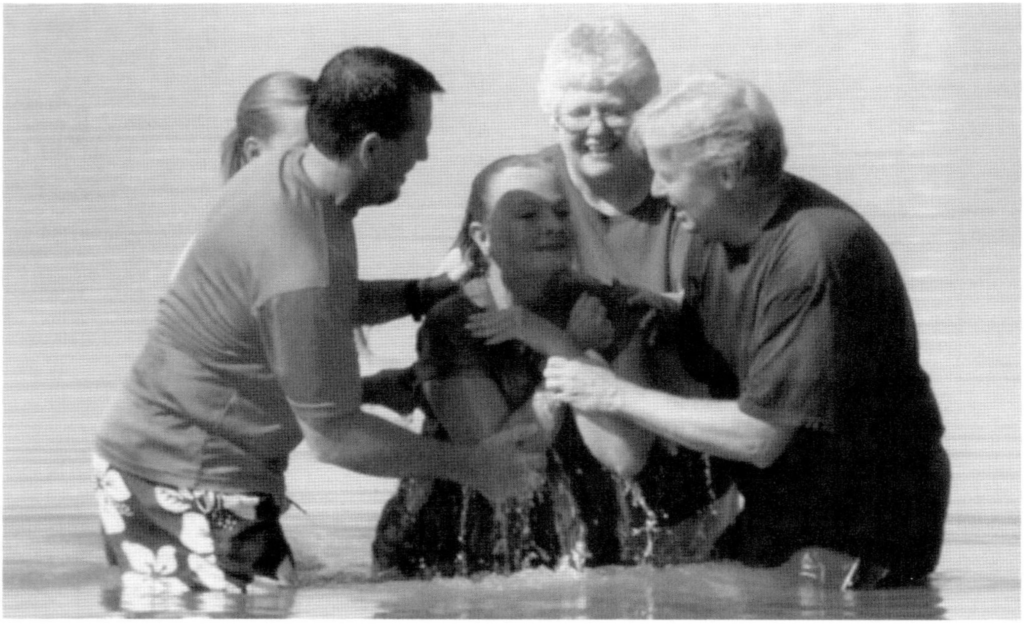

Baptisms and Holy Smokes
Cindy Bozart and her husband, Bob, still live in the lovely lake house that once belonged to her step grandfather James E. Parker. They have raised their three children in this residence.

They sometimes host baptismal events in the Lake Worth reservoir behind their legendary home for those in the church wishing to have immersion. In the photograph above, Frank Briggs, pastor of the Lighthouse Fellowship Church, immerses a young woman with the assistance of other unidentified persons. The Holy Smokes Barbeque Pit, sometimes used by Bob Bozart for cooking for Lighthouse Fellowship Church, sits on the drive of their home in the photograph below. (Courtesy Cindy Bozart and Lawana Mauldin.)

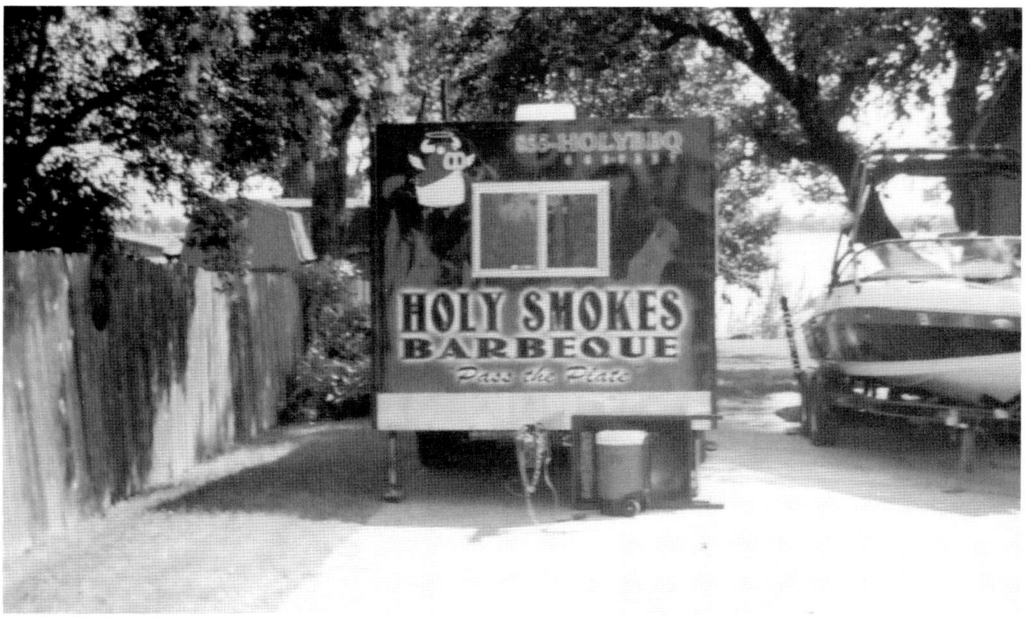

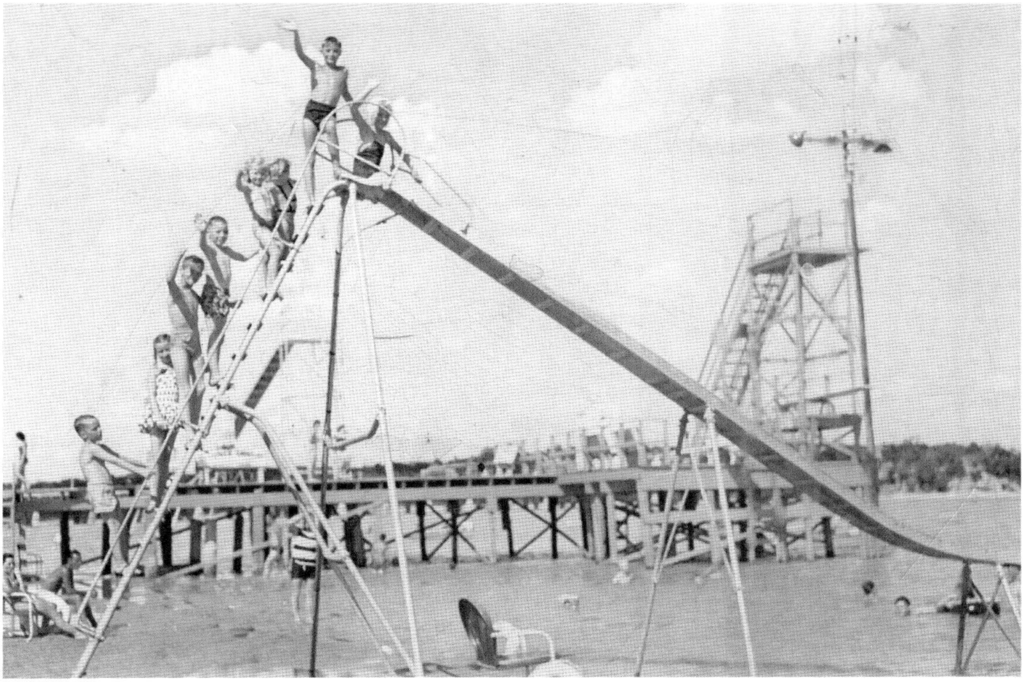

Beach Fun
Unidentified children, climbing the ladder to slip down the slide, paused for this photograph, believed to have been taken on the beach in the early days of Lake Worth Reservoir. Looking at the photograph likely stirs thoughts of many who look forward to the proposed new plans for this area. (Courtesy Carol Wright Baskin.)

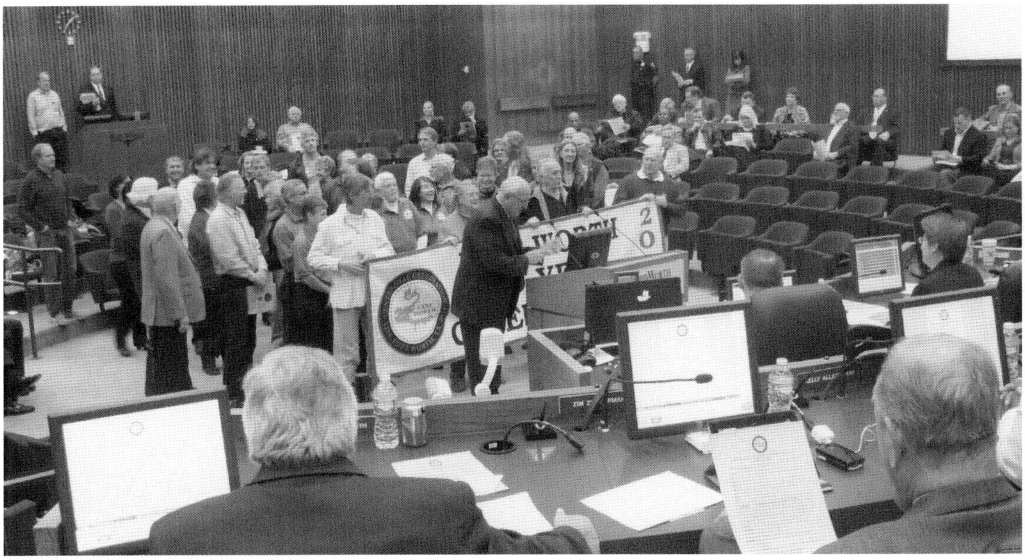

Centennial Celebration of Lake Worth
In early March 2014, the Lake Worth Centennial kick-off event took place at Fort Worth City Hall. The mayor of Fort Worth and the Fort Worth City Council presented the Lake Worth Centennial Committee the Centennial Proclamation Plaque for their work on events for 2014 honoring the Lake Worth reservoir's completion. (Courtesy John DeGroat.)

INDEX

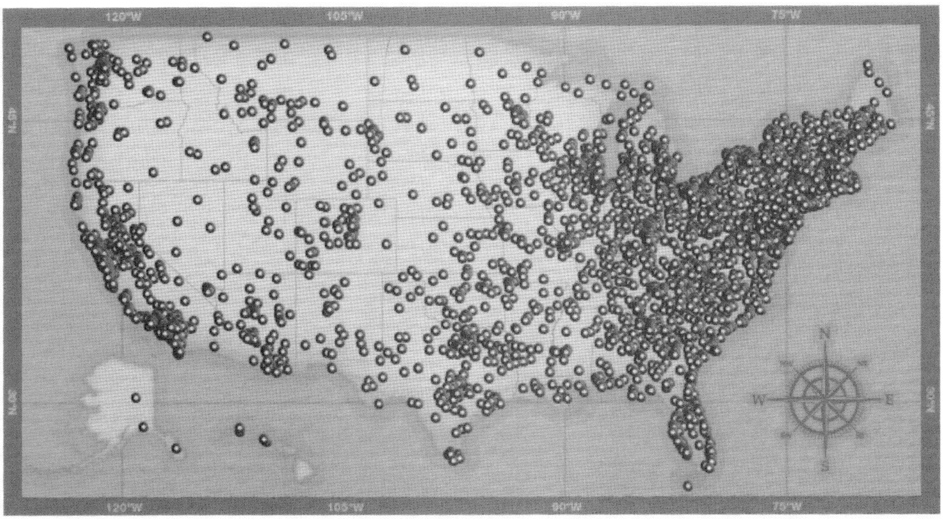